THE
PEOPLE'S
PROPERTY?

THE
PEOPLE'S
PROPERTY?

Power, Politics, and the Public

LYNN A. STAEHELI AND DON MITCHELL

Routledge
Taylor & Francis Group
New York · London

Routledge
Taylor & Francis Group
270 Madison Avenue
New York, NY 10016

Routledge
Taylor & Francis Group
2 Park Square
Milton Park, Abingdon
Oxon OX14 4RN

Printed in the United States of America on acid-free paper
10 9 8 7 6 5 4 3 2 1

International Standard Book Number-13: 978-0-415-95523-2 (Softcover) 978-0-415-95522-5 (Hardcover)

Library of Congress Cataloging-in-Publication Data

Staeheli, Lynn A.
    The people's property? power, politics, and the public / Lynn A. Staeheli and Don Mitchell.
        p. cm.
    Includes bibliographical references and index.
        ISBN 978-0-415-95522-5 (cloth) -- ISBN 978-0-415-95523-2 (pbk.)
    1. Property--Social aspects. 2. Right of property. 3. Privatization. 4. Public spaces--United States--Case studies. 5. Community power--United States--Case studies. I. Mitchell, Don, 1961- II. Title.

HB701.S68 2007
306.3'20973--dc22   2007001860

Visit the Taylor & Francis Web site at
http://www.taylorandfrancis.com

and the Routledge Web site at
http://www.routledge.com

CONTENTS

LIST OF FIGURES

ACKNOWLEDGMENTS

It has now been more than ten years since the project at the root of this book was hatched as the result of an argument we had over the nature and meaning of public space and the relevance of geography. We don't know if we are any closer to resolving the argument, but we do know that over the past decade we have accumulated many debts from funding agencies, colleagues, friends, and family, as the ideas that follow have germinated and developed in new ways.

Support from the National Science Foundation (BCS-9819828) allowed us to undertake the research, but the opinions expressed in this book are not those of the Foundation. Fellowships from the Rockefeller Foundation to spend a month at its Bellagio Study and Conference Center allowed us to do much of the writing. Both grants are gratefully acknowledged.

For administering our grants, but especially for making our everyday work lives easy by doing all those things that typically go unnoticed and too often un-thanked (especially as we traveled hither and yon for research and conferences), we would like to make partial amends and publicly thank Sugandha Brooks, Marcia Signer, and Marcia Richardson at the University of Colorado, and Janet Brieaddy, Christine Chapman, and Jackie Wells at Syracuse University.

Over the past decade we have drawn on the knowledge, expertise, and just plain hard work of a whole army of research assistants. We would like to thank Bruce D'Arcus, Kristina Gibson, Wendy Juniper, Jim Ketchum, Mike Longan, Katie Reed, Jim Russell, Nicel Saygin, Amy Sumpter, and Dan Trudeau. Unfortunately Judy Ball, our transcriber, passed away before she could see the final result of her work. We deeply appreciate the hours of hard work she did for us. A special thanks to Joe

Stoll of the Syracuse University Cartographic Laboratory for his excellent and speedy maps.

From the beginning of this project Nick Blomley has served as a sounding board, critic, idea generator, and friend. He read, either as a favor to us or as a critic enlisted by one editor or another, innumerable drafts and proposals. If this book reads in part like a dialogue with Nick's own ideas, that is no accident, as he has laid the groundwork and set the standard for all research on property in geography. Michael Brown, Susan Clarke, Matt Hannah, Jane Jacobs, Sallie Marston, and John O'Loughlin, like Nick, all provided intellectual friendship, as well as letters that got us through the gates of Villa Serboloni at Bellagio. That is a debt we can never repay except, we hope, in kind.

As noted below, the case studies brought together for this book originally appeared (in different form) as journal articles and book chapters. The advice and criticisms of our reviewers and editors have been invaluable. Even earlier presentations of these ideas at conferences were made possible by Bruce D'Arcus who organized a special Association of American Geographers (AAG) session on protest and public space (where we first aired our Washington, DC study); Mike Lamb, Setha Low, and Neil Smith who organized the Politics of Public Space conference at the CUNY Graduate Center where the San Diego research got its first workout; Jon May and Jürgen von Mahs put together a stimulating session at another AAG where we tried to refine this San Diego work. Michael Levine, Kristine Miller, and Bill Taylor organized a Workshop on Law, Landscape, and Ethics at the International Institute for the Sociology of Law in Oñati, Spain. Special thanks to Kristine for her valuable comments on our work, and, also at that conference, to Alex Scherr and Anna Secor who encouraged us as we began jabbering about turning all this into a book, and to the rakish Ken Olwig for his comments and for organizing a special issue of *Landscape Research* in which our Santa Fe chapter first appeared. Lorraine Dowler and Doris Wastl-Walter co-organized (along with Lynn) a conference in Rome on "Rights to the City," where we laid out our research from New York. The Syracuse case study was originally prepared for a special issue of *Urban Studies*. Thanks to Jon Bannister and Nick Fyfe for their encouragement and ideas. Ideas in the latter part of this book have been long in gestation. Of particular importance was the advice and encouragement of Audrey Kobayashi as we worked out our arguments about the relevancy of geographic research. Thanks too to all those geographers, named and anonymous, who we interviewed for this part of our work.

Our interviewees in San Diego, New York, Washington, Santa Fe, and Syracuse gave generously of their time and expertise. We thank them all, but especially want to thank, once again too late, Joe Ferguson who not only gave us great insight into what it is like to live in the midst of (or really just across the street from) constant protest at the Supreme Court, but also into the changing geography of the city. Joe was on board the plane that crashed into the Pentagon on September 11, 2001, and he is greatly missed.

Dave McBride encouraged and commissioned this book for Routledge. He was exceptionally helpful in shaping it. We appreciate especially the breakfast in Chicago, but we are not sure if he liked it as much as we did. At one point it looked like we were going to do something never before done in the history of academic publishing—deliver our manuscript early, under the word count, and to the same editor who commissioned it. Alas, we were two weeks late, and Dave had moved on; we are, however, still under the word count. Dave's imprint on this book remains strong and the way he shaped the geography list at Routledge will not soon be forgotten. We are grateful that he left us in such good hands; Angela Chnapko, Anne Horowitz, and Judith Simon have all been a great help in seeing the book through production. We want to thank especially our copy editor, Rebecca Condit.

Ideas are always rooted in specific places and circumstances. We outlined our overall project at a coffeehouse in Boulder (not to be named to protect our credibility), but the ideas were nurtured in (among others): Croces in San Diego (with special thanks for the bicycle cop for making the nature of public space in that city so clear); Herald Square in New York (ditto to the private security guard); a dark abandoned corner of the lobby in the late, great Gramercy Park Hotel; the wine bar at the Palmer House in Chicago; the veranda of the Dancing Ground of the Sun Hotel in Santa Fe; the Plaza in Oñati (with special thanks to its waiters bearing gin and tonics); the old square in Bilbao (ditto); the beach in Donestia/San Sebastian (ditto); the Home of Geography and the Villa San Pio in Rome (this time the bartenders brought beer and wine); the Villa Maranese with its espresso machine, the amazing (and amazingly tolerant) Susanna Coffee, and the great Laura and her colleagues who looked after us; the Villa Serboloni and especially Pilar Palacia who made our stay so fabulous. Thanks too to all our new friends there with whom we shared ideas, cocktails, ping-pong, and so many laughs: Toi, Brian, Donna, Sir Tony, Nancy, Charles, Pamela, Elliot, Norma, Geoff, Maryl, Amy, Bob, Pam, Steve, Lee, Jill, Rumina and Shelly. We hope that all are pleased with the product. We are just happy to be able to say at last, "Tit fu!"

Nel, Dan, Topher, and Susan have lived with this project for the last decade too, tolerating endless travel, our obsession with the public and relevance, and the endless delays on our promised San Juan to San Juan transect. Susan, in particular, should be praised for her persistent perusal of the pictograph dictionary in search of words that begin with "p." We hope the period in Bellagio—and the gelato—partially made up for this.

Chapter 1 is a revised version of Don Mitchell and Lynn A. Staeheli, "Permitting Protest: Constructing—and Dismantling—the Geography of Dissent in the United States," *International Journal of Urban and Regional Research* 29 (2005), 796–813. We thank Blackwell Publishing for permission to reuse this material here.

Chapter 2 is a revised version of Don Mitchell and Lynn A. Staeheli, "Turning Social Relations into Space: Property, Law, and the Plaza of Santa Fe, New Mexico," *Landscape Research* 30 (2005), 325–342. This work is reused with the permission of the publishers, Taylor & Francis.

Chapter 3 is a revised version of Don Mitchell and Lynn A. Staeheli, "Clean and Safe? Property Redevelopment, Public Space and Homelessness in San Diego, California," in S. Low and N. Smith (eds.), *The Politics of Public Space* (New York: Routledge, 2006), 143–175. We thank the editors and Routledge for permission to reuse this material.

Chapter 4 is a revised version of Lynn A. Staeheli and Don Mitchell, "USA's Destiny? Regulating Space and Creating Community in American Shopping Malls," *Urban Studies* 43 (2006), 977–992. This work is reused with the permission of the publishers, Taylor & Francis.

Chapter 5 is a revised version of Lynn A. Staeheli, Don Mitchell, and Kristina Gibson, "Conflicting Rights to the City in New York City's Community Gardens," *GeoJournal* 58 (2002), 197–205. It is revised with the kind permission of Springer Science and Business Media.

The Bailie
Stockbridge, Edinburgh

PREFACE

Friday, March 10, 2006, Chicago, Illinois. More than 100,000 immigrants—both documented and undocumented—marched with immigrant rights activists, union members, and other supporters into Chicago's downtown Loop and filled the Federal Plaza (Figure P.1) They came to protest the passing of the so-called Sensenbrenner Bill by the U.S. House of Representatives. The Sensenbrenner Bill (HR 4437) represented a drastic, and for many, highly anti-immigrant, reform to U.S. immigration and naturalization laws. Among its many provisions were new criminal sanctions against those, including humanitarian organizations, who aid and abet people who cross the border illegally. It also sought to make undocumented status a felony and ratcheted up penalties on employers of undocumented labor. The masses who gathered in Chicago opposed these changes, and by their presence, sought to make the scale of that opposition known. They were not alone. Within weeks protests spread across the United States, with more than one-half million people marching in Los Angeles and Dallas, tens of thousands in San Francisco and Philadelphia, and innumerable marches and rallies in small towns and cities across the whole of the United States. The marches were often in places like Rochester, New York or Birmingham, Alabama—places not strongly associated in the national consciousness with the latest wave of immigration.

But in Chicago (and all these other cities) protesters were doing more than just showing their opposition to the Sensenbrenner Bill. They were showing *themselves*. Gathering in their thousands, filling the Federal Plaza and the surrounding streets of the Loop, immigrants and their supporters were making an important claim: they were asserting

Figure P1 Immigrants and their supporters demonstrating in Chicago's Federal Plaza, March 10, 2006. This was the first of the large immigrants' rights rallies held across the United States in the spring of 2006 and it attracted more than 100,000 people to Federal Plaza—a traditional site for demonstrations in Chicago—and the surrounding streets. Photograph by Giuseppe Alcoff; used by permission.

themselves as part of the public—the *people*—of the United States. By filling public space they were making themselves visible, unavoidable; by their very presence, they were saying, "we are every bit as much a part of this city and country as you are." In so doing, they were making it clear that they were part of the public not despite, but *because* of their difference. And they were making political claims as members of that public, endowed with certain rights as members of the United States.

As activists and organizers have long known, being present in public space—making claims to and becoming visible in the streets, sidewalks, squares, and parks of the city—is a vital, necessary step in making claims *on* the public and *as part of* the public. Indeed, the wave of mass protest that began in Chicago has been remarkably effective in changing the nature of the debate over immigration in the United States, bringing to the fore tough questions of economy and belonging, of struggles over what constitutes "home," and of what the face of America looks like. For immigrants, making a claim to be part of the public has required, inevitably, the occupation of public space: it is in public space, such as the Federal Plaza, that movements become visible and thus must be reckoned with. Public space, in this protest, served its traditional roles: as a foundation or place for the struggle for inclusion, for promoting particular visions of how the public should be constituted, and promoting the rights that members of the public carry.

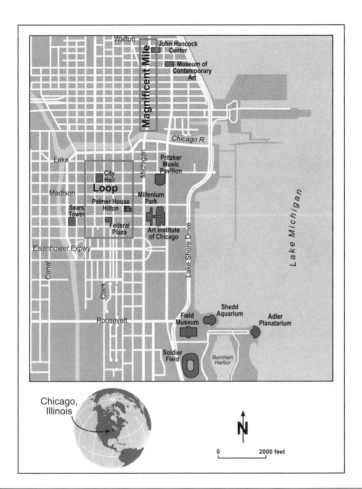

Figure P2 Map of downtown Chicago, showing Federal Plaza, the Palmer House Hilton, Millennium Park, and the Magnificent Mile. Cartography by Joe Stoll, Syracuse University Cartography Laboratory.

As the rally broke up in the late afternoon, many protestors, carrying their American and Mexican flags and chatting joyously among themselves, made their way down Monroe toward the entrance to the El on Wabash or buses waiting in Grant Park (Figure P.2). As they passed the entrance to the Palmer House Hotel, they mingled with some of the 5,000 or so academics stepping out from the annual meeting of the Association of American Geographers. Inside the Palmer House are public spaces of a very different kind (Figure P.3). The ornate lobby was filled with chatting, gossiping faculty and students, crisscrossed by anxious soon-to-be wedding parties wondering if the facilities were

Figure P3 The ornate lobby of the Palmer House Hotel in Chicago, where the Association of American Geographers held its annual meeting in March 2006, while the immigrants rights protest was going on only a few blocks away. Photograph by Don Mitchell.

adequate to their needs, and staffed by uniformed bellhops, maids, and customer service representatives (some of whom, no doubt, wished they could have been out at the protest). While many different kinds of people were visible in the lobby, it might better be called a "publicly-accessible" space, rather than public space per se, since it is, after all, privately-owned and controlled. Though somewhat limited by restrictions imposed by public accommodation laws that make it illegal to bar people from the lobby merely on grounds of race, gender, or creed, the managers of the Palmer House have an a priori right to exclude any and all from its property; unlike the streets, the public does not have a basic right to be present in the hotel. The lobby, thus, is a more highly controlled space of interaction, wherein a different kind of public, and a different segment of the people, can form and be seen. The filtering of this public occurs in many ways, ranging from the very high price for food and drinks in the flanking bars and restaurants, to the watchful glare of the bellhops and doormen who make it clear, for example, that the lobby is not an appropriate place for the indigent seeking refuge from the cold surrounding streets. Here the overriding ethic is, in fact, one of exclusion. It is not a random or chance exclusion, however. It is intended to create a space of comfortable interactions—comfortable, at least, for the people with a "legitimate" right to be in the lobby as conferred by the owners of the hotel.

Upstairs, in the conference rooms, practices of exclusion were even stronger. Though not evenly enforced, there was a ticket for admission, purchased with the conference fee. Possession of the ticket was most visible in the badges that the geographers wore; it was also apparent, for those who are initiated and know what to look for, in the style of clothing, hair, and ornamentation, the bearing, and perhaps most of all the *language* of the conference goers, which itself is the symbol of highly specialized training and socialization. While the scholars attending were varied in their interests (ranging from climate change to the changing geography of world religions, and from military terrain analysis to, well, the geographical analysis of public space), they all spoke more or less fluently in the coded languages of their fields. The spaces of the conference rooms are a very different kind of "public" space: they are the space of discourse, where ideas are tried out and contested, where debates (at least ideally) flourish. Though public in the sense of being relatively open and being defined by public debate, they are also highly restrictive. In this sense, they are little different from the public spaces of experimental science described by Shapin and Schaeffer (1985) in their analysis of the creation of early modern science, the legislative chambers of a statehouse, or a courtroom. Each is subject to written and unwritten rules that open the space (and the discourses in it) to initiates while closing it to others, structure the form of the debate and who may engage in it, and create the conditions for the production of knowledge. Here, no less than in the lobby, inclusion and publicness *depend* on exclusion; only by excluding and heavily regulating the space can the space be made open to public discourse and debate.

Back out on the street, some of the protesters and some of the geographers made their way over to the new Millennium Park, a couple of blocks to the northeast. (Figure P.4). This is yet another kind of public space. Recently built on government-owned land, much of the park (but certainly not all of it) was paid for by corporate and foundation donations, and the park boasts signature architecture from the likes of Frank Gehry. Hardly a square inch of the park is not sponsored by some private interest or another. Bricks in the walkways indicate corporate and individual donors; whole plazas and squares are named for their corporate patrons (SBC Plaza, Exelon Pavilion, BP Bridge, etc.); monuments proclaim their allegiance to their benefactors. Art installations are copyrighted—they remain the property of the artists. Sections of

Figure P4 Millennium Park, Chicago's new and highly popular public space. Barely a square inch is not sponsored by a corporation, local foundation, or wealthy individual. Special rules govern use (including photography) of the park, and the markers of security, roving guards, surveillance cameras, are omnipresent. Photograph by Don Mitchell.

the park—the Chase Promenade, for example, or the Pritzker Pavilion—can be rented for corporate or charity events, closing them off to the rest of the public. Police presence is heavy, and the park closes each evening at 11:00 p.m.

Designed specifically as a space of rest and recreation, Millennium Park is a public space of yet a different kind. Its role is not necessarily that of the Federal Plaza, a fairly open space in the heart of the city where the houses of state power (the federal and city governments most prominently) may be directly faced, thus making it such a crucial gathering place for political demonstrations. With its heavy corporate sponsorship and curfew, Millennium Park seems like some confusing hybrid space. It *is* publicly-owned, but the trappings of private ownership and commerce are woven into the fabric of the place. Yet it is not like the private, but still publicly-accessible space of the hotel lobby, or the restricted space of debate of the conference room. Like any space it is, no doubt, highly exclusionary in intent and function, but it is also welcoming. The official website of Millennium Park declares that the "park was created for the enjoyment of the people of Chicago and its visitors and its guests."* Yet it is clear that what is possible here is a quite different expression of what it is to be part of "the people" than that being struggled for a few blocks away in the streets near the federal

---

* Millennium Park website, http://www.millenniumpark.org/generalinformation/rules_ safety.html (accessed 20 April 2006).

building. A different *kind* of public can form here. It is a public in which the rules by which a public can gather and what the people can do are in many ways set by private, or at least not publicly accountable, entities.

Continuing north from Millennium Park, up North Michigan and across the river, protesters and geographers might have found themselves on the Magnificent Mile, a strip of swank department stores, hotels, and restaurants, where they would have joined a throng of Friday evening shoppers, happy hour bar-hoppers, and tourists on one of Chicago's destination streets (Figure P.5). Had they been there only a month earlier, however, the street scene would have looked, and more importantly, sounded, quite a bit different. For only a month earlier the Chicago City Council voted to ban all street musicians from a four-block stretch of the Mile, supporting local residents' and business owners' contentions that the noise was a public nuisance. Elsewhere in the city, street performers faced lowered decibel limits and higher permit fees. According to the president of the Greater North Michigan Avenue Association, the street musicians decrease "office workers' productivity and annoy customers in stores" (quoted in Keen 2006, 6A). The new regulations, instigated at the behest of local property and business owners, significantly transformed the experience of the sidewalks in the Magnificent Mile; in so doing, they altered the nature of public space.

Such distinctions in understanding urban public space, such "fine parsings of the geography" of inclusion and exclusion, control and struggle (to appropriate the felicitous phrase of one of our informants from Chapter 1), are now commonplace in contemporary cities, but scholars still struggle to understand them. For nearly twenty years, debate has raged over the nature of public space, its meanings and functions, and especially its transformations in the contemporary city. How should we make sense of the sort of "privatization" of public space evidenced by the corporate influence in Millennium Park or the rise of even more fully privatized festival marketplaces, such as Boston's Faneuil Hall or San Diego's Horton Plaza? Are "traditional" spaces like streets, sidewalks, parks, and Chicago's Federal Plaza really public in any substantive sense in light of regulations governing the time, place, and manner of protests? If shopping centers and malls (and indeed tourist hotels and conference centers like the Palmer House) are becoming something like the "new town squares," what kind of public can form in those squares? And what of policing and state-sanctioned violence in keeping spaces "safe for the public?" For what kind of public is it being kept? How are homeless and other indigent people to be incorporated into public spaces and the public? *Can* they be incorporated if other members of the public feel intimidated or wary of going to those spaces? What is the

Figure P5 The Magnificent Mile, Chicago, a strip of swank stores and boutiques, restaurants, and hotels—considered one of the destination streets of the city. Photograph by Don Mitchell.

relationship between urban public spaces and political public spheres in the changing geography (and geographic relations) that characterize cities today? All these have come under intense scholarly—and, in fact, activist—scrutiny in the past two decades.

This book seeks to intervene in these debates and discussions. It does so with a bifocal approach centered on the relationships between spaces as organized by property and as given meaning—and imbued with power of particular sorts—by people. While much research has centered on, and argued over, the nature of public space as *space*, comparatively little has focused on it as *property*. Yet as we will argue throughout this book, understanding public space as a set of property relationships is foundational; property is a crucial set of relationships that structure the role, function, and nature of public space as space. Even more, focusing on property opens up not only new ways of analyzing and understanding public space, but new fronts in the ongoing struggles over and interventions in it. A close attention to property and property relations helps us to better see how public space is so vitally relevant to everyday life, and what we can do about it. At the same time, close attention to the people *in* spaces and those who occupy and use property can help us understand the ways in which politics, power, and publicity are constituted and enacted in the formation of political communities; these configurations of community hold different possibilities for citizenship, democracy, and justice.

Consider that early March day in Chicago. Protesters marched through city-owned and regulated public streets, gathering finally at the Federal Plaza, which surely would be considered a "traditional public forum." Courts generally understand traditional public forums to be those spaces that "have immemorially been held *in trust* for the use of the public and, time out of mind, have been used for the purposes of assembly, communicating thoughts between citizens, and discussing public questions" (*Hague v. CIO* 1939, 515–516, emphasis added). That is, they are public spaces in the most basic sense. But, interestingly, in its founding decision, *Hague v. CIO*, the Supreme Court was careful to point out that *ownership* was less important than *customary use*, arguing that customary use created public spaces "wherever the title of the streets and parks may rest" (515). In reality, however, this designation of "traditional public forum," where the ability of the state to regulate public political activity is most highly circumscribed, has been reserved only for publicly-owned property, and a small set of it at that. For many, Millennium Park may seem much like Federal Plaza. Its deed is held by the city; it is policed by city officers; and except when rented out, it is open to all the public. Yet property rights and relations govern it, too, and sometimes in surprising ways. For example, copyright of the sculptures has been retained by the artists. In particular, commercial photographers are banned from photographing "Cloud Gate" (more affectionately known as "the bean" and one of the premier attractions of the park), since doing so would usurp the property rights of the artist. Such commercial photography bans do not obtain for the sculptures of Federal Plaza, but they are common in publicly-accessible spaces like the Palmer House's lobby. At Syracuse's Carousel Center (Chapter 4), in fact, even amateur photography is banned by mall management. And on the newly quiet Magnificent Mile, as in San Diego in the redeveloped Gaslamp and Horton Plaza districts (Chapter 3), it is perhaps not actual ownership in and of itself that matters, as much as it is the sets of relations among property owners that are so crucial for regulating the nature of street life. The relations and rights of property, and the questions of who owns publicly-accessible property in any meaningful sense (Chapter 2), matter deeply to what public space *is*, what it can be, what it is not, what it cannot be; they matter critically to who is and who is *not* included in the public.

Property is not the end of the story, however. People still gather in public spaces to make statements to the government and to the polity about who *should* be in the public and what rights members of the public should hold, whether it is in the streets of Washington, DC (Chapter 1) or in the Plaza of Santa Fe (Chapter 2). People who do not *belong* in a space, still transgress those spaces (Chapter 3). The private corporations that own the "new town squares" encased in shopping malls still have to confront the efforts of governments and of activists to unsettle the social and political relationships they attempt to create in the mall (Chapter 4). And sometimes, people who feel marginalized in the spaces of the city attempt to reclaim space—attempt to transgress or to squat space—in order to make new places that are suitable to publics that might challenge the power relations of the city and that create new ideals of citizenship and democracy (Chapter 5).

Rarely, however, is the public nature of space settled; it is continually made and remade. The public sphere is, thus, located and relocated, constructed and transgressed, in the streets, the plazas and parks, the government buildings, the shopping malls, and the hidden spaces of the city (Chapter 6). In physically locating the public sphere, publicly-accessible property shapes "the people," determining who does and who does not appear to be legitimate citizens or to be persons with legitimate claims on the polity (Chapter 7). Yet the relationship between people and property is never static, and as the immigrant rallies of 2006 showed, people, by taking and using public space, actively remake the public (in all its senses). Public space may, in some ways, be foundational in establishing who the people are, but the people—or contending segments of it—likewise use public space to which they have gained access as a source of power.

The People's Property? starts from the assumption that the nature of a space is critical to how it is used and therefore how it conditions political, social, and cultural activities. This is an assumption shared with much of the academic literature on public space. The argument commonly followed goes something like this: the regulation of public space sets the boundaries of the public by regulating terms of access, including the people and behaviors that are accommodated within it. We will talk about these issues in terms of property relationships. In so doing, we ask: what *kinds* of people populate publicly-accessible property? In what ways is *any* property a *people's* property? In what ways is public space really public in any normative sense? We answer these questions by focusing on the interplay between property (in its geographical sense, as a parcel of owned space) and people. By putting people and property in relation to each other—by putting them in tension—we explore how negotiations over ownership, control, and the peopling of public space are central to the quality of publicity, citizenship, and democracy in urban areas in the United States.*

By focusing on property in relationship to the structure and transformation of the public, *The People's Property?* grounds theories of public space in the actual workings of law and regulation, and in the actions of those subject to law and regulation as they seek to make a space for themselves in the urban realm. As hinted in the descriptions above, property rights are often defined as the "right to exclude" (Blomley 2004b; Macpherson 1978; Singer 2000). Property rights, and the struggle over them, powerfully condition the nature of accessibility. Property rights and property regimes are not static and the outcomes of these rights and regimes are not inevitable or fully determined. It is important, therefore, to understand who (which individuals or corporate entities, governed by what regulations and restrictions) owns publicly-accessible property and what actions are taken to either ensure or to contest the meaning of that ownership. Property and space more generally only exist as a tissue of relations— relations to other property, relations to various users, and relations to those who might be excluded. In that sense it is important to understand the changing bases for excluding some people and classes of people from otherwise publicly-accessible property and how these exclusions are challenged. That is to say, it is important to understand how possibilities for association in publicly-accessible space vary for different people—people who carry diverse identities, norms, and values—if we are to understand the role public spaces play in shaping democratic possibilities.

As such, we need to understand the power relationships that operate in public space. By controlling space, individuals and groups create the power to shape other relationships, including relations between people who aspire to be included in the public. Perhaps the most obvious power

---

* Our focus in this book is exclusively on the United States. This is both for practical reasons (our empirical case studies concerned controversies about public space in American cities) and because we understand that national legal regimes make a difference in how public space is used, how property relations operate, and in the kinds of resources people have access to when they seek to transform relations of power. National legal norms and practices are different in the United States than they are in Canada, the United Kingdom, or the countries of the European Union, to say nothing of sub-Saharan Africa, the wide range of countries in the Middle East and Asia, or post-dictatorship Latin America.

relationship in public space comes from the ownership of that space and the ability to reduce the abstract concept of *public space* to the more grounded concepts of "property" and "ownership." Part of this relationship also involves the removal of people from space, whether through the removal of homeless people or of the idea of people as inherent to spatial relationships. Rarely do we stop to consider who owns and manages publicly-accessible spaces (and for what reasons), but property ownership is a powerful tool in the regulation of space and, thereby, of the public. Court decisions governing First Amendment uses of public spaces, such as streets and sidewalks, frequently discuss the role of governments as owners and are explicit about the ways in which governments are (or are supposed to be) neutral in their treatment of people, of members of the public. Similarly, when the managers of publicly-accessible, but privately-owned spaces regulate the behaviors of people within those spaces (e.g., malls), it is understandable because property rights are abstracted from public politics in common discourse, and so they seem naturally to trump speech rights in those settings. These positions, however, elide questions of public ownership, thereby hiding the power relations that construct public spaces and neutralizing their political potential. Unasked are questions such as: Which portions of the public effectively own putatively public spaces? What portions of the public have a priori rights to access? Who is largely there by sufferance? In which public's interest does the government govern, even when it is being formally neutral?

Yet we do not support a linear view of the relationships among property, the regulation of space, and the production of publicity. There is a certain inevitability that permeates the academic literature on public space that follows a logic that Joseph Singer (2000; see Blomley 2004b) characterizes as an "ownership model." In this model, property is either owned publicly (taken to mean owned by the government) or by private individuals or corporations, and ownership is singular and appears largely uncontested. Each owner engages in attempts to regulate space, and this in turn sets the conditions for the development of citizens and people with particular political values, views, and subjectivities. Much of the literature focuses on the shifting balance between public and private ownership and argues that publicly-owned property is increasingly regulated and controlled as though it is private. One reason this seems so problematic for democracy is because such shifts too readily appear (including in law) as the simple prerogative of the property owner, even when that owner is a public entity. As the Supreme Court has made clear (see Chapter 2), as a property owner, a government has an obligation to "act like a landlord" (an owner) and not only as a "sovereign" (a representative of the people).

One of the major concerns in academic research in this vein is that the public quality of space seems to be diminishing, leading to further concerns about the shrinkage of the public realm, the privatization of politics, and the neutralization of citizens and citizenship. Yet millions of people took to the streets in spring 2006 precisely to claim their rights as members of the American public. Furthermore, oppositional politics are all around us—in the streets, in parks, on private property, and in academic and public debates—even if they frequently seem ineffectual. Often missing in the debates over the regulation of public space as property are the *people* who constitute the abstract public. These are people who are marked by gender, race, ability, age, religion, class, values, goals, ideas, and aspirations. These people are every bit as important as property, space, and ownership in the struggles for public space and for the quality of publicity, democracy, and citizenship.

In *The People's Property?* we attempt to understand the interplay among public space, property, politics, and power in the construction of publicity through an examination of five case studies involving controversies over public space. The case studies demonstrate the ways in which people—people variously positioned with respect to resources, identities, and values—imagine the kinds of publics they want to achieve. We start with what may be the most obvious struggle in public space: protests in the streets and parks of Washington, DC. We then shift to studies of the Plaza in Santa Fe, New Mexico, to the redevelopment of downtown San Diego, California, to the ways in which ideals of community have come to substitute for publicity in the Carousel Center in Syracuse, New York, and to the reclaiming of public space through the establishment of community gardens in New York City. In each case, we look at the ideals for public space held—or in some cases *not held*—by participants in these controversies and the ways in which the relations surrounding the nature of public space as property shape the resources that various participants use in their struggles. Property becomes one of the *tools* that some participants are able to wield in their efforts, while it is an *object* of struggle for other participants. Because of this, the nature of ownership itself becomes contested. In all cases, we focus on property and the relations that constitute it insofar as property is involved in the advance of various participants' efforts to create spaces for publicity and for citizenship with various qualities and normative visions of political membership.

From these case studies, we then attempt to synthesize the academic, policy, and political debates over public space and publicity in an attempt to identify the competing forms of publicity and democracy that various agents hope to achieve in and through public space. The case studies, however, only take us so far, as they isolate one struggle from the fabric of the cities in which they are situated. In highlighting the regulation of protest in the streets of Washington, DC, for example, we do not consider the ways in which the streets themselves are being encroached upon through redevelopment. In thinking about attempts to reclaim abandoned lots as gardens and as places of democratic potential, we do not consider the ways in which parks in New York have been partially privatized through corporate sponsorship. In cities, none of these struggles exists in isolation, and so the construction of publicity and citizenship are structured by the complex interplay between these struggles, by the point and counterpoint that is the rhythm of daily life and of political relationships. In the last two chapters of the book, therefore, we consider the cases together. We discuss the places or spaces where various participants in the struggles over public space (in the cities, in the governments, and even in the academy) locate publicity and thus how they seek to intervene in what could be called a *regime of publicity*. We discuss the politics of property that underlie the possible forms the public might take, the resources people might use in their struggles, and the power of people to reshape this regime of publicity, democracy, and citizenship.

1

PERMITTING PROTEST IN WASHINGTON, DC*

Perhaps the most obvious function of publicly-accessible space is to provide a place for gathering, a place for crowds to form. Chicago's Federal Plaza, and the streets around it, made it possible for immigrants and their supporters to, literally, *see* themselves by coming together in the same place, and thereby constituting themselves as part of "a public." Traditional public spaces like the Plaza and streets are, in this sense, where dissent and affirmation become visible. Even so, in order for protesters to gather in the Plaza in the first place, protest organizers had to apply for a protest permit from the city of Chicago. That is, the protest had to be approved, legitimated, sanctioned. The public had to be given permission by the state even to appear. In this regard, Chicago is like every other city in the United States. In traditional public spaces such as the Federal Plaza, governed as they are by permit systems, it is therefore worth asking: What are the conditions under which visibility becomes possible? How is this public "located?" By what rules and regulations? Who exercises the power to define this public? As this public is located and defined, what sort of politics becomes possible?

In this chapter we will argue that the politics *of* public space—and public property—are critical determinants of the politics *in* public space. By extension, the politics of public space play a role in how the public is constituted. We will argue that this is a locational struggle in that political possibilities are shaped by banning political activities

---

* This chapter is revised from: Don Mitchell and Lynn A. Staeheli, "Permitting Protest: Constructing – and Dismantling – the Geography of Dissent in the United States," *International Journal of Urban and Regional Research* 29 (2005), 796-813. (Blackwell Publishing).

in particular places while allowing the same activities elsewhere. Our chief example will be how cities (in this case Washington, DC, which might be called the "protest capital" of the United States) have adopted and developed permit systems as a means of regulating protest. Demonstration planners must apply for permits from city (or other) police departments, and these permits specify where protests can happen, how long they can last, and special restrictions on behavior—so-called *time, place, and manner restrictions*. By closing key sites to protest, we will argue, permit systems can have the effect of silencing dissident voices, while at the same time giving the appearance that public space is politically inclusive. Protest permits are the means by which the "right to exclude" in public space is effected; they are a means of determining what kinds of people have voice, how that voice is to be raised (or not raised), and presumably to what effect. This right to exclude, in turn, shapes just who can appear as part of the public, and whose voices can be heard as part of the polity. *Locating* the public, by designating the spaces in which and the conditions under which it can meet, is a primary means of *defining* the public.

LAW AND THE POLITICS OF AND IN PUBLIC SPACE

Dissent in the Liberal State

The history of mid- and late-twentieth-century policing of protest in liberal democracies such as the United States can be told as a progressive history of the incorporation and normalization of public dissent *within* the liberal state (Smolla 1992; Stone et al. 1992). As Gary Marx (1998, 254) has argued, in the wake of the upheavals of the 1960s, "there has been a leavening of police response to protest, regardless of the country. Rather than taking an adversarial and intentionally violent approach, police seek a more neutral stance. The policing of protest has become more normalized." This is in part because protest itself has become more normalized. In the United States, several commissions examined urban unrest and protest in the wake of the riots of 1964 through 1969 and the campus unrest and antiwar demonstrations of 1964 through 1973. The findings of these commissions, together with police forces who increasingly questioned the efficacy of repressive policing of protest, led to a system of what McPhail et al. (1998, 50) call the "negotiated management" of protests. In this negotiated system, permits, meetings between police and protesters, and the intervention of judges and other authorities allows for what could be called a co-production of protest between the state and protesters. That is, "to a greater extent than ever before, police view their job as managing, rather than repressing, protest, protecting the right to demonstrate and guaranteeing (even to those whose views they find intolerable) due process of law" (Marx 1998, 254).* During the 1970s, 1980s, and for much of the 1990s, protest was brought more and more under the aegis of the state itself, and the policing function concomitantly evolved from repression (or pacification though "escalated force" [McPhail et al. 1998, 50]) to one of management.

Such a managed incorporation of dissent has been one means for liberal democracies to draw the line more firmly between dissent that is productive (that is, dissent that allows for a range of voices to be heard, decisions to be evaluated, and mistakes corrected) and dissent that is, at least potentially, destructive to the state. Shifts in policing, in other words, have been a means not just to incorporate dissent, but also to actively shape it. Indeed, shaping dissent, rather than just quashing it outright, has been one of the main historical tasks of the liberal state (Gramsci 1971). In this project, traditional public space—the "people's property" in seemingly the most basic sense—has assumed a central role, as material public spaces have become venues for shaping dissent and constructing alternative publics.

Negotiated management of public protest is, of course, shaped by law: dissent in liberal democracies is constituted by a legal geography that establishes the bounds of the acceptable for both protesters and the police. "Law," Blomley (2000b, 436) has written, "is not confined to the statute book or the law courts but [can be] seen as a much more pervasive (and important) medium through which society and politics are lived, whether in constrained or libratory ways." Law is thus a codification—a set of rules that underlie behavior, including the behavior of the police charged with enforcing the law. And law is a powerful force for normalization in that we all internalize it and mold our behavior accordingly (even if in conscious defiance of the law). Whether based in common law or statutory legislation, law serves to define the boundaries of social relations and confer authority to the state and its agents.

Law, therefore, is a significant site of social struggle and as such is complex. Among other ways, it is geographically complex because it is jurisdictionally complex, with nested and sometimes overlapping hierarchies of territorial authority (cf. Blomley and Clark 1990; Blomley et al. 2001). In Washington, DC this is especially the case as the federal

---

* Of course, and as we shall discuss, much depends on the definition of "management." Even before the terrorist attacks of September 11, 2001, local and federal police forces had sent undercover agents to infiltrate various protest groups in order to secure intelligence in advance of both small and large demonstrations. Some officials argue that this is nothing more than a tool of protest management.

government plays a larger jurisdictional role than elsewhere (about 25% of the land is controlled by the National Park Service) and because the city is made up of a patchwork of public property controlled by different federal and local authorities, each accountable to different political constituencies and bound by different legal rules and cultural norms.

The geography of dissent in Washington, as elsewhere, is framed by such jurisdictional geographies. But it is also framed through legal categorizations of space, or more accurately of property, with the deeds to various public spaces held by a range of local and federal authorities. Law is sensitive to such variations in property (Blomley 2004b). What is legal on one kind of property might be illegal next door. Privately held property is subject to one set of legal rules and determinations; public property another. But the law also makes distinctions among different kinds of private and different kinds of public property. The geography of rights—rights to speech and political assembly, which are the cornerstone of dissent's incorporation into liberal democracy—is a function of this spatial sensibility of law, and of how both police and demonstrators interpret the nuances of geography.* To understand how, it is worth briefly reviewing the development of a liberal regime of protest in the United States, especially as it has developed in relation to First Amendment law.

Permitting Dissent

Before the First World War, the United States evidenced little interest in First Amendment jurisprudence. Policing dissent was left largely to the states and localities, and it was often violent (Preston 1963; Marx 1988). If the federal government got involved, it was usually in the form of authorizing the National Guard to break strikes and disperse rallies. During the First World War, however, the Supreme Court decided four landmark First Amendment cases, three concerning speech critical of the newly instituted draft, and one concerning protest against U.S. intervention in Russia after the revolution. It upheld the conviction of the dissidents in each case, but in doing so began to lay the foundation for a theory of free speech that incorporated rather than suppressed

---

* In the U.S. context, rights are predominantly understood as individual rights. Even though the First Amendment to the Constitution asserts that the rights of "the people" to free speech and assembly shall not be abridged, this is almost always interpreted in terms of rights held by individual persons (even though those "persons" are sometimes corporate bodies). In Constitutional law, therefore, the people are generally conceived of as a collection of persons, not as a collective. There are important implications in this for how *the* or *a* public can and cannot form, implications that will be developed throughout the book.

dissident speech.* By 1925, the court had furthered the incorporation process by finding that the First Amendment limited the actions of states and localities, as well as the federal government. And in 1939, a deeply divided Supreme Court finally declared that "the people" really did have a right to assemble in public spaces for political purposes (*Hague v. CIO* 1939).

The *Hague* decision introduced a set of practical considerations related to how public dissent was to be incorporated into the American state. The Court held that "wherever the title of the streets and parks may rest, they have immemorially been held in trust for the use of the public and, time out of mind, have been used for the purposes of assembly, communicating thoughts between citizens, and discussing public questions" (*Hague v. CIO* 1939, 515). Importantly, the Court held that "the use of the streets and parks for the communication of views on national questions may be regulated in the interests of all . . . [but] it must not, in the guise of regulation, be abridged, or denied" (515). Indeed, regulation was important because speech and assembly in public space, according to the Court, needed to be "exercised in subordination to the general comfort and convenience . . . peace and good order" (515). The practical issues raised by this ruling concerned how to allow for the use of government-owned streets and parks for political assembly while also subordinating that use to the demands of comfort, peace, and order. In other words, the specific geography of protest was clearly at stake.

To define this geography, the Court developed, and continues to refine, what is known as "public forum doctrine." Public forum doctrine holds that in "traditional public forums" (the streets and parks of the *Hague* decision) speech and assembly cannot be banned outright, but its "time, place, and manner" can be regulated, just so long as regulations are content-neutral and serve a compelling state interest. However, not all public property is a traditional public forum. Most public property, such as military bases, the inside of government office buildings, school grounds, large tracts of national forest or Bureau of Land Management (BLM) lands, and dams and the reservoirs behind them, are not public forums at all. Free speech and assembly rights simply do not obtain on this kind of public property, and their deed holders (branches of the military, the BLM, the Corps of Engineers) may choose to allow or disallow public assembly and speech as they see fit. Still other public properties are considered to be "dedicated public forums." These properties have not been held or used from "time immemorial" for political

---

* For a geographical review of these cases, see Mitchell (2003a).

activities, but nonetheless a government agency has specifically allowed speech and assembly. Free speech areas on public university campuses are the classic example of dedicated public forums. Regulation of dedicated public forums is bound by the same rules as apply to traditional public forums, but government agencies may revoke the dedication and ban First Amendment activities altogether, just so long as it does so for all groups and in a content-neutral way.

Public forum doctrine thus creates a broad legal context for regulating peoples' political activities on public property. This point is key: while the traditional public forum of the streets and parks is held in trust for *the people*, it can be regulated to serve the interest of *the state*. Within this context, a massive amount of legal wrangling occurs. Much of this wrangling concerns the minutiae of time, place, and manner restrictions in traditional and dedicated public forums. Since the 1940s, the development of public forum doctrine has led local government and police agencies to develop intricate local rules governing protest, making some sites off limits (removing dedications), encouraging the use of others, and setting limits on size, timing, noise, and so forth. The broad context of public forum doctrine has legitimated the construction of an intricate geography of rights in American cities. And, in particular, it has encouraged the development of protest permit systems in almost every city in the United States as a means to enforce that intricate geography.

The near universal acceptance of such permit systems is ironic. In *Hague v. CIO*, the Court struck down just such a system, finding it to be a form of prior restraint on expressive activity. "Prior restraint" refers to the government suppression of communication before it has a chance to take place. In 1931, the Supreme Court developed a "prior restraint doctrine" (*Near v. Minnesota* 1931) that holds that "there is a heavy presumption against" the constitutional validity of any prior restraint (*Bantam Books, Inc. v Sullivan* 1963, 70). This means that the validity of any prior restraint practice cannot be assumed by lawmakers or courts; validity has to be proven. Even as it has recognized protest permit systems as a kind of prior restraint, however, the Court has nonetheless encouraged their development as a means of balancing the right to protest against the need for comfort, order, and convenience. Only two years after the *Hague* decision found Jersey City's permit system to be a form of prior restraint, the Supreme Court upheld the constitutionality of a New Hampshire law that required a license for any "parade or procession on a public street" (*Cox v. New Hampshire* 1941, 570–571). The Court held that parades were different from rallies and could be regulated both to maintain "good order" and to keep streets free for traffic. But if the court here seemed to limit the validity of permit systems to parades in public streets, a dozen years later it made it clear that narrowly tailored permit systems could be used in other spaces—like parks—and for stationary as well as moving protests (*Poulos v. New Hampshire* 1953; see also *Cantwell v. Connecticut* 1940; *Shuttlesworth v. Birmingham* 1969).

Any regulation of speech and assembly—whether through permit, law, or injunction—the Court has held, must be "justified without reference to the content of the regulated speech, [be] narrowly tailored to serve a significant governmental interest, [and] leave open ample alternative channels for communication of the information" (*Clark v. Community for Creative Non-Violence* 1984, 293). This three-part test of constitutionality gives great scope to governments to limit and even deny the right to protest. At the very least, the adoption of permit systems means that it is now simply illegal in the United States to have a protest of any significant size without first getting the state's approval. "Free speech" is really "permitted speech;" prior restraint is alive and well in America. But, significantly, prior restraint is exercised primarily *geographically*; by defining the location and the permitted activities at a demonstration, march, or protest, states attempt to define publics and how they will appear and behave.

Policing Dissent

Prior restraint, in other words, is the means by which protest—dissent—is accommodated and incorporated into liberal democracy. Laws, injunctions, and permit systems provide the set of ground rules for protesters and police alike, and in the process they tend to normalize, and therefore shape, protest activity. Indeed, with such legal frameworks at hand, acts of civil disobedience are often now highly scripted: protesters agree with police in advance how specific aspects of public forum law will be broken, by whom, and with what penalties. Much of the groundwork for protest takes place in pre-protest meetings involving protest organizers, police representatives, and lawyers for both sides, as they wrangle over the ways that permits will be written, and even the plans to exceed or ignore aspects of the permit.

Even so, such bureaucratic pre-protest planning is never complete, and sometimes fails. The police in Seattle in 1999 during the World Trade Organization meeting, for example, were caught off guard, and a radically *different* kind of public from what city officials anticipated quickly appeared. While permits had been issued for dozens of protests and parades around the city, some 20,000 unpermitted protesters gathered downtown and overwhelmed a police force that was able to do little to keep traffic flowing, escort WTO delegates to the conference, or deter acts of violence against property. The mass mobilizations against the International Monetary Fund (IMF), World Bank, World Economic Forum, and the G8 and European Union (EU) summits that quickly followed—in part because of the shock of recognition so many people felt in seeing the radical public that appeared on the streets of Seattle—have encouraged police in the United States and elsewhere to supplement their pre-protest permit systems and negotiations both with "emergency rules" (banning protest altogether in some spaces) and with undercover infiltration of activist group meetings (Montgomery and Santana 2000b; Phillips and Trofimov 2001; Mendoza 2003; Archibold 2004). In 2001, at the request of then attorney general John Ashcroft and numerous police agencies, federal courts relaxed restrictions on police spying on domestic political organizations. These actions predate September 11, 2001, but have intensified since then.

Restrictions on police spying in the United States stem from public anger over FBI (Federal Bureau of Investigation) and local police infiltration of progressive and radical groups during the Civil Rights and Vietnam eras (Cole and Dempsey 2002). They stand as stark recognition that "the people" and "the state" are never totally coterminous. Yet in the wake of September 11, many can now be heard arguing that such restrictions are a hindrance in the prosecution of the war on terror (Powell 2002). As critics like Jim Redden (2000) argue, however, the current debate over police spying represents a form of historical amnesia. As Redden (2000) details, restrictions on spying implemented across the United States in the 1970s frequently led to a sort of privatization of spying rather than its elimination. Police turned to private security and detective firms to gain intelligence on political organizations; such private actors tend not to be bound by the same strictures as public police agencies. Police argued that they needed to turn to private intelligence, or to expand police infiltration of activist groups after Seattle to better anticipate how protests might develop (and thus guarantee good order and the general convenience of "the public") and to "protect themselves" from violence and charges of police abuse (Mendoza 2003, A10). In Washington, DC, however, such police infiltration of protest groups has led to a number of lawsuits by activists seeking to curb such actions. Activists argue that exceeding the bounds placed on protest by the normalization of dissent—the sorts of excess that the police hope to guard against with their reinvigorated spying—is essential to the extension of democracy (Monbiot 2004). The geography of dissent is shaped by this kind of legal wrangling, too. But the question remains: What effect does all this—the prior restraint of permit systems and the infiltration of some protest groups by state actors, and even private actors working on behalf of the state—have on the politics of and in public space?

FINE PARSINGS OF GEOGRAPHY: NEGOTIATING WASHINGTON'S PROTEST LANDSCAPE

Both the American Civil Liberties Union (ACLU 1982) and the National Lawyer's Guild (NLG n.d.) publish guides to protest in Washington, DC. The ACLU guide explains:

> The District of Columbia is unique in that demonstrations are governed by a variety of rules depending on whether the location is under the control of the D.C. Government, the National Park Service, the Capitol Police, or some other federal agency. The location will also control who issues the permit, if one is necessary, who will provide police protections, whose set of rules control, and where you are taken if arrested. (ACLU 1982, 4)

The National Lawyer's Guild picks up on this last point and adds, "there is a difference between what you are legally entitled to do in a theoretical sense, and what the police on a particular occasion are going to let you do" (NLG n.d., 2). As the ACLU indicates, what you are entitled to do, at least in a theoretical sense, is logistically complex (see also McCarthy et al. 1996). The ACLU guide thus seeks to demystify the process by which protests are regulated and policed. Its guide explains the rules that govern public space in the city's different jurisdictions, when permits are required, where they can be obtained, and how to work within the system to exercise speech and protest rights. Though out of date, the ACLU's pamphlet tries to make the ground rules for demonstrations clear, so that at least as far as ordinary protest goes, the Washington "system" can remain (as Art Spitzer*, a representative of the ACLU, put it in an interview) "pretty well-oiled." The National Lawyer's Guild, by contrast, helps clarify what will happen if things get a bit sticky. It explains the logistics of policing in Washington and advises readers about the various charges that could be pressed against demonstrators, how the police might behave at different kinds of protests,

---

* Respondents were offered the right to maintain confidentiality for themselves and their organization. When names are used in this chapter and the rest of the book, it means that respondents waived that right. When they chose to maintain their confidentiality, we did not use their names or identify their organization. See also the methodological appendix for the book.

what the arrest procedure will likely entail, the options demonstrators might have for posting bail, the means to secure legal representation and contest charges, and so forth.

Taken together, the two guides present a good overview of the protest landscape in Washington, but it is a landscape that is constantly shifting. "Going back to the '60s and '70s and '80s there was a lot more litigation than we have had recently," Spitzer says. This litigation concerned everything from restrictions on the size of demonstrations allowed in Lafayette Park (across the street from the White House), to whether protesters demonstrating against homeless policies could sleep in that same park as a means of dramatizing their point, to whether it was permissible to hand out leaflets on the grounds of the Capitol. And while time, place, and manner restrictions may work smoothly in Washington, it is also the case, according to Spitzer, that rules and restrictions on protest in public space "never decrease. . . . For example, if there is all of a sudden a fear of terrorism during the Persian Gulf War [of 1991], they'll put new restrictions in place. Well, they never turn out to be temporary restrictions." Negotiating these restrictions can be a challenge. Special rules govern protest at the Supreme Court, a different set governs the Capitol grounds. With dedicated public forums and non-public forums incorporated into nearly every federal building and property in the city, the ACLU has found it necessary to engage in what the ACLU's Fritz Mulhauser calls "very fine parsings of the geography" of the city.

Although the ACLU describes the protest system in Washington as "well-oiled," it is clear that it is a system of many moving and complex parts. As Mulhauser notes:

> This city is very complicated, because of overlapping and cooperative jurisdictions. For someone who has a benign goal—the socialists want to put up a table with literature on a street corner for two hours some afternoon or somebody wants to hand out leaflets in one place or at one time—it is not a simple question. Or it is a simple question but it is not easy to find the answer to [it].*

---

* We know firsthand that getting answers to where protest is possible, and who regulates it, can be difficult. Repeated phone calls to the Supreme Court to find someone to interview about protest on and around its grounds (the Court has distinct rules and a separate police force from the rest of the government) finally led a Court phone receptionist to declare in exasperation: "I guess no one around here knows anything about protest!" Calls to the Secret Service were finally returned by a spokesman who blithely declared that the Service never involves itself in planning for protests.

The former commander in charge of protest policing for the Washington, DC Metropolitan Police says that for most demonstrations and other expressive activity, things really are not so complicated: "It's a very easy process," he told us. For parades, "It's a one-page application for a . . . permit." The permit has to be requested fourteen days in advance and "If a parade is for an issue under the First Amendment . . . we just do the safe flow of traffic to get you from one point to another." Large rallies that might block a sidewalk, disrupt traffic, or block an entrance have a similar application process. Other sorts of demonstrations—picketing, leafleting, street speaking—do not require a permit if they occur on DC-controlled property. But much of the property in DC is not DC-controlled. The National Park Service controls about 25 percent of the land, and there are dozens of other jurisdictions, each with its own rules, and sometimes with its own police force.

On National Park property (most of the parks and monuments in the city, as well as the Mall), any protest activity by more than 25 people requires a permit. Permits for protests larger than the limits set for Lafayette Park (3,000 people) or for the sidewalk in front of the White House (750 people) must be applied for 10 days in advance. All others can be applied for as late as 48 hours in advance according to the ACLU and representatives of the National Park Service. If the Park Service does not act on a permit within 24 hours, it is considered presumptively granted; the Park Service may, however, withdraw approved applications if done in a content-neutral way (ACLU 1982, 7). On National Park property, a whole section of the Code of Federal Regulations (36 CFR 7.96), extending to some twelve pages, regulates the location of protests and the kinds of allowable actions, such as standing and moving. The rules are intricate, in part because many of them are the result of lawsuits.

On both DC and National Park property, a distinction is drawn between a demonstration and a special event. According to the commander of the Metro Police (as the DC city police are called), a "special event is usually a sponsored event, a celebration of some sort, or a parade of some sort that's not a First Amendment issue." Organizers of special events have to pay for logistics and special policing, but organizers of demonstrations do not, and the line between the two is often difficult to draw. But it is an important line since it determines who will bear the cost of political expression. The line becomes especially difficult to draw when demonstration organizers draw on celebrities to help boost crowds; according to the ACLU's Art Spitzer: "If you get Stevie Wonder up there . . . you're going to get another 30,000 young people from DC coming to your demonstration, maybe more than that. . . . And yet the Park Service would say, 'Well, you've got Stevie Wonder and you've got this other group and you've got this other group, you're putting on a concert. You're not doing a demonstration.'" Costs associated with both demonstrations and special events can be steep, and so a representative of the National Park Service joked, "As far as we're concerned, they're all special events!"

To parse the fine geography of the District and to assure that the complex regulatory fabric woven around protest and special events is properly understood and negotiated, both Park and Metro Police try to work closely with event and demonstration organizers. According to a former commander, the Metro Police has:

> a squad that does nothing but plan presidential movement, digni-
> tary routes, special events, and demonstrations. They meet with
> organizers. If it's large scale, involving multiple jurisdictions,
> there's a joint meeting with the Capitol Police and the Park Police
> to meet with the organizers and plan out the march or demonstra-
> tion or whatever it is. A lot of times you are going from Capitol
> territory to Park territory, and so all these agencies work together.
> We can't issue a permit to go on the Capitol territory unless we
> know Capitol is going to issue a permit. So there's lots of coordi-
> nation among the agencies.

According to a Park Police commander, the Park Police meets with demonstrators and event organizers "when they apply for their permits. . . . If it's a group we think we might have problems with, we might have a lawyer there . . . to deal with them. . . . [W]e try to work it out as best as possible for the convenience and safety of all." Demonstration and event organizers "basically tell us what they want to do, and we'll explain what the law allows them to do. And there's a lot of compro-mise. Certain things we just can't allow. Certain things maybe we can allow, and we end up helping them plan a lot."

The jurisdictional and regulatory complexity of Washington has led to the professionalization of protest organizing. Like wedding or con-vention coordinators, professional consultants are now often employed to negotiate the permit process, meet with police, arrange for stages and a sound system, and coordinate preparation and clean up—"everything that they need within the confines and laws of the District of Columbia to perform [an] event," according to one event coordinator. A lot of groundwork thus goes into many of the protests, demonstrations, and special events in Washington. Protest appears to be fully regularized, fully incorporated into the business of the nation-state. Indeed the very complexity of protest organizing in DC has been a significant factor in the drive to routinize—and normalize—it.

An additional incentive toward routinization has been a desire, both on the part of police and protesters in the wake of the violent riots and demonstrations of the 1960s, to find ways to minimize the threat of violence (Marx 1998, 253). A National Park Police captain observes that routine helps protesters better understand how to make their protest known and visible without undue disturbance to themselves or others:

> They want to know, "What do I have to do to get arrested and minimize the impact against the police or against property?" and what's going to happen to them. So we explain it to them. Like in front of the White House, if you sit down in the center portion holding a sign, that's illegal, you'll be arrested. There are times where they'll time their arrest to make sure it gets on the evening news and stuff like that. And we will explain to them exactly what steps they can take to minimize the disruption in their lives. If they have a valid ID, and they don't have any contraband on them, and they cooperate fully, you can probably be processed pretty quickly.

The Metro Police commander also speaks of the symbolic importance of arrest:

> A lot of people come to us and say, "Well we want to march, we want to demonstrate, and we want fifty people to be arrested." And we will work that out beforehand, and what the charge is going to be, and where they're going to be taken so they can have their legal people there and ready to post bail and get them out.

Standard protest logistics and organization, to summarize, now often include consultation with police, negotiation over who will get arrested (and for what), and compromise over where protests and parades can occur, what sorts of signs can be carried, what kinds of costumes can be worn, and so forth.

For the police, this planning also includes finding out such things as the number of buses chartered in distant cities (to gauge protest size), and contacting police in other cities to gain intelligence about political organizations coming to town for demonstrations. It may also involve undercover work or drawing on informants to learn about those parts of protest plans that organizers do not divulge directly to the police. And police agencies expend considerable resources to learn from protests elsewhere. The former commander of the Metro Police, for example, recalls: "I went to Prague and Switzerland when they had their protests there, and we sent people to Seattle. I went to Los Angeles when the Democratic Convention was out there. We just sent somebody to

Quebec. . . . So we try to follow them [the protesters] around to see, because it [the nature of protest] changes."

The routinization of protest in Washington, however, has come at a cost. ACLU lawyers believe that protests have become so routinized as to be prosaic. They argue, "With so many demonstrations in Washington, if you really want to be on the front page, you almost have to break the rules, unless you've got 100,000 people coming." The Metro Police commander concurs: "Washington is so sanitized with demonstrations, I don't think people pay them any mind anymore. I mean they're just everyday." Perhaps protest politics have run their course. "My wife has been involved in the women's movement for thirty years," an ACLU lawyer says. "And now, any time someone would come to her and say, 'We're going to do a march,' she would say, 'That's just not an effective way in this day and age to make any points. Think of a better idea.'"* The incorporation of public dissent into the liberal state has perhaps led to its neutralization. In many cases, police have greater expertise and knowledge of the advantages and disadvantages of protest sites than do protest organizers; holding this expertise sometimes allows police to contain protest or to minimize its impacts without organizers understanding the implications of site decisions (Fillieule and Jobard 1998).

Some activists still hold to the importance of public protest, but they have begun to reject the permit system: "Look, I'm always going to challenge the permits. . . . So many of the Constitutional rights disappear," said one activist. Indeed, the former Metro Police commander worried that "demonstrations are changing because some of them are becoming more volatile, more uncooperative with the police. This is sort of sad for us, because we have always prided ourselves on working with them and letting them express themselves."

If the police see a rise in violence as a consequence of failing to abide by the protest system in Washington, some activists see matters differently. As Adam Eidinger, who has been in numerous protests in the city recalled:

> I remember this summit meeting, and the police show up and they start going on television and telling people if they go out in the streets they might get beat up. . . . And really the violence stems a lot from how the police view our right to public space. They are losing in the courts. They cannot justify what they have been doing against us, because it's been proven to be their real crimes. There are very, very few convictions [of protesters].

---

* For a fuller analysis of the changing efficacy of protest in the media age, see D'Arcus (2005).

The routinization and incorporation of public dissent through the permit system was perhaps most thoroughly tested in the large demonstrations that rocked the city in the wake of the Seattle protests of 1999. The experience in these protests, which are the subject of the next section, suggest that perhaps dissent is not as easily incorporated through the "very fine parsings of the geography" as many would hope. It may be the case that the form of "soft" prior restraint embodied in the permit system has reached the end of its usefulness, and that new geographical strategies of control are required, strategies that redefine the meaning of public space, its uses, and the conditions under which people can be in it.

PROTEST BEYOND THE PERMITTED

The National Park Service has long designated certain events in the capital as "National Celebration Events" (ACLU 1982, 7). During such events—the Cherry Blossom Festival, Independence Day celebrations, presidential inaugurations—the space designated for the event is off limits to protest, but protest is permitted nearby. In January 2001, however, for the first time the Secret Service designated George W. Bush's inauguration not a National Celebration Event, but as a National Special Security Event. This terminological switch meant that the Secret Service was in overall charge of security arrangements. Because of the contested 2000 presidential election and the judicial rather than electoral decision that installed the president, and because of the general upswing of protest nation- and worldwide, massive protests were expected along the route of the inaugural parade. The Secret Service and the DC-area police agencies sought to "ensure that the swearing-in of the next president, the parade, and other inaugural events [were] not 'tainted by' protesters" (Santana 2000, B1).

The Secret Service and police were particularly concerned because undercover operations had indicated that "[s]ome likely demonstrators . . . [were] veterans of the violent 1999 protest in Seattle. Others were among the 1,300 arrested in Washington in April" at the 2000 IMF/World Bank meeting demonstrations (Santana 2001, B1). Because of these concerns, much of the Mall was surrounded by a two-meter-high metal fence and entirely closed on inauguration day; six checkpoints complete with metal detectors were established for the few thousand ticketed guests allowed into the parade viewing area in front of the White House; police were stationed every two meters along the parade route with hundreds of other police in riot gear posted nearby; subway stations were closed; Secret Service snipers were deployed on rooftops; and several dozen buses stood ready to transport arrestees to mass arraignment sites away from the inauguration area (Rosenbaum 2001; Santana 2001; Wildermuth 2001).

The National Park Service argued that the intense security represented a general ratcheting-up of security over the previous four years. But against this ratcheting-up, police planners had to contend with a 1997 court ruling that said protesters could not be barred entirely from inaugural parade routes (Davis 1997; Aigen 1998). In anticipation of President Bill Clinton's second inauguration, Secret Service and police announced that all protest would be banned from anywhere near the parade route. In response to a suit contesting this, the DC District Court ruled that permitting Clinton's supporters to hold signs at the parade, but not detractors, constituted a content-based restriction on speech. The court also held, importantly, that the National Park Service's standard practice of making *itself* the permit-tee for the parade route (and thereby blocking other users because of a first-come, first-served rule) was impermissible. Demonstration at the 1997 inauguration had to be accommodated; so too in 2001, security concerns notwithstanding.

In response, the Park Service and the city granted a blanket permit for the entire parade route to the Presidential Inauguration Committee (PIC), and then granted protest groups permits only for places agreeable to the PIC's parade planners.* While individual protesters and very small groups had to be allowed access to the parade route, larger protests were sequestered in official "protest zones" approved by the PIC. As it turns out, individual protesters made a strong showing and jeers were often louder than cheers for the president (Rosenbaum 2001, 1.17). The protests throughout the day were peaceful, a result that police attributed to their stepped-up security, but that protesters said only indicated how unnecessary the extra security was (Barker and Montgomery 2001).

Despite the few arrests, the Partnership for Civil Justice and the National Lawyer's Guild filed suit in March 2001, charging that police had violated a court order requiring protesters and supporters to be treated equally along the parade route, and that control of at least one of the checkpoints was handed over to a representative of the PIC, who then blocked a group of protesters from reaching a plaza for which

---

* This strategy had been successfully field tested at the 2000 Republican National Convention in Philadelphia the previous August. Its constitutional legitimacy is dubious at best; see Janiszewski (2002).

they had a protest permit. Elsewhere, the suit claimed, police simply detained more than one hundred protesters in a preemptive action, and did not allow them to reach the parade route. In addition, the suit provides evidence that police *agent provacateurs* were working among the protest groups seeking to spark violence (Montgomery 2001).

Whatever the validity of these claims (and many have been substantiated as the case has made its way through the courts), they make clear the limits of the permit system to incorporate dissent. Indeed, in September 2004, in response to a Partnership for Civil Justice request for a preliminary injunction, the District of Columbia announced it would no longer arrest people for parading without a permit,* recognizing, perhaps, that many aspects of the permit system had long been untenable. Already by April 2000, at the protests of the IMF/World Bank meetings, the police themselves seemed to acknowledge that the routinization of protest evidenced in the general acceptance of protest permit systems was inadequate. Engaging in what the *New York Times* called "a pre-emptive show of force" (Kifner 2000), Metro police and other forces in Washington worked assiduously before and during the meetings "to ensure," as the *Washington Post* put it, "that the world doesn't change too dramatically on the streets of Washington" (Montgomery and Santana 2000a, A1). Metro Police monitored the Internet sites of protest groups, infiltrated meetings, and showed up at key activists' homes just as they were getting ready to leave to hang posters announcing demonstration events (Montgomery and Santana 2000b).

Two days before the IMF/World Bank meetings began, police arrested seven people for possessing "instruments of crime" —PVC pipe, duct tape, gas masks, and heavy chains (Goldstein and Santana 2000, B1). The crime for which they were instruments was presumably engaging in acts of civil disobedience. Activists complained the arrests were "pretextual" and "preemptive," concerns that seemed to be borne out the morning before the meetings, when police raided a warehouse "convergence center." Claiming suspected fire code violations, a police Emergency Response Team, assisted by the Secret Service (an organization not usually involved in fire code infractions) and accompanied by a police helicopter hovering overhead (likewise rather extraordinary for a building inspection) ordered protesters out, sealed the building, and searched it thoroughly, finding "numerous" violations. They declared the warehouse indefinitely closed (Hendren 2000; Kifner 2000; Kornblut

---

* See the Partnership for Civil Justice website, http://www.justiceonline.org/site/News2?page =NewsArticle&id=5093&news_iv_ctrl=1003 (accessed 22 May 2006).

2000). Among other things, police claimed in the press to have found a Molotov cocktail; it later turned out to be an unfinished soda.

Later that day, police made a "display of force" (Kornblut 2000, A31), as "a line of police officers in riot helmets stamped their feet rhythmically and pumped their nightsticks in front of their chests and . . . moved in on . . . protesters a few blocks away from the [World B]ank headquarters" (Kifner 2000, 1.6). Protesters had been marching down sidewalks, with police escorts, causing "little serious disruption on the city's streets" (1.6). Though Executive Assistant Police Chief Terrance Gainer had earlier declared, "if [protesters] exercise peaceful demonstrations in areas that don't block vehicle or pedestrian traffic, then everything is fine" (1.6), police decided to block the roadway in front of the marchers and then surround them on all sides, refusing to allow them to either continue their march or to leave. Protesters and bystanders pleaded and chanted to be let go, but police refused. Eventually they arrested some 600 of them on charges of failing to disperse (!) and parading without a permit (Kifner 2000; Kornblut 2000). Lengthy arraignment procedures kept protesters locked up through much of the following day, the main day of the protests (Kifner 2000). Washington's mayor made no bones about why the arrests were made: they were a "matter of prudence" (quoted in Kifner and Sanger 2000, A1); they were "preventative" and "proactive" (quoted in *Fifty Years is Enough et al. v District of Columbia et al.* n.d.). While it may be true, in other words, that the streets, from "time immemorial" have been used for communicating ideas, police seemed determined that any communication was going to be on *their* terms.

This did not go uncontested. Police Chief Charles Ramsey praised the preemptive arrests, the accompanying creation of a no-protest zone around the World Bank and IMF headquarters, and the performance of law enforcement officers because "[w]e didn't lose the city, so as far as I am concerned, it was worth it." Activists, however, filed a class-action suit, claiming the city police "success" was bought at the cost of violating the First, Fourth, and Fifth Amendment rights of peaceful protesters. In particular, the plaintiffs asserted:

> Defendants planned and implemented a strategy to disrupt the plaintiffs' exercise of First Amendment rights to speak and assemble. In furtherance of this unconstitutional disruption strategy, defendants prevented protesters from demonstrating near IMF-World Bank meetings; preemptively arrested hundreds of persons, including plaintiffs, journalists and tourists, without cause; . . . closed plaintiffs' Convergence Center on pretext;

seized, confiscated, and refused to release thousands of pieces of plaintiffs' political literature, signs, banners, puppets and related property and items; harassed and intimidated plaintiffs; deployed unwarranted "pop-up police lines"; deployed an *agent provocateur*; disseminated misinformation falsely portraying plaintiffs as violent; and used excessive force and brutality against non-violent protesters (*Fifty Years is Enough et al. v. District of Columbia et al.*, n.d., Introduction para. 2).

In addition to asserting that the protest exclusion zone was overly large, was not narrowly tailored to serve a legitimate state interest, and did not leave open adequate alternative channels of communication (all parts of the test for legitimate time, place, and manner restrictions), the suit alleged that pop-up police lines "well outside the 'no-protest zone'" would converge on and trap peaceful protesters, who would then be arrested. "The use of police lines, arbitrarily established and at times mobile, vaguely, arbitrarily and capriciously created no-protest zones on public sidewalks" (*Fifty Years is Enough et al. v. District of Columbia et al.*, n.d. "Deployment" para. 10).

Such policing suggests that, from the police perspective at least, prior restraint exercised through the permit system was insufficient for maintaining public order during large demonstrations. It also throws into question the standard assumption in some of the academic literature that police are now more interested in managing dissent than repressing it. A more accurate assessment would be that repression is now one tool among many for controlling public space, and determining how it is populated, and under what conditions. A return to an "escalation of force strategy" (McPhail et al. 1998) is now perhaps a crucial adjunct to the negotiated management strategy that seemed to mark the late 1970s and 1980s.

CONCLUSION: PUBLIC SPACE AND THE GEOGRAPHY OF DISSENT AFTER SEPTEMBER 11

Large-scale protest is, of course, still possible, as the immigrant rights demonstrations of 2006 made clear. Even in the immediate wake of the terrorist attacks of September 11, 2001, huge demonstrations were not out of the question. In mid-April 2002, for example, as many as 100,000 people rallied on the grounds of the Capitol in support of Israel, its policies in Palestine, and the Bush administration's support for these policies. If the police were present at this rally, they kept well to the background (Schemo 2002).

Yet only a week later, citing security concerns, police activated a network of 1,000 cameras in downtown Washington to keep tabs on protesters gathering in advance of the 2002 IMF/World Bank meetings. Fearing First Amendment problems, camera operators were ordered not to focus on fliers or handbills protesters might be carrying (Hsu 2002). While anti-capitalism was still high on the agenda for the protests, much of the protest weekend was given over to rallies against Israel's stepped-up occupation of Palestine, the United States' continued paramilitary presence in Colombia, and the continued operations of the School of Americas (a training ground for Latin American military officers). While this time the city and National Park Service did not erect a fence around key sites and create official no-protest zones, police did delay issuing a parade permit to anti-capitalist activists for several weeks, finally approving a protest permit quite different from the one for which protest organizers had applied. Organizers wanted to march in front of the headquarters of global corporations such as Coca-Cola, Monsanto, and Citibank. Rather than just attending to the safe flow of traffic, as our police interviewees said was standard practice, police denied protesters a permit for their chosen route. Instead, they issued a permit for protesters to gather outside the IMF and World Bank buildings before marching along a route to Freedom Plaza that steered clear of the multinationals' headquarters. At Freedom Plaza, the anti-capitalist protesters would be allowed to join up with protesters concerned about other issues (Fernandez and Dvorak 2002). Even though there was no credible evidence that the anti-capitalist protesters who had applied for permission to parade near corporate headquarters had ever engaged in violent or destructive behavior (the only legitimate reason for denying a permit [ACLU 1982, 5]), police worried that splinter groups might do so this time (Fernandez and Dvorak 2002).

During the protests themselves, "an overwhelming police presence" was visible on the streets (Morello and Fernandez 2002, B1). The Partnership for Civil Justice among others complained that this presence was intimidating. In addition to the uniformed officers on the streets, police infiltrated protest groups and masqueraded as protesters during the marches (Dvorak 2002). In essence, the police created a constant, moving barrier between protest groups and the rest of the city, hemming protesters in on all sides and keeping them moving along routes the police themselves preferred.

In advance of the semiannual IMF-World Bank meetings the following September, police returned to a strategy of fencing off the World Bank and IMF sites, establishing a four-block no-go zone that was expandable as necessary (Fernandez and Fahrenthold 2002a). Officials created a 3,000-member police force with recruits from as far away as Chicago, outnumbering protesters about three to one, and using their numbers to engage in a series of preemptive arrests on the first day of the protest (Fernandez and Fahrenthold 2002b). Once again, police forced protesters into a plaza, refused to let them leave, and arrested about 600 for failure to obey police orders to disperse. In fact, an internal police report leaked to the press in March 2003 admitted that the order to disperse was never actually given. With this leak, even middle-of-the-road commentators began to call the Metropolitan Police a "paramilitary operation" and wondered if the city government was operating more like a "junta" than a "civilian authority" (Milloy 2003, B1). Such comments give pause, to say the least, about whether Washington's permit system was still "well-oiled" in quite the way that ACLU's Art Spitzer thought less than two years earlier.

It also gives occasion to wonder about the ways in which the control of public space—both its regulation through negotiated management and its policing through escalation of force—is exercised as a means of controlling politics. Beginning in 1939, the Supreme Court created the rules, or constructed a regime, for the regulation of government-owned property—public property—and thereby clarified the nature of the rights of those who use it. In publicly-owned public space, classified as a traditional or dedicated public forum, people presumably have an a priori right to gather, to protest, to parade, to speak out. But just as the Court has learned to differentiate types of public property in law (constructing a whole category of "non-public" forums, for example), so too, it seems, is the *public* who populates public space differentiated. If we are used to thinking of public space as something like the "people's property," then the tales of protest policing in Washington outlined in this chapter suggest that there still remain different rules (formal or informal, legitimate or seemingly illegitimate) for different people, even as all those people, as individuals, presumably possess the same bundle of rights. Some, perhaps those engaged in a politics of affirmation, seem to have greater purchase on the space of the public than others, such as those engaged in a politics of dissent. The power of the state to decide who can and cannot be in particular spaces can be a powerful force limiting the voices that can be heard and the people who can be seen.

This power affects not only the exercise of individually held rights, but also the entry of individuals into a more collective entity—the public. If the only people who can exercise their rights without fear of arrest are those who affirm state policy (perhaps even by accepting and affirming state means of "normalizing" dissent), then it seems that "freedom of speech" becomes "freedom of state speech." Dissent is made safe for democracy more than democracy is transformed by dissent. Citizenship and the kind of democracy that is visible in public space become limited and degraded. It is true that the struggle to open speech and publicity in traditional public forums continues and the reaction against heavy-handed state tactics has sometimes moderated repressive practices. But as important as these struggles are, they do not, and likely cannot, eliminate the ability of the state, through its control of property, to limit who appears in public and to shape the nature of the public. The state retains powerful, if contested, tools for determining who *belongs* in public space.

Yet the state is not the only determiner of belonging. Property rights, including rights over and in public property, exist within a set of relations that are complex, multifarious, and often diffuse. In the next chapter we continue our exploration of the relation between public property and public space by exploring the complex politics of belonging in the Plaza of Santa Fe, New Mexico.

2

PROPERTY, LAW, AND THE PLAZA OF SANTA FE, NEW MEXICO

*Turning Social Relations into Space**

Property seems like such a tangible thing—and it is. The plazas and small parks of Washington, where police penned in protesters, are as real as can be. As publicly-owned spaces, they are governed by a set of rules and laws, such as those making it illegal to parade without a permit. The rules governing those spaces are in fact quite different from the rules governing privately held property right next door. But saying that makes clear another point: as tangible as property is, it is also a set of relationships. Indeed, property is, in many ways, *primarily* a set of relationships. Consider Chicago's Millennium Park. While it is true enough to say Millennium Park is owned by the city of Chicago, it is also inadequate because all those corporate sponsors, as well as the artists of sculptures like "Cloud Gate," have definite rights to the space, too—rights that are rights of ownership in many respects. The key questions, therefore, have to do with just how those relationships (relations among different entities with ownership rights, between them and other users, and between these and others who might make other kinds of claims, such as claims of affect or of belonging to the space) are turned into something tangible, something real. Just how are social relations turned into space? And what happens when they are?

* This chapter is revised from: Don Mitchell and Lynn A. Staeheli, "Turning Social Relations into Space: Property, Law, and the Plaza of Santa Fe, New Mexico," *Landscape Research* 30 (2005), 325-342. Taylor and Francis Ltd, http://www.tandf.co.uk/journals

How are relations of power solidified on the ground and made as real as the space that encapsulates them and gives them form?

These are questions of particular importance on the Plaza of Santa Fe, New Mexico, where the process of turning social relations into space shows just how contested ownership of public space really is. It is quite inadequate, we will show in this chapter, to understand public property as having a single, simple owner. Conceptually, it is difficult to imagine how one owner—even an owner such as the state, which is ostensibly the manifestation of the body politic (Olwig, 2003; Rasmussen and Brown, 2005)—can represent the people in all their diversity who constitute the public. Ownership is a complex issue, fraught with all manner of contradictions, even as it often appears only to be a question of whose name appears on a deed.

THE PLAZA OF SANTA FE

Laid out in partial conformance to the Law of the Indies, the Plaza in Santa Fe was surrounded in the 1850s by key administrative buildings and the homes of the city's elite. Part commons, part ceremonial ground, part military drill field, the Plaza served as the political, social, and symbolic heart not only of Santa Fe, but also the region of which the city was capital. Over the years, the mud-or-dust open space of the Plaza was planted with shade trees and grass, laced with walkways and benches, and reduced by half in size. In 1866, the territorial assembly voted to erect an obelisk—the Soldiers' Monument—at the center of the Plaza, directly in front of the Palace of the Governors (Figure 2.1). The obelisk was to memorialize the men who died in New Mexican battles during the Civil War. But before the obelisk

Figure 2.1 The Santa Fe Plaza in 1882. By this time the Plaza had been reduced to half its original size (the cathedral is just out of the picture to the top left) and the obelisk had been erected at its center. Note the bandstand to the lower left of the obelisk. Source: Library of Congress.

Figure 2.2 The obelisk at the center of the Plaza. The plaque in front reads: "Monument texts reflect the character of the times in which they are written and the temper of those who wrote them. This monument was dedicated in 1868 near the close of a period of intense strife which pitted northerner against southerner, Indian against white, Indian against Indian. Thus, we see on this monument, as in other records, the use of such terms as 'savage' and 'rebel.' Attitudes change and prejudices hopefully dissolve." Photograph by Lynn Staeheli.

was erected, the Assembly voted to also memorialize "the brave victims who have perished in various wars with the savage Indians," which, with some alteration, was duly inscribed in the marble plaques at the monument's base (Figure 2.2). In 1974, in daylight and in front of a number of onlookers, a young man stepped over the low fence around the monument and chiseled out the word "savage" (Figure 2.3). Looking just like any number of war monuments around the United States, the hole he made gives the obelisk much of its distinction, and ensures that the monument will remain a lightning rod for controversy. At least since the 1950s, periodic calls have been issued for the removal of the monument, and each time

Figure 2.3 The altered text on the obelisk. Photograph by Lynn Staeheli.

they have been rebuffed (Wilson 1997, 315–316). The most recent agitation to have the monument removed was in 2000 when the Santa Fe branch of the National Association for the Advancement of Colored People (NAACP) began a movement to have it replaced by a monument that would "make public space sacred," as Wanda Ross Padilla, the president of the Santa Fe NAACP put it.

The monument is a lightning rod because the Plaza remains the symbolic heart of Santa Fe, and the monument is the symbolic heart of the Plaza (Figure 2.4). But there is more to the story than that. The degree to which the Plaza remains, and should remain, the social and political center of the city, depends on whose social and political life one is talking about. As the chiseling out of the word "savage" indicates, the Plaza is a contested space: contested between Hispanic locals and "Anglos"; residents and tourists; non-Indian street merchants, the New Mexican Historical Society, and surrounding stores; teenagers and the city government; and those who want to be rid of the obelisk and the historical preservation establishment that likes to point out that the obelisk is almost the only thing of historical value left on the Plaza.

Given the range of controversy, is should be no surprise, therefore, that the Plaza is the object of a great deal of regulatory attention. The Santa Fe City Code—the laws and regulations that say what can and cannot be done in the city—devotes ten pages to describing the ways the Plaza should be governed and maintained and the kinds of activities that can occur there. Nearly two pages are given to definitions alone.

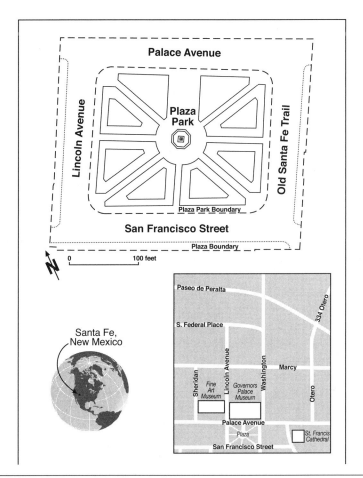

Figure 2.4 Map of the Santa Fe Plaza redrawn from Santa Fe City Code, Ordinance 1981-39. Note the two different boundaries: The interior line indicates the legal limit of the Plaza Park; the outer line indicates the legal limit of the Plaza as a whole, which includes the Plaza Park, the four surrounding streets, and a portion of the sidewalks across the streets from the Park. Cartography by Joe Stoll, Syracuse University Cartographic Laboratory.

Both Plaza and Plaza Park are defined, as are skateboard, recreational object, flower peddler, artist, business, handicraft, commercial use, civic non-profit organization, major commercial event, and more. The proliferation of definitions gives a good hint about the intensity and the nature of controversies in the Plaza. Other subsections of the Code for the Plaza govern: the issuance of permits for major commercial and non-commercial events; the selection and regulation of Plaza vendors; the range of prohibited activities; and those activities that must be confined to specific locations such as hacky-sack,* which can only be played "in the southeast quadrant of the Plaza Park as long as due care for the safety of the public is exercised" (Section 23-5.4(D)). Hacky-sack is the only ball game permitted on the Plaza.

Given the extent of these regulations, their intent comes as something of a surprise. Section 23-5 of the City Code begins with a preamble that outlines this intent:

> The Plaza and the Plaza Park are the heart of the city. Its usage should be creative, evolving, and non-institutionalized. Standards should encourage variety, equity in usage, and respect for the important role the Plaza and Plaza Park play in the life of Santa Fe.

At the heart of Santa Fe, in other words, sits a contradiction: the very space in the city that is supposed to be the least institutionalized—because of its social and symbolic importance—is in fact the most highly regulated.

This contradiction can best be explained by exploring the Plaza as a *public* property, in which *different* publics have a claim to the space, with a differential relationship with regard to access to that space, and a different conception of what rights they may possess in it. Conceptually this is clear enough, and practically, the Plaza of Santa Fe seems to bear out the contention. But if we stop the story there, we do not in fact gain much purchase on why certain controversies over publicly-owned and publicly-accessible space unfold as they do, why certain activities and not others come to be regulated, what the social effects of such regulation might be in terms of access and exclusion, and the effect of all this on the formation of a public. How, for example, is the "right to exclude" struggled over and by whom? To address these kinds of issues we need to focus on how spaces such as the Plaza in Santa Fe function as a *property* that is both a thing (a place with definite boundaries and a clear spatial extent) and a *set of social relationships* that are not necessarily confined by those boundaries. In this chapter, therefore, we focus on a set of controversies over the Plaza of Santa Fe and explore the complex and contradictory dynamics of law and property as they intersect to shape and define a critical public space that is the symbolic heart of Santa Fe's public sphere.

---

* Hacky-sack is a game using a small, soft ball. It is played with three or four people in a circle who attempt to bounce the sack off various parts of their bodies before passing it to another player.

THE CONTRADICTIONS OF PROPERTY,
THE COMPLEXITY OF LAW

What does it mean to examine Santa Fe's premier public space as property? That depends on what we take "property" to be. As Nick Blomley (2004b) details, no matter how solid it may appear, property is never just a thing. It is also a set of relationships of a particular kind: a "network of social relations that governs the conduct of people with respect to the use and disposition of things" (Hoebel 1966, 424, quoted in Blomley 2004b, 2). In these relationships, ownership appears to be primary. This is the "ownership model" (Singer 2000, in Blomley 2004b, 3) that takes it as self-evident that ownership determines use, and that ownership is singular. Ownership is as clear as the deed upon which it is recorded. "The ownership model," Blomley (2004b, 2) says, "assumes a unitary, solitary, and identifiable owner, separated from others by boundaries that protect him or her from nonowners and grant the owner the power to exclude." It seems simple enough. The City of Santa Fe owns the Plaza; the City of Chicago owns Millennium Park; the federal government owns the Mall in Washington. Period. And yet, as Blomley (2004b, 3–4) makes clear, and as is obvious in Millennium Park no less than the Santa Fe Plaza, the ownership model is more a normative description of how things ought to be under capitalism than the way they really are. To see property in terms of the ownership model is to occlude the way property is always also a network of social relationships.

What kind of relationships? Property involves relationships between people and entities with specific rights and claims to the place in question. First, not only the deed owner, but perhaps others too, will have the right of use. Streets and parks, according to the Supreme Court, are held in trust for people to use to communicate thoughts. But other kinds of uses might be important too: utilities might be granted easements, or the public might have access for recreation or transportation. Second, while one entity might own the land, another might own the things on the land, and be under no obligation to do with them as the landowner pleases. Third, formal deed restrictions, zoning rules, and restrictive covenants might give third parties rights to limit how property is used. Fourth, there might be competing claims of ownership, not explicitly recognized in current law, as when native groups retain or reassert claims to land expropriated from them, throwing into question the very right of ownership and how it was derived (see Blomley 2003; Harris 2003; Sparke 1998). And finally, there are the less formal, but still important, rights claims of those who, as members of the public, assert a different claim on property: a right to *be* on a particular parcel of property. All these issues are important for both private and public property, but the last one is particularly important in the case of public property, which is held in trust by the state for "the people." The struggle over who can *be* on public property is a struggle over who *is* and *is not* to be included as part of "the people."

Despite their importance for defining "the people," struggles over the nature of (public) property often remain invisible, precisely because they often appear to be "settled" (Blomley 2004b), part of what we will call in the next chapter a property *regime*. The status of property-as-property—as single and unified under the ownership model and within a relatively stable and coherent regime—is often taken for granted. But when property claims become contentious, they burst into visibility through the institutions of law. The law is both the means to mediate disputes over property and is written as a result of disputes. Land-use laws that restrict how property owners may make their buildings look, how big they can be, and what can be done in them, are the result of contentious claims of some members of the community over the way the totality of property forms a landscape, and thus over the ways that individual owners' rights must be restricted in order to preserve the rights of other landowners. Formal rules over the use of a park result from competing rights and use claims by different groups who seek to *belong* in a park and often to exclude those who they feel do not belong. Court decisions that determine the activities that may occur in the park, that restrict some actions (taking wedding photographs near "Cloud Gate," for example), or that adjudicate ownership disputes literally shape the lands to which they pertain (Olwig 1996, 2003). One purpose of law, that is, is to negotiate how the social relations that *are* property get transformed into the regulated space that *is* property.

And in Santa Fe, the complexity—and the sheer volume—of that law, especially as it relates to the Plaza, gives a good indication of just how contentious those social relations are, and thus how difficult that negotiation is.

WHO OWNS THE PLAZA?

It ought to be easy to answer the question of who owns the Plaza in Santa Fe, but it is not. In the first place, property always exists in relation to other properties, and in Santa Fe it is not just the case that the Plaza is the symbolic center of the city; it is also *literally* the center of property. On 9 April 1900, a dozen years before New Mexico became a state, the U.S. Congress decreed the tip of the Soldiers' Monument to be the starting point for a survey and the mapping of all property in the city. Every property deed in the city is keyed to the obelisk, and it is not unusual to hear arguments that it must be preserved in its present location for just that reason. Removing the monument, as some activists advocate, is seen by some people not just as an assault on history, but also an attack on the sacred rights of property (Simmons 2000).

The obelisk itself is owned by the state of New Mexico and nothing can be legally done to it unless the state agrees. The actual Plaza is city property, but what can or cannot be done to this property is closely tied to the monument, since the monument is the anchor of the Plaza's designation as a national historical landmark. Any alteration of the monument, even if the state approved it, could threaten the historical status of the Plaza and thus significant financial aid for the landscape maintenance and restoration. This is not an idle threat. In 1973, following a short campaign against the monument by American Indian Movement activists, the Santa Fe City Council voted unanimously to remove the obelisk. The National Park Service responded by threatening to withdraw Plaza renovation funds. The monument stayed (Navrot 2000).

By not removing the obelisk in 1973, the city remained eligible for a 1974 grant from the federal government to renovate the Plaza, and in accepting the grant, it traded away some of its ownership rights (see Hummels 1998). Conditions attached to the grant stipulated that any changes to the Plaza—from changing the walkway paving materials, to uprooting trees, to building a bandstand, to paving over the grass lawns that in any event needed to be resodded every year—had to be approved by both the New Mexico Historic Preservation Office and the National Park Service. Part of this agreement stipulates that any changes to the Plaza must be in accordance with a historic preservation plan prepared by the famed Santa Fe architect John Gaw Meem. The city may formally *own* the Plaza (except for the monument), but it cannot *do* with the Plaza just as it pleases.

In these terms, the question of who owns the Plaza is not easily answered. On the one hand, and in terms of the ownership model, the city owns the Plaza (except the monument); it holds the deed to the Plaza and in that regard it is like any other property in the city and regulated as such. But on the other hand, the Plaza is *not* like any other property in the city. The ownership rights of the state of New Mexico considerably complicate what the city can do with the Plaza. Equally, the historic preservation agreement of 1974 in essence creates a permanent easement or deed restriction. And because it fronted the money for renovations in the 1970s, the federal government claims certain rights over the property of the Plaza. Property is a relationship among different kinds of rights claims, in this case fought out among different governmental agencies. The Plaza in Santa Fe is as jurisdictionally complex as the protest landscape in Washington. If the Plaza is somehow the "people's property," then it is less than clear which governmental agency is the people's representative—which "fictive individual" (Blomley 2004b, 7) is to have the preeminent claim.

Nor is it clear just which "people" the owners of the Plaza represent. Property is often defined as the right to exclude—the ability to determine who does and does not belong in a particular space (Blomley 1998, 2000a; Macpherson 1978). For Wanda Ross Padilla, the president of the Santa Fe Chapter of the NAACP, the monument, with its heroic description of white conquest, is symbolic of this right to exclude in a different way; it in part determines who feels welcome in the Plaza and welcome in the heart of the city. To Padilla the monument is "just offensive. . . . Every time I go down there [to the Plaza] that was what was on my mind: 'Look at that thing, look at that thing.'" Like many we interviewed, Padilla worried that the Plaza was no longer a place for locals. "A lot of the native Hispanics in this town feel like the Plaza has been taken away from them . . . everything has been taken away from them [and] they don't feel comfortable going downtown."

The Plaza, in this sense, is a metonym for the larger transformation of downtown Santa Fe. The Plaza area—the shops and streets around it as well as the park itself—is the historic center of commerce as well as government in Santa Fe. In 1997, the last store on the Plaza that really catered to local needs closed. "The biggest thing that has happened to the Plaza," according to former city councilor and tour bus operator Frank Montaño,

> is that it has changed in terms of its commerce quite a bit. There were a lot of local people that came to the downtown area because of the services. And now you come down because you have someone that's visiting, you come down because your granddaughter or your daughter or your niece or your nephew is performing in an event that's downtown.

While, as one city employee told us, "those of us who work near the Plaza have a chance to go down [to the Plaza] . . . and sit and have our lunch or walk around, take a little stroll," she also argued, "I think it probably meant something a little bit more in the past where it was more like a social gathering place." For many local people, in other words, downtown is no longer an everyday experience, and the Plaza has increasingly become a place for spectacles and special events. "It used to be the heart of the community," lamented one city planner.

This sense of wistfulness is important. It is more than nostalgia, and it is more than the voice of "stakeholders" (as those with claims on property are often called). The structure and meaning of the surrounding landscape creates a sense of belonging *in* the Plaza. "I think tourism saved the Plaza," says city planner Anne Condon. But as she quickly adds, this "saving" is double edged. In the 1980s, according to Chris Wilson (1997, 9), the city embarked on an intensive campaign of tourist promotion, using "the manipulation of the myth" of Santa Fe— the myth of Santa Fe as an authentic outpost of New Mexican culture, made from centuries of Indian and Hispanic mixing—"as a tourism marketing image." The city sought to project "Santa Fe as a Tahiti in the desert, bathed in rosy sunsets." The campaign was quite successful. "The magnitude of the subsequent boom (millions of tourists and thousands of amenity migrants who came and stayed)," Wilson (1997, 9) continues, "was more than a city of sixty thousand could comfortably absorb. In effect the entire community began to be gentrified, as more and more native residents could no longer afford the city's cost of living." As local residents were pushed out of the town, so too did many of them begin to feel pushed out of the Plaza.

As rents around the Plaza skyrocketed and the retail mix changed, shifting almost exclusively to national-brand boutiques, galleries, and shops selling Santa Fe–style jewelry, furniture and crafts, many in the city came to feel they were not welcome in the posh stores surrounding the plaza. As one planner commented:

> Locals do feel . . . they're getting the message when they're in some of the stores that they're not wanted. Unless you have money and look like you have money, you're not really wanted. Browsing is discouraged. People follow you around stores. My kids get thrown out of stores all the time and they're not shoplifters.

She further argued that while "the Plaza itself is democracy," there is nonetheless

> a practical exclusion because of housing costs [and] the local people are moving further and further out all the time because of the cost of housing. Our historic neighborhoods tend to be our most beautiful and they're the most regulated because of our Historic District Ordinance, so they're the biggest guarantees that they're going to stay nice, that redevelopment isn't going to make them awful. And we're talking about million dollar and half million dollar houses surrounding here, so as the locals move further and

further out . . . as a practical matter they feel excluded because they have to make a special effort to come down here.

Or as another planner put it: "a lot of the locals feel like maybe we've relinquished too much of Santa Fe to tourism. . . . We've been over-glamorized. The over-glamorization of Santa Fe is too much like Aspen." Another longtime resident said:

I think [downtown] really has been lost. And not only to the local people but to the people who would come here to visit. Santa Fe used to offer something that was really special that a lot of other places didn't. And my perception of it was that it offered something that was plain and funky and down to earth and nobody cared who you were. Nobody cared if you had a lot of money. It wasn't important. That's all different now. Now it's glitzy, and there's almost been an attitude of snobbery that's evolving.

In what sense, then, has tourism saved the Plaza? According to city planner Condon:

One time all [the commercial property abutting the Plaza] was local service retail, a little bit of tourists but not a whole lot, and my feeling is that it would have died out when the malls were built and Santa Fe would have gone the way of so many other downtowns, been kind of boarded up, vacant, maybe even some disastrous urban renewal.

But at the same time, the Plaza saved Santa Fe for tourism. Former city councilor and tour operator Frank Montaño argues, "the Plaza has actually probably made Santa Fe the destination that it is. It is a very vibrant space and has always been a very active space of social gathering and commerce." In other words, there is a dialectic of property at work in downtown Santa Fe. On the one hand, the maintenance of the Plaza as a vibrant and open public space is essential to the survival of the commercial businesses that surround it and for the collection of rents on the properties that host these businesses. Regulating the use of the Plaza is thus essential to the survival of surrounding businesses. On the other hand, the collecting of rents, together with the spiral of gentrification of which it is a part, transforms the kinds of people who use the Plaza, who have easy access to it, and who feel they belong. So while the "the Plaza itself is democracy," it is not necessarily a space of democratic inclusion.

THE PLAZA AS COMMERCIAL SPACE

The question of who "owns" the Plaza is significantly complicated by just this dialectic, just this role property plays in defining the democracy of the Plaza. But the struggle over ownership—over what sorts of social relations of property will prevail—has rarely been engaged directly. Rather, it has tended to surface in a series of skirmishes over the "proper" use of the Plaza, over its role as a social center. This dialectical relationship between commercial and social functions of property is written into the ten pages of the City Code that govern the Plaza.

Santa Fe City Code section 23-5.3, entitled "Plaza Vendors; Permits Allowed; Requirements Selection Process; Conditions of Operations," alone covers some four and one-half pages. The code is explicit. Licenses to engage in commercial activity are "privileges of the holders," and they "are not and shall not be construed as rights in property or otherwise" (Section 23-5.3(A)). Yet such licenses nonetheless significantly limit what the city, as property owner may and may not do. Licenses, together with the code, outline a very strict set of rules and procedures that bind the city every bit as much as they bind the licensees.

For decades, Indian artisans have sold their goods across the street from the Plaza under the portico of the Palace of the Governors. The Palace of the Governors is owned by the state of New Mexico and serves as the home of the Museum of New Mexico. The Indian vendors are considered a "living exhibit" of the museum and thus are not regulated by either commercial law or the rules of the Plaza. In the early 1980s local (predominantly Hispanic) artists, upset that the Indian artists had an exclusive right to sell merchandise on the streets, began illegally selling their work on the Plaza. Realizing that controlled vending on the Plaza encouraged rather than hindered tourism, the city implemented a program to provide a limited number of vending licenses for non-Indian vendors. Until 2003, artist vendor licenses cost $350 annually (when they were raised to $700), and portrait artist licenses cost $75. A condition of the license was that all goods sold had to be "handcrafted by the applicant or the applicant's spouse, their children or one (1) relative" (Section 23-5.3 (C6-7)). Each application is scored by the city administrator in charge of the vending program on the following criteria (beginning in 2003 a jury of local art educators was employed to rank the applications):

(a) compatibility with Plaza activities;
(b) experience of the applicant;
(c) addition of diversity to the Plaza services;

(d) residents of Santa Fe County shall be granted an additional 20% to their ranking;

(e) applicants who hold a permit at the time of the application shall be granted an additional 5% to their ranking for each year they have held such a permit, but not to exceed 50% (not applicable to rotating vendors' licenses);

(f) applicants who currently hold a permit for permanent tables on the Plaza [when this version of the system was implemented in 1995] shall be granted an additional five years to hold a permit on the Plaza;

(g) artistic quality. (Section 23-5.3 (D2))

No vending is allowed during major events on the Plaza, such as Fiesta, Fiesta Market, Spanish Market, and Indian Market, when the Plaza is given over to massive arts and crafts fairs organized by specific Santa Fe institutions, such as the Southwest Institute of Indian Arts.

The licensing program is highly controversial, and the tortured syntax of the subsection of Code that regulates it gives a good sense of how difficult it has been for the city to accommodate different interests. The program has led to struggles among Plaza vendors that have ranged from name-calling to fistfights to lawsuits (Mac-Donald 2001; Sharpe 1996, 1997). It has required constant review and revision from city officials as they seek to create an equitable system for awarding licenses. It has also called up significant opposition from local, store-based merchants, many of whom sell much the same kind of jewelry and craftwork as is available on the Plaza. Merchants argue that the vendor program undercuts their ability to make sales and threatens their viability. After all, the fixed costs of Plaza vending, from property tax to heating and electricity, are almost non-existent, and the ready access that Plaza vendors have to strolling tourists provides what some merchants see as an unfair competitive advantage. As one Plaza vendor put it: "The Plaza vending ordinance, as the former city manager said, is a piece of crap. . . . Even though I am part of it, I recognize what a special interest law it is."

Despite its controversial nature, Plaza vending has been maintained because it helps sustain the sense of life and informality that is meant to define the Plaza, and it helps create a sense of the Plaza as a heart of commerce. But the question of how and for whom the Plaza is to be commercial is unresolved. The *Santa Fe New Mexican* (2002, A7) is scathing in its evaluation of the ongoing attempts to revise the vending ordinance. "So ignore the dusty ordinance under which vendors were to have been jury-reviewed and given the hook if they were peddling schlock," the *New Mexican* editorialized in response to one proposed change in the law that would have increased the number of vending licenses and changed how they were awarded:

> Ignore that City Hall is handmaiden to the merchants cheapening the Santa Fe experience for visitors thinking they're buying fine work because it carries the municipal imprimatur. . . .

> So why have restriction at all? Why not turn the Plaza into one big open-air market, replete with plastic toys, plastic shoes, stuffed animals and made-in-Malaysia souvenirs?

> We have the makings of a souk, and [city council member] Heldmeyer wants to make it a monopoly for a mere 16 merchants.

> ¡No, doctora! First, let's research, and build a monument to, the councilors who first opened the Plaza to vendors. We could hold a special annual fair in honor of those politicos. Then let's fill every square inch of our central square with anyone who wants to sell anything legal.

The *New Mexican* advocated removing all the vendors. But it did not advocate completely decommercializing the Plaza. It supports the continuance of the large art fairs that are held on and around the Plaza each year, the selling of refreshments during fiestas, and the rights of Indian merchants under the portico of the Palace of the Governors. And, as we will see, it also supports partially privatizing the Plaza through the creation of a "conservancy" similar to one that now governs much of New York's Central Park. What concerns it, apparently, is class.

Similarly, the Santa Fe bureau of the *Albuquerque Journal* (2002, 4) "would like to hear a fresh City Council discussion about whether the vendors should be permitted on the Plaza at all." In part, the *Journal* would like such a discussion because "[s]elling goods on the Plaza is a privilege, and we bet a valuable one. It might not be a bad idea to require vendors to disclose how much they make from streets sales and adjust fees upwards again, if necessary." In other words, not only are vendors unsightly (the *Journal* refers to the vending area as "cluttered"), and perhaps purveyors of cheap goods, but they continue to compete unfairly with what the *Journal* sees as the legitimate merchants downtown.

Here we reach, once again, the heart of the contradiction that defines the Plaza as a public property. First, trade is based in property, in the ownership of things. This requires a certain level of order and thus the policing of property; it is particularly important to guard against *impropriety*, such as bogus goods and unfair practices. And yet a market in goods requires a certain level of "anarchy"—that is, impropriety—in order to be "free." The dialectic of this contradiction gets worked out in code, in that vending licenses are "privileges" that may be "revoked by the city manager at any time" (Section 23-5.3(F)). And it may also explain why the local newspapers so frequently comment on the quality of the art for sale on the Plaza, and rarely raise similar issues about the local boutiques. Plaza merchant John Coventry, for example, came in second to last in a recent vendor application process, and the *New Mexican* (2002, A7) made a point of noting that he is primarily known for "using his license to set up displays of headless Barbie dolls and peanuts in a cash register on his table in the Plaza," leading to exactly the sort of unsightliness that both the *New Mexican* and the *Journal* complain about in their editorials. Nor is the city ordinance governing vending in the Plaza silent on this count; recall that it requires vending license applications to be judged partly on "compatibility with Plaza activities" and "artistic quality," both notoriously slippery concepts that immediately raise questions about who, how, and in whose interest, such judgments are made.* While John Coventry argues that his work is original art and therefore of intrinsic value, planner Anne Condon says more generally:

> I wonder why we don't have some other uses on the Plaza like flower stalls and tomato stands and things like that, that you see in Portland and New York that add a lot of color and beauty. There's not much added by having the [current] vendors here, in my opinion. Not much of any real charm or character.

GIVING A GIFT HORSE A ROOT CANAL: AFFLUENCE, INFLUENCE, AND COMMERCE ON THE PLAZA

Issues of unsightliness, charm, and character have come up in other ways, too, and are central to discussions of who and what belongs in the Plaza. Before the monument was erected in the nineteenth century, a wooden Victorian-style bandstand stood at the center of the Plaza. To make room for the obelisk, the bandstand was relocated closer to the Palace of the Governors. In 1910 it was removed to Fort Marcy Park a

---

* And so local officials and newspaper writers seem not to know how to respond to Coventry, who, when denied a license in the most recent round, testified at a hearing: "I've never been in this program for the money. I'm in it for the validation and the pride. I'm even proud I got one of the lowest scores. At least I am doing something artistic on my own" (quoted in Sharpe 2003d, B1).

few blocks away and eventually dismantled (Herter 2002; Wilson 1997, 186). Sometime later a Santa Fe–style stucco stage was built on the Plaza, but was removed before the 1974 preservation agreement. Since that agreement made permanent alterations to the Plaza difficult, the city has erected a "temporary" stage—made of pipes, plywood and tarpaulins—every summer. While planner Condon worries about the lack of charm and character provided by the vendors, she is more sanguine about the bandstand: "It doesn't look like it's got this design aesthetic that's elite. It's just real funky." Its very "klutziness" helps the Plaza "work as a space," she says.

Others feel differently, and there was a lively and long-running debate about how to replace the temporary stage with something permanent. Many hoped a permanent stage or gazebo could replace what Condon calls "a war monument of dubious distinction"—the obelisk. Frank Montaño, who at one time chaired the Plaza Renovation Committee for the city, thought a permanent gazebo would serve as a "gathering place for both locals and visitors," but did not think it would be possible to remove the obelisk. "It would be too controversial of an issue to try to tackle." The Renovation Committee thus recommended putting a gazebo where the temporary stage was typically erected.

In fall 2002, the Santa Fe Community Foundation established a Plaza Community Stage Fund to raise money to pay for the construction of a permanent gazebo. It hired local architect Beverley Spears to design a gazebo "that was unobtrusive without being drab" and "sufficiently 'jewel-like' to merit placement in Santa Fe's premier public space" (*Journal*, Editorial 2003, 4). In May 2003, the plans for the gazebo were approved by the Historic Design Review Board of the city and six months later by the State Historic Preservation Division. Work on the bandstand commenced in February 2003 and was completed in early summer. In between there was much wrangling over size, exact location, and the kind of events for which it should be used.* The architect at times worried that all this second guessing of design would ruin it and that perhaps "it would be better not to build it at all" (Sharpe 2003b, B1).

Complicating matters was the question of who would control the design process. The gazebo was funded and built by the Santa Fe Community Foundation and then gifted to the city, which was to "assume

---

* The city now sponsors an annual eight-week-long Santa Fe Bandstand summer concert series featuring national artists, and drawing global tourists as well as local residents to the Plaza. See http://www.outsideinproductions.org/summerbandstand/index.html (accessed 23 May 2006); Santa Fe Economic Development Division (2005).

ownership and liability . . . [and] maintain it and provide enough electric power and ongoing essentials for its multi-faceted use" (Herter 2002, F7). But if the city was eventually to own the gazebo, it was clear it did not own the design process. As city councilors debated the project, they were warned by the newspapers that they were playing with fire (see, for example, *Journal* Editorial 2003), and were threatened by representatives of the Santa Fe Foundation: "The president of the Santa Fe Foundation . . . said [in a public hearing] if the design or locale of the gazebo is changed significantly, she would have to submit the new plan to each of the 150 people who have donated so far" (Sharpe 2003b, B1; 2003a). "If the design starts looking different from what the (Foundation) donors approved and designed, then I think we will start seeing donor disinterest," the president later added (Huddy 2003, 3). In December 2003 the wife of the New Mexico governor intervened, telling the council that "she and Gov. Bill Richardson have 'personally supported' the gazebo project from the beginning," and that "some of the donors to the gazebo project 'are getting real frustrated' and may pull out if the project was further delayed" (Sharpe 2003a, B1; *Journal* Staff Reports 2003). Or, as one donor to the project put it in comments before the city council: "Because the gazebo is to be built with private funds, questioning its design 'is a little like giving a gift horse root-canal surgery'" (Sharpe 2003c, A1).*

Though opposed to private vendors engaging in commercial activities in the public Plaza, it was just this infusion of private money and private control that the two main newspapers in Santa Fe liked about the gazebo project. As the *New Mexican* editorialized: "Best of all, this project is a gift to the city from the Santa Fe Foundation" (*New Mexican* 2003a, F6). It was best of all because it provided a model for "dress[ing] up the down-at-the-heels Plaza." The Foundation involvement in the gazebo, the *New Mexican* (2003b, A5) wrote, was "reminiscent of a flag we ran up the pole a few years ago: the creation of a Plaza Conservancy, modeled roughly on the Central Park Conservancy, which keeps New

---

* In fact, the final design did not even satisfy the other big private players on the Plaza. The organizers of the Spanish and Indian Art Markets, the biggest tourist attractions in Santa Fe, were dissatisfied with the plans because the gazebo would not be big enough for the entertainment at their events. The city agreed, therefore, that a second temporary stage would be set up for each of the markets and for Fiesta. The city would pay the cost of this additional stage. It is not clear from news reports whether the city would purchase the temporary stage ($106,000, plus $4,000 for each time it is erected) or rent from a private company (about $6,000 each event). In either event, the gift of the gazebo, together with the Santa Fe Community Foundation's inability to incorporate the concerns of the big private Plaza players in its design, brought with it a high corollary cost to the city (Sharpe 2003a, B1).

York City's greensward in such good condition. When Santa Feans see what a private-public partnership can accomplish with the bandstand . . . the idea might gain fresh momentum."* But if, in this model, public changes to private gifts are seen as gift-horse root canals, then what might such a development (in essence transferring property rights to private organizations) mean for community or for public regulation of a place that is both Santa Fe's premier public space and the heart of its symbolic landscape? Who *then* might the Plaza be for? Exactly this question was raised by two Santa Fe City Council members concerned about growing private influence over the park:

> Councilors Matthew Ortiz and David Pfeffer said that by allow-ing private funds to build a gazebo where a temporary stage had been located for years, the city is displacing the traditional uses of the Plaza.

> "I know that when affluence and influence converge on behalf of this particular project, that it is very hard for the community to be able to hold onto what they have." (Sharpe 2003a, B1)

Pfeffer said, "Something will be irrevocably lost on the Plaza." And, added Ortiz, "we are losing the center of the Plaza. We're being kicked in a corner" (*Journal* Staff Report 2003, 1).

PLAZA RATS: YOUTH, TRANSIENTS, TOURISTS, AND THE POLICE

Also being kicked in the corner are hacky-sacks (little bean bags), which by rules laid out in the City Code (Section 23-5.4(D)) can only be kicked "in the southeast grassed quadrant of the Plaza Park," and only so long as "due care for the safety of the public is being exercised." That a whole paragraph of the City Code needs to be devoted to hacky-sack, which is only one "recreational object" among an infinite variety, might seem odd. The paragraph derives from the early 1990s when downtown business owners and city officials worried about the large number of youth—Plaza Rats, as they are called—hanging out in the Plaza, riding skateboards, playing hacky-sack and other games. As Frank Montaño, the sponsor of a bill that outlawed all these things later put it, the youth were "experimenting with their freedoms . . . assert[ing] themselves and let[ting] it be known that they're young and free and they're going to be

---

* We examine the nature of such private-public partnerships and their transformative effect on public space more fully in the next chapter. For critical analyses of the Central Park Conservancy, see Katz (1998, 2001, 2006) and Kohn (2004).

Figure 2.5 "Plaza rats," hanging out at the obelisk. Note the skateboard. Photograph by Lynn Staeheli.

whatever they want to be" (Figure 2.5). Skateboarding and ball games intimidated some visitors to the park, especially the elderly, according to Montaño. For skateboarders, a new skate park was built a few blocks away. Hacky-sack players, however, turned out to be a thornier problem, and one that makes clear just how hard it is to regulate a public property as a space of sociability.

Hacky-sack is usually played with three or four people. The goals in passing the sack from one person to another are to keep it off the ground, but to do so with style. It is a relatively passive game, both a game of skill and a time killer while hanging out. It is necessarily sociable. When the ban on skateboarding and ball games went into effect, local youth interpreted it as "an attempt to drive young people from the Plaza" (Neary 1994, A1) and reserve it instead for "financially well-off transients," as Anne Condon defined tourists, only half in jest.

After much lobbying by area youth, the city council backed down and voted for a specific exception for hacky-sack to its prohibition against "project[ing], throw[ing], kick[ing] or strik[ing] any type of recreational object" in the Plaza (Section 23-5.4(A3)) (see Hummels 1999a, 1999b). Even so, as one planner put it, "for all practical purposes we threw our teenagers off" the Plaza. And as another said, "There's nowhere for teenagers. It's terrible." For Condon, the lack of youth on the Plaza is an indication that it is underused and thus an inviting place not for well-off, transient tourists, but for transients of the other kind: "when a public space is unused, people take it over, like transients." Pushing youth out of the Plaza, making them feel like it did not belong to them, Condon suggested, had the effect of making the Plaza more open to homeless people.

From the perspective of another city planner, however, the youth are, and remain, the problem:

It seems like [the Plaza] doesn't include everybody or there are certain groups, and those groups change, I think, who seem to kind of take over the Plaza and especially those groups [that] seem to be participating in some activities, they're playing some games out there. It discourages others because of their little hacky-sacks in the air and it sort of makes people want to stay away from it.

The City Code is both a result of this tension among different groups who want to feel that the Plaza is "theirs" and a means to mediate it. It is evidence of the simmering controversies that not only occasionally erupt in and over the Plaza, but actively *shape* it as a public space.

But law is not everything. The Plaza is also policed, both formally and informally. Perhaps one of the most remarkable things about the Plaza is that although heavily regulated in terms of formal law, it appears to be quite lightly policed. There are no prominent signs on the Plaza indicating what is and is not allowed, when the Plaza is and is not open, or how visitors should or should not behave. And while police are not absent, they are also not very obtrusive. "We have usually a couple of policemen on bicycles whose basic beat is the Plaza to make sure nothing happens that shouldn't, because we don't want to scare the tourists off," Condon says. "If somebody is very obviously drunk, the police will suddenly materialize and hustle the person off . . . but we're not aggressive about it. No. There aren't a lot of rules and there is not a lot of oversight. There's more behind the scenes." Perennial city critic John Coventry agrees. While he thinks policing during the big tourist events is heavy-handed, he says "on a daily basis, the presence of a patrol officer who everyone knows [provides] a wonderful, lowest level of control." The Chamber of Commerce's vice president for public relations thinks that, on the Plaza, "A lot of times you can achieve a result without an ordinance, you know, with sensitive enforcement," which he argued the city has, but largely because the cop on the beat is a "good guy. And he's very good at balancing all these different things. So it all comes down to one person and one personality. If you had a real jerk down there, it could be real trouble between people."

This informal level of control is apparently quite important to the "success" of the Plaza. But it also serves as a reminder of the inherent contradiction that defines the Plaza as a property: the informality as it is lived and policed in fact is formed through a quite elaborate and formal, if behind the scenes, regulation—regulation that itself is the result of near constant battles over who, literally and figuratively, *owns* the Plaza. That is, those ten pages of City Code that regulate the Plaza as the city's preeminent public space are the result of constant attempts to answer the questions: "To whom does the Plaza belong? Who belongs to the Plaza?" For now the answer seems to be that vendors, tourists, and hacky-sack players belong, but poor transients, skateboarders, and maybe even long-time residents do not.

CONCLUSION: CITY AS LANDLORD, CITY AS SOVEREIGN, BUT WHERE IS THE PUBLIC?

There is another way to phrase those questions of belonging that get right at the status of the Plaza as a public property. Legal scholars, advocates, and judges often distinguish between a government's role as "landlord" and "sovereign."* As landlord it is an owner of property with many of the rights that pertain to such a status. As landlord, it can determine who is and who is not allowed on the Plaza, and what activities are permitted there. As sovereign, it is the embodiment of power—in democracies, presumably of the people's power (Rasmussen and Brown, 2005). Between its two roles lies a contradiction. The state's role as landlord assumes something like the ownership model of property. Its status as sovereign recognizes that property is always produced through social relations and, as such, reflects a balance of power.

This contradiction between the state as landlord (its ownership of property) and the state as sovereign (its accountability to the public) is crucial for shaping the nature of property and thus of public space. Law—the pages of rules and regulations that make up the City Code—both reflects and mediates this contradiction between landlordism and sovereignty. In so doing it not only reflects "the public"—the people who comprise the sovereign—but in fact creates it.

Henri Lefebvre (1991) has argued that any social order, any society, "excretes" space. Space and social relations are produced out of the social relations that make social life. Space and social life are coproductions. Similarly, any society or social order "excretes" law and regulation. The form and functioning of the Plaza of Santa Fe is perhaps best understood as involving the excretion of both space and law. As government-owned property, over which any number of contending groups stake claims, it is produced through the contradictory dialectic of landlordism and sovereignty. Something like the ownership model of

---

* Most recently, the U.S. Supreme Court has addressed this issue in *Virginia v. Hicks* (2003). For an analysis see Mitchell (2005a).

property tells only part of the story. Deferring to "ownership" to settle disputes over public property is, clearly, insufficient. Indeed, if the evidence of Santa Fe is anything to go by, the ownership model does not do a very good job on its own terms, since even the ownership *per se* of the Plaza is so occluded. Legitimate, codified rights claims by those who are not landlord, but who still must be represented as part of the sovereign complicates the story of public property. In its role as sovereign, the city government must write the rules governing the use of the park; it must adjudicate conflicts between rightful users; it must police the park. All these activities, attendant upon the state as guarantor of social order, hem in its power as landlord, as legal owner of the property. The more than ten pages of City Code dedicated to regulating the use of its own property are not mute, but are in fact exceptionally loud testimony to just how hard it is, in the words of the City Code, to institutionalize "non-institutionalization"—to formalize informality. Or, as we put it earlier, they are loud testimony to how hard it is to transform the social relations that *are* property into the space that *is* property.

Those ten plus pages do one more thing too. They raise the question of what happens when a state abdicates its responsibility as sovereign, as the *public* mediator of all these different rights claims on public property, and hands it over to a private organization. This, in essence, was what the Santa Fe newspapers were advocating in their calls for a Plaza conservancy. In the next chapter we explore this question in the context of San Diego, California's struggles over how to manage its homeless population in a time of rapid gentrification and redevelopment.

3

PRIVATELY PUBLIC

Property Redevelopment, Public Space,
*and Homelessness in San Diego**

The power of property owners, businesses, and residents of Chicago's Magnificent Mile was obvious enough. They prevailed over the buskers who performed there in legitimizing their own, in many ways private, interests in governing the streets and sidewalks. This is not unusual. But it is important. *How* particular private interests prevail in public space is a crucial issue for understanding how publics are formed, and for understanding what is and is not legitimate to do on publicly-owned property. Likewise it is crucial for understanding how, and especially by whom, public spaces are governed, even though they may remain publicly-owned property. Examining how particular private interests predominate, in other words, is important for understanding the restructuring of downtowns and the changing mix of people who can and do populate them.

In this regard, San Diego, California is not very different from other American cities. Over the past two decades, its downtown has gone through a massive redevelopment, with a new baseball park, convention center, festival marketplace, gentrified Gaslamp District, loft conversions, and new condo construction remarkably altering the face—and the feel—of the city. And like other American cities, San Diego is faced with a recalcitrant, and perhaps growing, population of homeless people

---

* This chapter is revised from: Don Mitchell and Lynn A. Staeheli, "Clean and Safe? Property Redevelopment, Public Space and Homelessness in San Diego, California," in S. Low and N. Smith (eds.), *The Politics of Public Space* (New York: Routledge, 2006), 143-175.

who find themselves squeezed out of the traditional public spaces of the city. These changes have presented San Diego with a significant problem of governance. For many, the city government is simply incapable (for all manner of structural and constitutional reasons) of managing the homeless. This, they argue, threatens the very "success" of downtown redevelopment. The answer to this problem, they further argue, lies in finding ways to privatize the policing and maintenance of downtown streets, sidewalks, and parks.

When asked how he would characterize downtown San Diego's redevelopment, Father Joe Carroll, the president of the St. Vincent de Paul Villages and the largest provider of social services for homeless and other poor people in the city, responded:

> I think it is exciting. I moved downtown. There's so much going on downtown. I think it's exciting. I think you have to begin to look at new approaches. Public spaces should be privately-owned, not publicly-owned.

Why?

> Because private people can enforce the rules. Cities can't. Everything becomes an entitlement. So if you build a beautiful park and the homeless move in, you can't move them out.

One way that "private people" can enforce rules is through the construction of the sorts of public-private partnerships for which the Santa Fe newspapers argued. In downtown San Diego, this has taken the form of a Property-Based Business Improvement District (P-BID) that cleans streets and parks, hires "ambassadors" to direct tourists to attractions, and often, to convince the homeless to "move along" and not populate the public spaces of downtown. In so doing the P-BID in particular, and San Diego's history of redevelopment in general, raises a question pointedly put by Henri Lefebvre (1996) back in 1968: Just who has the right to the city? Who has the right to be—and be seen—in public, and under what conditions?

In this chapter we focus on public space, property redevelopment, and homelessness in San Diego to provide a case study exploring the complexity of that question as it relates to the governance of publicly-owned and accessible property. San Diego's redevelopment cannot be understood outside an examination of the role that homelessness has played in it. For proponents of downtown redevelopment, one of the crucial issues has always been, and remains, the homeless and other street people. As Dave Allsbrook, the head of Centre City Development Corporation (CCDC), put it "The homeless population continues to frustrate us and we're not unique in this. It's a problem in most major cities." The argument of many is that the city has to actually *remove* the homeless population if redevelopment is to take hold. Yet at the same time, redevelopment itself exacerbates and causes both visible and invisible homelessness as single-room occupancy (SRO) hotels are destroyed or converted to more expensive apartments, rents rise, shelters are relocated, and services such as public toilets or drop-in centers are closed down (Miller 1985). This contradiction—that redevelopment both causes and is hindered by homelessness in downtown—has led to a contentious politics of property, public space, and the people who have a legitimate right to be in downtown San Diego.

The relationship between property and public space is particularly crucial for understanding how the changing geography of homelessness has both shaped and been shaped by downtown's transformation. For, we will argue, it is in *that* relationship that the fate of homeless people, and thus downtown, is determined. The next section therefore stakes out a set of claims about why the politics of public space and its relationship to homelessness under conditions of redevelopment should be understood as a politics of property—or at least of changing property regimes. In these changing regimes, we will show, a new definition of what the public is—and thus who has a legitimate claim to be part of the public (and therefore a right to the city)—is being worked out.

REDEVELOPMENT, PROPERTY, AND PUBLIC SPACE

Redevelopment in San Diego

Considered on its own terms, the redevelopment of downtown San Diego has been a spectacular success. Its success can be glimpsed in this recollection of a downtown worker connected to the Horton Plaza Mall development, which opened in 1985 and which is considered the cornerstone of redevelopment in San Diego: "I was [working] at University Towne Center [in La Jolla, north of downtown] . . . when Horton was being developed. And there was no reason to come downtown . . . unless you got called for jury duty . . . [I]t was all x-rated movie houses, sailors, homeless people. It was no place you'd want to be at night." Storeowner Bill Keller concurs: "Downtown was perceived as a dangerous place with nowhere to park."

But now that has all changed. Keller was one of the original tenants in Horton Plaza and later served as the president of the Gaslamp Quarter Association, a business group dedicated to the preservation and redevelopment of downtown San Diego's historic and entertainment district.

He now sounds almost incredulous as he describes the "intense activity" along the sidewalks of Fifth Avenue—the heart of the Gaslamp—on a Friday or Saturday night. With thousands of people out bar hopping, strolling, and sitting in sidewalk cafes, "it's just buzzing, it's just amazing." Horton Plaza Mall is now one of the leading tourist destinations in San Diego (along with the zoo and Marine World), and the nearby Gaslamp Quarter is filled with people taking a break from the new convention center, and with college students and other young people who find it the best place in the city to party. In the words of the downtown worker quoted above, with the mall's opening "all of a sudden, in 1985, you had people gathering together in a downtown environment that people thought would never be successful. But it worked."

Mitch Mitchell, vice president for public policy at the San Diego Chamber of Commerce, thinks San Diego is the "crown jewel" of redevelopment around the country, and to support his argument points to a boom in downtown residential construction, the development of a new, and quite fancy, downtown supermarket, and the fact that property redevelopment, including both gentrification-type upgrading and large redevelopment-authority-led projects, has not been confined to a single district but is expanding throughout the whole of the downtown area. For Mitchell, the success of redevelopment is directly linked to the city's ability to create a vision for the whole of downtown, and to undertake redevelopment in phases, not just piecemeal bits (see also Acuña 1990). The latest phase of redevelopment has now extended into the old warehouse and social services district east of downtown, an event marked, perhaps inevitably, by the elimination of its historic name, Center City East, and its rebirth as "East Village." Indeed, East Village is now the site of extensive redevelopment pressure as a large ballpark district centered on the Padres' new baseball stadium has been created at its southwest edge (Figure 3.1).

San Diego's current phase of redevelopment can be traced to the early 1970s when the city focused redevelopment efforts away from areas north of Broadway (the skyscraper core) to the south and the area around the old Horton Plaza Park, and then down along Fifth Avenue (the Gaslamp) where a wealth of old, architecturally significant buildings still stood and which had long been a key, if seedy, entertainment district.* Indeed, Horton Plaza Park itself was a longtime gathering point for homeless people, the elderly poor, and other marginalized

---

* Early efforts to redevelop Broadway, Horton Plaza, and the Gaslamp hinged on the relocation of the Rescue Mission, and the closing of numerous massage parlors, topless bars, single-room occupancy hotels, and card shops (Schacter 1985; Schwartz 1985; Serrano 1988). That is, redevelopment proceeded through a sanitation of urban space. And as redevelopment continued, the *cordon sanitaire* extended outward (Frammolino 1986).

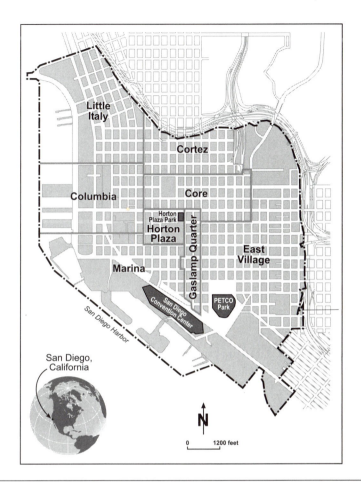

Figure 3.1 Map of Downtown San Diego showing the main redevelopment districts. Broadway separates the Horton Plaza area and the Gaslamp District (Fifth Avenue) from the skyscraper core. Petco Park is the new San Diego Padres baseball stadium. Cartography by Joe Stoll, Syracuse University Cartographic Laboratory.

people. With its underground public toilets, benches, and proximity to the bus station, shelters, inexpensive bars, and so forth, the park served as a gathering place, something of a social center, and a hub for essential services (Cooley 1985; *Los Angeles Times* 1985). Fourth and Fifth Avenues, indeed much of the south-of-Broadway area, contained a large number of inexpensive lodgings. Besides shelters such as the Rescue Mission, numerous single-room occupancy hotels and cheap bars crowded the area. Horton Plaza Mall was built at the edge of the historic center of the city, Horton Plaza (Figure 3.2). Designed as a festival marketplace, the architect Jon Jerde sought to recreate the

Figure 3.2 Horton Plaza Shopping Center. Many mark downtown San Diego's renaissance to the development of this festival marketplace at the edge of Horton Plaza Park. Photograph by Lynn Staeheli.

feel of a confined European street, with its "exuberant sense of public life," while also drawing on "an abstraction of indigenous architectural language" so as to reflect something of "San Diego's rich history."* As its developer, Ernest Hahn, declared on opening day, "It's not a shopping center. It's a street, it's a happening, it's a festival marketplace" (Harris 1985, 2.1). But it was a happening that turned its back on the city: three sides consisted of blank facades or large parking garages, and the fourth, fronting Horton Plaza Park, sought to draw people out of the park and into the precincts of the shopping center. The "center was built like a fort with very little interface to the area around it," according to a source involved with its development, a strategy that allowed suburban tourists and visitors to "feel safe. Security was heavily emphasized at this particular center." For Bill Keller, the construction of Horton Plaza as a privately owned and controlled, publicly-accessible space was critical to the success of downtown redevelopment: "I think Horton Plaza created the first public space in downtown for people from the suburbs to . . . begin the process of coming back into the neighborhood."† This

---

* See Jon Jerde's website, http://www.jerde.com/flash.php (accessed 24 May 2006). Jerde is perhaps best known in the United States for his designs for the 1984 Los Angeles Olympics and for Universal Studio's CityWalk in Los Angeles. For brief critical reviews of Jerde's mall architecture, see Betsky (1991) and Ouroussoff (2000).

† We examine the kinds of public activities possible in, and the types of policing of, the "public space" of malls in the next chapter. For now our point is only that this sort of encapsulating of public space in private property was perceived as critical to the redevelopment of public properties in surrounding areas, even as the mall turned its back on those very spaces.

process of "coming back" to the city has been greatly aided not just by the construction of publicly-accessible private property such as Horton Plaza Mall, but also by significant transformations in the nature of publicly owned property, such as the streets and parks. To see what kinds of transformation, it is worth examining (in a bit more detail than we have so far) just what we mean when we talk about "property."

Property Rights, Property Regimes, and Public Space

Property regimes—by which we mean prevailing systems of laws, practices, and relations among different properties—determine who may be excluded from particular spaces and under what conditions. As we saw in the last chapter, how this right is exercised, and over which segment of "the people," is always a vexed issue. It is vexed in part because, as Blomley (2000a, 88) makes clear, the property right to exclude necessarily implies a violent act:

> Expulsion . . . entails a right. The powers of the state can be invoked to assist in that expulsion. Police can be called to physically remove a trespasser; injunctions prepared, criminal sanctions sought. As such, expulsion is a violent act. Violence can be explicitly deployed or (more usually) implied. But such violence has state sanction and is thus legitimate.

At stake are the rules and reasons for expulsion, and the interests through which and for which the powers of the state are invoked.

Under capitalism, the powers of the state are often arrayed to protect a property's value. As a fungible, delineated *thing*, landed property's use value is, to a large extent, equivalent to its exchange value. The purpose of owning property is to have it increase in value. But since landed property can only exist in relation to other properties (it cannot be separated from neighboring properties) every owner of property has an economic interest in every other owner's property. The right to use and the right to exclude, therefore, are limited by exactly those same rights held by others. Property thus exists as a *regime* of practices, laws, and meanings that formally and informally determine the exact nature of a property right and that significantly complicate the ownership model of property. In a city, private property (and the values it contains) is necessarily determined in part by practices, laws, and meaning that also determine the use of public property.

These are critical issues in connection with redevelopment for a number of reasons. First, in San Diego, as is typical in American cities, redevelopment has been advanced as a means of increasing the value of private property, and therefore making it attractive to inward investment and a net benefit to its current owners.* Indeed, since San Diego's public-private redevelopment agency, the Centre City Development Corporation operates through property tax–increment financing, its very raison d'etre is to increase property values. With its powers of condemnation and taxation, and particularly with its power to promote or block the issuance of the conditional use permits (CUP) that allow particular kinds of businesses and services to operate or not, CCDC possesses certain rights to exclude people and uses, even from privately-owned property. But it can only legitimately do so if it is serving the interest of private property as a whole.

Second, redevelopment in cities like San Diego, as an incremental, expanding process, relies on a dialectic of public and private property. Public property is critical to redevelopment in several ways. Public and semi-public developments, such as convention centers or ballparks, are often key linchpins in the redevelopment process. This is certainly the case in San Diego where the convention center has long been seen as the basis of downtown's growth and success (Acuña 1988, Hamilton 1994; Showley 1994), and where a new San Diego Padres baseball stadium has become the center of an expansive new area of redevelopment in San Diego's East Village. In addition, public *spaces*, such as sidewalks, streets, and parks, are frequently cornerstones of redevelopment efforts. Publicly funded beautification of public spaces is used to jump-start private property redevelopment, partly because improvements in public space have a relational benefit to the value of surrounding private property. In this sense, private property redevelopment *relies* on public property redevelopment.

Yet at the same time, the redevelopment of private property frequently displaces poor and very poor populations. This has been the case in San Diego.† As poor people have been forced out of cheap lodg-

---

* Blomley (1998) explores some of the implications for understanding development as a narrative (and practice) of "upgrading" property, a narrative that entails the establishment of "good" and "bad" property. He shows that activists often operationalize normative judgments about property in order to rally opposition to gentrifiers. Without discounting the importance of that, the San Diego case shows that normative judgments about good and bad property have been just as essential for groups working in the opposite direction and favoring the closing, demolishing, removal or "upgrading" of housing, services, and establishments that either serve low-income people in downtown or that have long been ghettoized there.

† This point is borne out in reports commissioned by the city council in 1984 (Miller 1985) and a year later by the city's Housing Commission. The Housing Commission found that single-room occupancy hotel rooms declined by 1,247 units, or 26 percent, between 1976 and 1984 (Schwartz 1985, B1; Frammolino 1985). The Commission expected the number of rooms would fall by another thousand before 1988. Meanwhile, rents in remaining single-room occupancy hotels increased by 80 percent between 1980 and 1985 (Schraeger 1994, 41). It was apparent in both reports that the destruction of SRO rooms, and their increasing cost, were contributing to the growth of homelessness (Frammolino 1985).

ing, and as many of the indoor places in which they used to hang out have been closed down, the street presence of homeless people has grown (see Schacter 1985; Schwartz 1985; Serrano 1988). Many homeless people moved to open public space—Horton Plaza Park, sidewalks in front of newly opened bars and restaurants in the Gaslamp, or the spacious lawns outside the convention center—thereby threatening the very increases in value that would prove redevelopment's success. Homelessness in public space—on public property—was both a result of, and (many feared) a threat to redevelopment (Acuña 1989). Considerable effort has thus been expended (as we will detail below) in figuring out how to regulate homeless people on public property, or how to expel them altogether. This effort raises the question of just how much they can be excluded from property that presumably belongs to all the people. What new property rules are required? To what extent can public property be privatized—privatized either in the sense that rules of exclusion similar to private property can be enacted, or in the sense that private interests can directly control access to public space?

Those questions in turn raise a third important issue related to property and redevelopment. Private property owners, working as individuals, have a presumptive right of exclusion. The law scholar Jeremy Waldron (1991) has argued that in the American city, the only place homeless people can *be*, without being at the sufferance of another person, is on public property. They must have permission to be everywhere else. This holds true even in shelters and transitional housing where controlling agencies reserve the right to expel those who do not follow the agencies' rules. Waldron thus argues that in a "libertarian paradise" in which all property is governed by private property rules, homeless people would simply have no place to be, no place where they could live. Even if we do not follow Waldron to the dystopian extreme he so compellingly outlines, it remains the case that public property is the only place where homeless people, who otherwise have no other place over which they have property rights, can live or act autonomously. The nature of the laws that govern public space, therefore, also determines the sorts of autonomy homeless people may possess, even as these laws establish the rules by which people may be invited into or excluded from public space.

When, therefore, the maintenance and policing of public space is handed over to business and property owners organized into a Business Improvement District (as has been the case in San Diego), the means by which public space is regulated, and hence the relationships that constitute it as property, are transformed. A helpful way to understand the nature of this transformation is to see it as part of the transformation of the property *regime* operative in the contemporary city. Drawing on an argument by Krueckeberg (1995), Blomley (2004b, xv) argues that "urban land . . . needs to be recognized as land over which a legal regime of real property is operative." The term "regime" implies a relatively settled, fairly consistent, set of practices, ideologies, and social relations. A regime can be, at least metaphorically, mapped. Its contours can be drawn. Or, to abandon the metaphor, certain relatively settled relations and rules can be *institutionalized.* Roles—of owners and users, police and transgressors—are (again relatively) clear.

But this is not to say that property regimes do not vary over space and time. Indeed, as with regimes of accumulation or social reproduction (Boyer 1990; Katz 2001, 2004), property regimes are, in fact, dynamic and contested. They are, for that reason, both a shaper and an outcome of the exercise of power. When regimes undergo transformation, which is the case in San Diego, relations become unstable and are, at least to some degree, deinstitutionalized. They are up for grabs. Property becomes a site for social contestation, as we saw in Santa Fe. Since property regimes are necessarily relational, however, it is important to remember that they must necessarily exist beyond, and encapsulate, the specific relations and rights of property governing any specific parcel at any given time. Yet it is only by focusing on specific parcels, and specific times, that property regimes can be mapped.

Or, perhaps such mapping can only be accomplished by focusing on who is being excluded from public and private property—and how.

From Pseudo-Public Space to Pseudo-Private Property

In these terms the politics of public space can usefully be understood as a politics of property—a politics of the "people's property," wherein both the nature of "the people" and the nature of "property" are highly contested. This contestation often appears over the ways in which public spaces are preeminently spaces of sociability. Public investment in inner cities over the past two to three decades has increasingly focused on creating signature festival spaces: baseball stadiums, aquariums, redeveloped city squares and parks, urban marketplaces, and historic streetscapes. These signature spaces are meant to draw visitors and residents into the city to meet, mingle, and spend. Considerable investment has been made in making downtowns sites of spectacle (Harvey 1989; Hubbard and Hall 1998; Knox 1993; Sorkin 1992; Zukin 1991, 1995). Public space is seen, in this light, as the marker of urbanity. Lively streets, lively cafes, and lively spaces for gathering mark a city *as* a city.

Rapid suburbanization and white flight stepped up disinvestment in inner cities (see Sugrue 1996). The transformation of labor markets, the ravages of bulldozer redevelopment, and the decline of housing quality in the postwar period have all contributed to what has been widely perceived as the decline, and maybe even the death, of American downtowns (see Jacobs 1961). The reconfiguration of public spaces—reclaiming them from what are often perceived to be malignant uses (Magnet 2000)—has therefore become a central focus of urban redevelopment in hopes of reversing decline and repopulating the city. But to do so, it is almost universally held, the public spaces of the city have to be made "safe" for exactly that portion of the public that has fled the cities for the suburbs. Spectacle, in other words, needs to be carefully controlled to make it safe for people—or at least for some people, even at the expense of other people. Such control, developed over years of experimentation and never complete, has entailed rewriting the rules of public property, transforming the laws that govern it, and more and more frequently handing its regulation over to private entities (Zukin 1995). It has also entailed a literal privatization of public space, a moving of the space of sociability onto private property and in essence recreating the suburban mall downtown. For critics like Darrell Crilley (1993), such a privatization creates a "pseudo-public space," no longer really public in the sense of open access to all. But as Jon Goss (1996) argues, the production of pseudo-public spaces is not always regressive. It can open up opportunities for different kinds of sociability, and it can invite in those people who may be excluded from the public spaces of the city through the fear—and sometimes the exercise—of violence (see also Pain 1991, 1997, 2000; Lees 1998, 2001).

Public space in this sense (the sense of providing an open space of sociability) is possible precisely because the property is private and its owners can enforce exclusions of those deemed dangerous, deviant, or undesirable (see Chapter 4). The Horton Plaza Mall is a preeminent example of this kind of privately held, publicly-accessible space. But this kind of privatization is not the only means of securing "public" space. In addition to creating Crilley's pseudo-public spaces, cities are experimenting with the development of what could be called *pseudo-private properties*. These are properties that are formally owned by the city or another governmental agency, but that are subject to control and regulation by private interests. Examples include public sidewalks patrolled by business improvement district–hired security forces, and parks governed by conservatories or other private organizations. Such pseudo-private properties, we will suggest in the remainder of this chapter, have become necessary to the redevelopment of downtown under a system that makes *accumulation*—the increase in value—the primary reason for maintaining or improving the public spaces of the city, and in which sociability and spectacle are merely a means toward that primary goal. Under these conditions, the presence of homeless people on pseudo-private property becomes doubly problematic. Homeless people's very right to the city is thrown into question because as we noted, they simply have no claim on, and are not protected by private property and now have a decreasing claim on public spaces that are reconstituted as pseudo-private property.

Such an argument can be substantiated through a closer examination of San Diego's redevelopment, and particularly of its business improvement district–controlled program for regulating and maintaining the public spaces of downtown—a program called Clean and Safe.

CLEAN AND SAFE IN SAN DIEGO: CHANGING PROPERTY REGIMES

Horton Plaza and Horton Plaza Park

Horton Plaza Park was the historical center of San Diego, and it is likewise the physical, social, and political center of contemporary redevelopment efforts in the city (Figure 3.3). Even as redevelopment has spread south through the Gaslamp, west to the waterfront, north onto Cortez Hill, east into East Village, and to the new ballpark (see Figure 3.1), Horton Plaza Park remains the focus of discussions about the successes and failures of redevelopment. Deeded to the city in 1894 by Alonzo Horton, who stipulated that it forever remain a park, the half-block Horton Plaza quickly became the ceremonial and social heart of downtown.* By the 1960s, however, the park had become a gathering place for the elderly, the poor, and the homeless, and by the 1970s was largely avoided by middle-class workers from the nearby skyscraper core, and by visitors to the city. When redevelopment was first being contemplated, Horton Plaza's status as a *public* park posed a particular problem. Planners—together with the Hahn Corporation, the developer eventually selected to build the Horton Plaza shopping center—felt that the park's very publicness, and its growing association with the poor underside of the city, would threaten the success of the mall in particular and redevelopment more generally. As Mike Stepner, the former city architect, recalled, "The initial [redevelopment] plan call[ed] for a lot of

---

* A note on names: For ninety years, "Horton Plaza" referred to the public park on Broadway between Third and Fourth Avenues. With the development of the Mall just behind it, the name Horton Plaza was legally transferred to the Hahn Corporation (which then vigorously protected its rights to that name as a trademark). The public park is now legally called Horton Park, but is usually referred to as Horton Plaza Park.

Figure 3.3 Horton Plaza Park in the mid-1980s. Note the ample benches and the central lawn. These features were removed in the 1990s makeover. Photograph by Susan Millar, used by permission.

public space" because as redevelopment was getting underway, "there wasn't [much] public space in downtown." Besides Horton Park, there was only Pantoja Park just to the west (called Condo Park by many because it is surrounded by a cluster of townhouses and apartments and has the feel of being a private preserve more than a public park).

But this early interest in creating more public space, according to Stepner, quickly came to be seen as a problem, rather than a good. "When downtown redevelopment started," both public parks "were really homeless havens." While once the restrooms below Horton Park were a boon to shoppers downtown, they had "become real hell-holes" by the early 1980s (Jones 1985), inhabited by homeless people and drug users. More generally, redevelopment planners argued that the park would need, at the very least, a significant facelift, and new rules would have to be established limiting its use. Therefore, despite Alonzo Horton's deed stipulation, a portion of Horton Plaza Park was ceded to the Hahn Corporation in exchange for its agreement to reha-bilitate the park using CCDC funds. There was protracted discussion, in fact, about deeding the entire park to Hahn. According to Stepner, "The privatizing of that public square was a real issue."

Using three-quarters of a million CCDC dollars, the Hahn corpora-tion filled in the underground restrooms, at the time the last remaining public toilets downtown. The park itself was relandscaped, historic-style benches with armrests that prevented people from lying on them were installed, and the fountain was reconditioned. The lawns were resodded, and the bus stop, which "provided not only an audience for the many would-be preachers who wailed about sin and hellfire, but also targets for the pickpockets and panhandlers" (Cooley 1985, 2.1), was moved a block away. But one downtown worker associated with the redevelopment noted, "the homeless issue did not go away." The early results had seemed favorable, with a police captain reporting a few weeks after the mall's opening that "the transients have simply become less visible; I think there has been a dispersion of the transient population" (Cooley 1985). The transients, however, soon returned. By 1989, "tiny Horton Plaza Park" was once again "home to the homeless, the alcoholic, the misplaced, the recently released, the open-air preachers," and merchants were vocal in their complaints (Sutro 1989, 5.1). A *Los Angeles Times* architecture critic, drawing on the influential work of William Whyte (1988), lamented that "Horton Plaza is today a desolate place," suggesting that the new landscape plantings were used mostly as "urinals in what you might call the wee wee hours," and noting that although Hahn had once sponsored a noontime concert series in the park, he had long since moved it into the space of the mall itself (Sutro 1989, 5.1). The Horton Plaza Activities Committee, composed of local "business-types," sought to reinstitute entertainment in the park during the summer.

Instead, just before Christmas 1989, the city removed the park benches closest to the entrance of the Robinson's department store, the only large store that opened onto the park. The city justified this removal as an attempt "to 'normalize' the park, to get the transients to move and make the park more acceptable to legitimate shoppers, tourists and passers-by" in the words of a Parks and Recreation manager (quoted in Perry 1989, 2.1). The city promised to replace the benches the following June. It did not. Instead, the city council voted in June 1990 to remove *all* benches from the park, and to tear up the lawns and replace them with prickly plants and flowers (Horstman 1990; Johnson 1990; cf. Flusty 2001). In the words of City Architect Stepner's report to the city council on the changes, the goal was "to return the space to full public usage by all segments of the community" and to "dilute the influence of the so-called undesirables" (quoted in Johnson 1990, B2). Council member Bob Filner argued that the redesign was "an attempt to save the park" (B2) (Figure 3.4).

Practices of exclusion, to put the matter in property terms, were transformed through design—or at least that was the goal. The expectation was, once again, that the benches and perhaps even the lawns could be replaced a year later after the "undesirables" had learned to go elsewhere. This time, the cost of park redevelopment was to be paid entirely by neighboring businesses, prompting the *Los Angeles Times* (1990, B2) to complain in an editorial that the redesign "smacks of a classic attempt to sweep these people," whom the *Times* described as "the homeless and others who use the park peacefully," out of view of

Figure 3.4 Horton Plaza Park in 2001. Note the absence of anywhere to sit and how the lawn has been replaced with prickly landscaping to deter people from loitering, sleeping, or really spending any time at all in the park. Photograph by Lynn Staeheli.

tourists and shoppers rather than deal with "the more fundamental task of housing the thousands who live on the San Diego streets." A year later, the city followed through on its plan for re-landscaping by sending bulldozers in at 5:00 a.m. in order to "restore the dignity" of the park in the words of both John Roberts, the managing director of the U.S. Grant Hotel across the street, and Ron Oliver, president of the Central City Association. "The problem is the vagrants," Oliver added (quoted in Granberry 1991, B1).

Or as one informant connected to Horton Plaza shopping center recently put it, "until downtown can really come to grips with . . . [the issues of vagrancy], I think it's very difficult for the retail component to interface with the park and the [bus stop]." Dave Allsbrook of the CCDC recalls that while the 1985 design of the park was the result of "a fairly elaborate public process," the 1990 makeover that replaced the benches and the grass was the result of business and development lobby pressure. Hahn, the owners of the Horton Plaza, were very concerned because the dividing line between the public property and the mall's property was invisible on the landscape. Eventually, the Central City Association (the business wing of the Downtown Partnership) "weighed in on the issues and ultimately the park was reconfigured," according to Allsbrook. The redevelopment of the park was undertaken precisely to ensure and protect the interests of nearby property owners.

Nor does it seem that the timing of the redevelopment was accidental. The city first voted to make changes to the park as the Center City Planning Committee (CCPC), directed by Horton Plaza developer Ernest Hahn himself, was finalizing its redevelopment master plan. During debate over the plan, one of the CCPC members, Louis Wolfsheimer, a San Diego port commissioner,* "launched a tirade against the 'crazies' who populate downtown" (Acuña 1989, B2). According to the *Los Angeles Times*:

> Wolfsheimer is not the first person to complain about what many perceive as downtown's most glaring weakness. For several years, business owners, shopkeepers, office workers, downtown civic groups and others have warned that the area's future as a residential neighborhood and as the region's cultural focal point is jeopardized by the onslaught of peripatetic petty criminals, panhandlers, the mentally disturbed, drug users and dealers (B2).

Downtown San Diego's redevelopment was on "a collision course" with street people (B2). For his part, Wolfsheimer was careful to separate what he called the "crazies" from "the homeless or transients who live downtown," a distinction that became increasingly important in the discourse about street people and redevelopment downtown at the end of the 1980s.

For on that distinction hinged a set of policies and practices geared, on the one hand, toward *regulating* the "crazies," and on the other, toward *managing* the rest. And in the interaction between regulating and managing, new relations of property were developed.

Conditional Use Permits: Managing Homelessness

Throughout the 1980s and into the 1990s, redevelopment was having the effect of both increasing homelessness and making it more visible (Miller 1985; Frammolino 1985; Schwartz 1985; Schraeger 1994). This visibility led to numerous lawsuits and then, by court order, to increased spending of redevelopment funds on low-income housing and social services. The visibility of homeless people seemed to drive much social service development and business community support for a particular kind of social service provision, however. As the director of the Interfaith Shelter Network told us, the main impetus behind San Diego homeless policies seemed to be to make the "homeless invisible." According to another knowledgeable social service provider, Rachel's Center, a drop-in center for women in East Village, "grew out of the redevelopment of Horton Plaza because it displaced so many people. And women homeless who were formerly invisible were now very visible, and there was no place for women to go to the bathroom, [or] to

---

* The Port Commission provided the land that the convention center was built on, and is a major player in downtown redevelopment (Acuña 1988).

just have a safe place just to sit and spend the day." When speaking of the lack of places just to sit in downtown San Diego, this social service provider argued, "It's deliberate. It's an absolutely deliberate thing. It's a city of contrasts like St. Vincent's, Catholic Charities, Rachel's, . . . Salvation Army, and the works that we do, and yet [we] have such a mean spirit legislatively towards the poor."*

This legislative "mean spirit" and simultaneous charitable beneficence manifested itself in a number of ways in the 1980s and 1990s. For example, just before Horton Plaza shopping center opened, Ernest Hahn donated $1 million to James Rouse's Enterprise Foundation to build low-income housing downtown and in Barrio Logan, just to the southeast (Enge 1985). In 1987, following a multimillion-dollar gift from Joan Kroc (the McDonald's founder's widow), St. Vincent de Paul opened the first of its shelter and service facilities on its campus in East Village; other huge gifts followed, including ones from prominent downtown developers. Other services—the Rescue Mission, Rachel's Center, the Neil Good Day Center, and the Salvation Army—were similarly heavily supported. At the same time, CCDC and the city only reluctantly endorsed the expansion of social services and the construction of low-income housing. Father Joe Carroll of St. Vincent de Paul Villages complains that every time he tries to expand, CCDC raises objections and the city makes the acquisition of a required conditional use permit (CUP) nearly impossible.

Carroll was not alone in raising the problem of CUPs. CUPs are required of every social service in the city and they have become a key battleground in redevelopment. CUPs—also issued for trash dumps, adult bookstores, rock-crushing facilities, and dance clubs—set the ground rules for the operation of a facility. In the early years of redevelopment, the city encouraged the gentrification of the Gaslamp by refusing to renew the CUPs of social services, peep shows, and adult bookstores in the area. A lawsuit, and subsequent threats by a judge toward an uncooperative city government, forced San Diego to begin approving at least some CUPs for facilities for the homeless and poor, but the city government remained reluctant. In 2001, for example, a facility tried to get its CUP modified so it could serve as a nighttime drop-in center. Some of the nearby businesses objected and tried to block the new CUP. The dynamic at work in this controversy was interesting, but frustrating, to social service providers. The director of one facility complained that the center received "great donations from busi-

---

* The interview continues: Interviewer: "Is there any place to gather?" Respondent: "For the poor?" Interviewer: "Um-hum." Respondent: "Not that I am aware of."

nesses that are located blocks away," but that the relationship between the agency and the businesses on the same block as the facility "is not good, because these people feel that their business is threatened." Businesses located near homeless service providers fear the effects of street people hanging out near their businesses, and often fight the issuance or expansion of CUPs.

At its starkest, the CUP process means that social service providers are stymied in their work. Father Joe is perhaps the bluntest in his assessment, saying that "I" (as the embodiment of St. Vincent de Paul) "have no right to exist, absolutely no right to exist. None whatsoever. . . . I have to get a CUP for everything I do. . . . The little guys can't do it. And we need little guys at the shelters along with the big guys. It takes $100,000 to do a CUP process. So you end up [with] churches open[ing] up a shelter illegally and we get these long drawn-out battles in court." The property rights of social service providers, in other words, are highly constrained, largely because of the feared effects that CUP approval will have on other property. "Conditional use permits," says a social service provider, "are probably the biggest albatross on the social services' back that exists." While much of downtown is being made over for the benefit of private property owners, private social service organizations, which are also property owners, find themselves at the center of contention and ever greater public scrutiny.

Clean and Safe: Regulating Homelessness

If CUPs represent one angle on legislative mean-spiritedness, another can be seen in the ongoing debates about what to do about the street people—homeless people, panhandlers, idlers, and Wolfsheimer's "crazies"—who still remain on the streets of the Gaslamp, around Horton Plaza, or along the walkways that connect the convention center to the rest of downtown. The story of learning to regulate street people in San Diego is complex, contradictory, and vexing for those who are charged with promoting redevelopment. "The whole homeless population continues to frustrate us," says the CCDC's Dave Allsbrook, "and we are not unique in this. It's a problem in most major cities." Thus, as the *Los Angeles Times* put it, "Like other big cities, San Diego has alternated between the carrot and the stick for the homeless and panhandlers" (Perry 1993, A3).

For a century, California had a law that simply banned begging. In 1991, however, the California Supreme Court struck down the law, asserting that panhandling was a form of protected speech and so could not be banned on public streets. Cities around the state responded in diverse ways. San Francisco, for example, was one of the first to pass an anti-*aggressive* panhandling law that sought to control certain types of behavior associated with begging, but not begging itself.* San Diego, by contrast, at first relied on stepped-up enforcement of municipal codes that made it a misdemeanor to block a sidewalk, jaywalk, or be drunk in public (King 1993; Perry 1993). Since misdemeanors have to be witnessed in order to be cited, the San Diego Police Department published *A Citizen's Guide to the Control of Transient Related Crime* (n.d.) and distributed it downtown in hopes of encouraging people to make citizen's arrests.

San Diego police encouraged an "old-fashioned crackdown" and announced it was going after "panhasslers," citing them on any legitimate basis it could find.† A reporter for the *San Francisco Chronicle* found this crackdown to be preferable to San Francisco's 1992 anti-aggressive panhandling law, because it avoided an "ethical debate," and seemed to escape the notice of homeless advocates (King 1993, A1). The crackdown was in fact supported by some of these advocates. Father Joe Carroll was one. He opposed panhandling but thought it futile to try to outlaw it. Commenting on San Francisco's definition of aggressive panhandling, Father Carroll sardonically noted that it "sounds like my insurance agent" (quoted in King 1993, A1).

Nonetheless, then San Diego mayor Susan Golding began pushing for an aggressive panhandling law in August 1992. The law was passed three months later. Together with the aggressive policing of San Diego's streets, the law earned San Diego the distinction of being named among the five top cities with the "meanest streets" in America, as designated by the National Law Center on Homelessness and Poverty (NLCHP 1996; Vobejda and Haverman 1996). But it is not clear that the law had much of an effect on regulating homeless people in the public spaces of San Diego. When asked in 2001 about the importance and efficacy of the law, few of our informants could remember much about it, although

---

* Anti-aggressive panhandling laws are now common. See Amster (2004) and Mitchell (1998, 2005b).

† Most of the crimes listed in the Citizen's Guide could easily have been applied against Gaslamp revelers (exactly the target market for redevelopment)—public drunkenness, jaywalking, disorderly behavior, breaking noise ordinances—except for perhaps the charge of "molesting a trashcan," which was usually leveled against transients who searched the trash for recyclables. Street people charged with misdemeanors often fail to appear before a judge or pay a fine, and so their charges are turned into a felony. According to Steve Binder, a public defender, the high point for police citation of homeless people came in 1991, with some 8,700 misdemeanors charged. Two years later, when San Diego engaged in its "old-fashioned crackdown," there were only 118 citations (newspapers reported 42 citations the first day of the campaign). If Binder is correct in his numbers, the results can probably be explained by the police taking a more aggressive approach to moving homeless people along in addition to citing them.

it remains on the books. As the president of the Downtown Partnership complained, "the police do not really think it is their job to roust people when they're sleeping in doorways. Even though there's an ordinance that speaks to that, to the police that's not a biggie when they ought to be solving robberies."

The Downtown Partnership has therefore promoted a series of other, private means of regulating homeless people on public property. In the late 1990s, the Partnership, in conjunction with the CCDC, contracted with the Alpha Project to have formerly homeless men and women "patrol" the streets of downtown San Diego. The Alpha Project is run by Bob McElroy, who cultivates something of an outsider status among social service providers in the city. He says that many of the mainstream providers, like St. Vincent de Paul and Catholic Charities, enable homelessness rather than work to solve it. Solutions, according to McElroy's brand of conservative Christianity, require something like tough love, direct control over homeless people, and a program that will "challenge [the homeless] to get off [their] butt[s]." This is a philosophy that resonates well with the Downtown Partnership.

The CCDC and the Partnership thus asked the Alpha Project to "patrol" Horton Plaza Park and to report public drunkenness, urination, drug deals, and other "unsavory" behaviors. McElroy described Alpha's mode of operation as follows:

> Police can't do anything about [the homeless]. They have a constitutional right to be there [on the street]. . . . So they called us. I said . . . we're gonna go out there and offer these people help and we'll store their belongings and we'll give them transportation. . . . Anything a person needs, we have resources for. But you also can't stand in front of this business and harass people and run this guy's business into the ground. And ninety-nine percent of the people say, "I respect that." . . . Others will want to debate and espouse their constitutional rights, at which time we take people out on the traffic medians. If they want to do that, then we espouse our constitutional rights to inform the passing public that we're a social service agency and we offered this person everything that he's panhandling for, we offered him a job, we give him a home, we've offered him transportation, we've offered him sobriety, so what that does is dry [up handouts]—if people didn't give to panhandlers, there wouldn't be any panhandlers, correct? . . . So we blow their income and they move. That's how we get people to move. Don't harass nobody, don't pepper spray nobody, don't push nobody around. . . . Peer to peer. That's why it works.

McElroy admits that this usually just moves panhandlers from one place to the next—"that's what community policing is all about," he says—but it does have the effect of cleaning the streets in the targeted area, and then, perhaps, leads to stepped-up enforcement and community organization in the area to which homeless people have moved.*

CCDC was pleased with the results of the Alpha intervention (even if it was not entirely pleased with McElroy's management of it) and by summer of 2000 had regularized it as the Clean and Safe Program (Huard 2000; Millican 2000). Clean and Safe is the public name of a new P-BID that covers the whole downtown. The P-BID released the city's Parks and Recreation Department from responsibility for maintaining public spaces downtown and handed it over to a private concern: the Downtown Partnership. "On June 30th," the president of the P-BID organization recalls, "the city maintained [Horton Plaza Park, the sidewalks, downtown plantings and medians]. On July 1st they gave us the keys and said, good luck you guys." Besides good luck, the P-BID collects an assessment from area businesses so that all in the area may receive an "enhanced level of services." The P-BID, though regulated by state law, is a private organization, accountable to a privately appointed board of directors. It faces only minimal (largely accounting) oversight from the city.

According to the Downtown Partnership, which the city has charged with managing the P-BID, the impetus behind the P-BID's formation was a "general dissatisfaction [over city services], coupled with the rise of the homeless in downtown." The P-BID takes responsibility for "general cleanliness [on] a daily basis. Because of the homeless issue, there is constant defecating, urinating, wine bottles, on a daily basis. And if nothing else, if we can stay ahead at ground zero on that, we're doing superbly." The P-BID does "constant maintenance, constant cleanliness, constant power washing, because that stuff stinks."

Cleaning is thus an important part of the P-BID's work. Another part is making the streets and public spaces "safe" for residents, downtown employees, and visitors. In response to business and property owners' demands for more direct efforts at removing homeless people from the streets and parks, the second facet of the program employs "community ambassadors" to patrol downtown. The Partnership officially described its Ambassador Program (in 2003) like this:

---

* The Downtown Partnership's president confirmed this effect. "The Port [of San Diego] is complaining to us now because they are saying 'because you are rousting your homeless from your areas, they're coming across Harbor Drive to our areas. Stop.' . . . Little Italy, Hillcrest, they complain to us because they're saying 'you're doing a darn good job of rousting your homeless.'"

One of the primary goals of the Safety Ambassadors is to enhance and complement the City of San Diego's Police Department Services. Using two-way radios and patrolling on foot and bicycles, Ambassadors act as an extra set of "eyes and ears" for law enforcement and property owners, and can respond to Clean and Safe service calls in a matter of minutes.

Safety Ambassadors are proactively engaging homeless individuals and providing them with useful information about the various social services and where they can be found. Our Safety Ambassadors also:

- Deter aggressive panhandling and other nuisance crimes
- Work with the Homeless Outreach Team (HOT) to provide social service outreach referrals
- Assist with directions and information
- Maintain open communication with police to report ongoing issues
- Add a presence in Downtown to prevent vandalism and other undesirable behavior
- Conduct routine patrol of all Downtown parks (Children's Park, Gaslamp Square Park, Pantoja Park, Horton Square, and linear Park [sic])
- Provide emergency services*

The President of the Partnership, however, describes the Ambassador program differently:

There are two types of safety ambassadors. And I'd better be careful on this. One group are greeters. They walk around downtown in pairs and give directions, hand out maps, assist. They're not safety. They're welcome ambassadors, so to speak, and they all wear nice uniforms and caps, and you know, you can tell that's who they are. There's another part are the safety ambassadors that are a little meaner, a little rougher looking, so to speak. They stay out of the public view a little bit more. But they're not leg-breakers. Without being leg-breakers, they're the guys who will get in the face of the homeless people, and I don't want to say verbally abuse them by any means. We don't want to do that. But, you know, you send two girls out who are used to giving direc-

---

* Downtown San Diego Partnership, www.downtownsandiego.org/clean.asp (accessed 19 May 2003). The current description, which has been changed in only minor ways is at: http://www.downtownsandiego.org/index.cfm/fuseaction/clean.home (accessed 26 May 2006).

tions and smiling at people, they're not the people you want in the face of the homeless. So we've had to, in the last month, hire six additional people who are a little bit on the—I don't want to say rougher looking—but you don't want to mess with them is what it amounts to. So the police have given those people special training in terms of what you can and can't do. And our hope and our fear frankly is that they don't take it upon themselves to do things they're not supposed to in terms of keeping downtown safe. They don't get in fights. They're to be our eyes and ears out in the community, and with direct contact with the police department. But again that's a real fine line that we can't afford to cross.

It is also a line, apparently, that the designers of the Clean and Safe Program had to be convinced to draw.

When it was being debated, homeless advocates and social service workers called dozens of shelters around the United States to gauge the effects of similar programs elsewhere. According to Rosemary Johnston, the director of the Interfaith Shelter Network:

We got an earful. And we found out in some cities the ACLU had sued because the Clean and Safe ambassadors were harassing homeless people and depriving them of their rights, and of course none of this was shared in the initial unveiling of this vision. So, we went back to the committee with this information and we were hardly greeted warmly. The Downtown Partnership staff was very upset that we had uncovered this information and [that we had] got letters of support.

Eventually, Clean and Safe agreed that ambassadors would have to take a training program led by the ACLU and volunteer lawyers, and Johnston says, "I haven't really heard a lot of complaints about it."*

According to many interviewees, the program is very popular among business owners in the area, even if there are tensions over which parts of downtown are getting the most attention. One of its main benefits, according to the Chamber of Commerce's Mitch Mitchell, is that "they've sent a message which is that the business owners want to be sure the customers are safe and be sure the areas are clean." This, for many, is precisely the value of privatizing services.

But for others, that is also exactly its cost. One social service worker, for example, argued: "The beauty of downtowns in my opinion is that

---

* By partial contrast, Steve Binder, a public defender, calls Clean and Safe "a misallocation of resources" because "it belies the fact that [the homeless] need services, not law enforcement or a gentle prod to get out of town."

downtowns, any downtown, accepts what's there. If you are a little bit eccentric, a little bit crazy, people accept it. They don't single you out as they would in a suburb or a small little shopping center. You recognize it. You expect it in an urban area." While arguing that public spaces ought to be privatized, Father Joe Carroll also asserted that CCDC and other redevelopment players had "a purification mentality" that was seeking to create a city only for the "upper-middle and upper class." Rosemary Johnston added: "There were all these kudos about these BIDs in other areas of the country. You know they're called 'Clean and Safe.' And I had problems with . . . that name because it seems to me that the homeless population as a whole represents a greater threat to our complacency than to our safety."

CONCLUSION: PSEUDO-PRIVATE PROPERTY

The homeless, and the Clean and Safe–type programs that have been called up to regulate or remove them when they stand in the way of redevelopment, thus seem to herald a new property regime in downtown areas. Private entities are gaining control, even over public property. The traditional, at least partially democratic regulation of public property is replaced with a privatized set of rules of exclusion, and a form of violence (in Blomley's terms) that retains state sanction, even as the act is ceded to the hands of private individuals. As the president of the Downtown Partnership was so careful not to make explicit, downtown's new private ambassadors have a very set idea of who belongs and who does *not* belong in the public spaces of the city. Formerly public space is turned into pseudo-private property.

The new property regime changes the nature of public space downtown. Father Joe Carroll, who bemoans the "purification" of downtown, even as he is happy to have moved there, succinctly sums up the contradictions that lie at the heart of this transformation:

> Horton Plaza [Park] is owned by the city. Their solution was to make it unfriendly. But if they gave it to Horton Plaza [Mall], they could maintain it and keep people off. All of a sudden nobody has the benches now. Nobody has the privileges of what the Park used to offer. The city's solution is to make it so unfriendly no one will use it.

Perhaps Clean and Safe can be seen as a compromise, an innovation that does not fully privatize public *space*, leaving it to the whims of, say, a single corporation. But it is a compromise accomplished by changing how public property is regulated—and by *whom*. It is a compromise that sorts the public into the desirable (shoppers, tourists, condo owners) and the undesirable (the poor, homeless, and those with no other space to be).

The result is, perhaps, even more important than if Horton Plaza Park and similar spaces had been fully privatized, for it transforms the very nature of what is *public*. It transforms the meaning and practices—the regime—of property such that the very expectation that there is a "public good" is undermined. To the extent that there is a public in this newly sanitized space, it is a public that seems to be narrowly defined, both in terms of people (upper-middle and upper class residents and tourists) and in terms of interests (business, tourist industry, high-end retail, and property development). In this sense, what is at work is the neoliberalization of the city (see Harvey 2005; Leitner, Peck, and Sheppard 2006; MacLeod 2002; Smith 1996): *liberalization* because it is based on a presumptive equality of ownership and ownership rights in a world where exchange value predominates; *neo* because it does not eliminate the public entirely so much as it changes its meaning, and changes who has control over it. In this transformation, homeless people become pariahs, at once a symbol of all that is wrong with the public sphere and an ongoing hindrance to redevelopment and the good it brings in the form of increased property values. By turning over responsibility for maintaining and regulating public property to a private organization, homeless people find they have been even further stripped of any right to the city.

But so too have all those others who may wish to gather in public space and *not* consume—who may wish to use public space as a space of sociability, but not a sociability defined only, or primarily, by commodity exchange. For all along the Gaslamp now, no less than in Horton Plaza Mall itself, it is hard to imagine that people without money are welcome. On the Gaslamp's Fifth Avenue, according Dave Allsbrook, "on Thursday, Friday, Saturday night, it's amazing. It's wall-to-wall people up and down the sidewalks." The publicness on display now is something different than it was before redevelopment took hold. It is more akin to the kind of publicness possible in the entirely private—but publicly-accessible—property of the mall. So it is to there, to the precincts of the shopping mall as the site of a new kind of publicity, that we turn in the next chapter.

4

PUBLICLY PRIVATE

*Regulating Space and Creating Community
in Syracuse's Carousel Center* *

To jump-start its redevelopment, San Diego built a shopping mall. The goal of redevelopment was to attract a different *kind* of public downtown. To do so, redevelopment officials felt it was crucial to create a different kind of publicly-accessible space, one that was not bound by the same rules of open access as the other spaces of the city. By making an attractive gathering place on private property, a gathering place where new tourists, shoppers, and visitors would feel safe, San Diego sought to remake the downtown community, transforming it from one hospitable to "down-and-outs," to one desirable to a new class of people. In essence, it hoped Horton Plaza shopping center would become a new kind of town square, one quite different from Horton Plaza Park just outside.

In North American cities, shopping malls are often heralded as the new town squares, functioning in the public mind much as the Plaza in Santa Fe does. But just as the Plaza was constructed in and through the dialectic of property, shopping malls exhibit their own dialectic; in this case, it is a dialectic in which property rights of private landlords are used to justify the regulation of the space such that only certain members of the public under certain conditions are allowed into the new town square. Because malls are usually private property, exclusionary mechanisms can be utilized far more easily and with less oversight than

* This chapter is revised from: Lynn A. Staeheli and Don Mitchell, "USA's Destiny? Regulating Space and Creating Community in American Shopping Malls," *Urban Studies* 43 (2006), 977-992. Taylor and Francis Ltd, http://www.tandf.co.uk/journals

is possible (at least at this point in time) in downtown spaces, or the spaces of the "old town square."

As an example, on February 27, 2003, during the lead-up to the second war in Iraq, the management of the Carousel Center mall in Syracuse, New York informed a local peace group that they could no longer have a table in the mall (Gadoua 2003). No explanation of the decision was given by the mall owners. The owners may have felt it was clear that the status of the mall as private property meant they could welcome—or discourage—groups as they pleased. This principle was established during an earlier debate over access to the mall in 2000, when the Pyramid Companies argued that access to the mall had to be consistent with its primary function: consumption. "This is a building the public is invited to, not a public building," they argued (Brieaddy 2000).* Activists, however, disagreed, arguing that it was a de facto public space. And the editors of the Syracuse *Post-Standard* agreed with the activists, writing, "Carousel is, of course, within its rights. The mall is private property." The editorial continued, however: "Malls take the place of town squares, parks, streets, and other spaces that are publicly-owned. That should imply a heavy responsibility. Putting limits on speech—even when you have the right to do it—is dangerous" (*Post-Standard* 2003, A16).

But for mall owners, *not* putting limits on speech is often perceived as more dangerous. On the one hand, owners need to attract a large, and often diverse, public to their malls. On the other hand, they have to assure that this public is there to spend. Malls need to ensure that people feel welcome, that they will feel comfortable, and that they will feel safe. The solution is often to both ideologically and physically position the mall as the heart of *community*. As Margaret Kohn (2004 193) has written, "Community is an appealing alternative to public life. It promises to provide the pleasures of sociability without the discomforts of the unfamiliar." That is, the promotion of and making a space for "community" simultaneously creates a certain kind of public, one that is familiar and unthreatening and in which the distinction between public and private is ambiguous. The emphasis on community common to many malls (and that lurks behind many of the debates over how to remake and regulate publicly-owned gathering places such as

---

* Pyramid Companies is fairly aggressive in cleansing its malls of unwanted political messages. In early March 2003, security guards at Pyramid's Crossgate Mall near Albany ordered Stephen Downs to remove a T-shirt reading "Give Peace a Chance" or leave the premises. When he refused, they called the police and had him arrested. Apparently he was not the first to be ordered out of the mall for wearing offending T-shirts. See Kohn (2004, 1–2).

Santa Fe's Plaza or Horton Plaza Park) creates a moral justification for the regulation of space within malls in ways that blend public ideals with particular forms of public control and private accumulation that many Americans believe cannot be accommodated in the traditional public spaces of the city.

The debates over public access to the mall, over its function as a de facto public space—over the kind of speech rights that pertain to the mall and over who does and does not belong to the community constructed within it—point to the importance of space in sustaining and in some cases shaping the sense of "publicness" that defines a *civitas*.* These are debates that have been raised in almost every city in the country. What is at stake is the kind of public that is created in publicly-accessible, but privately-owned property. We will examine this issue through a consideration of the "publicly-private" property of Carousel Center Mall in Syracuse, New York.

SYRACUSE, NEW YORK: THE CENTER OF USA'S DESTINY?

Carousel Center Mall opened in October 1990 on a brownfield site north of downtown Syracuse, New York (Roberts and Schein 1993; Short et al. 1993) (Figure 4.1). Built by the Pyramid Companies, an important Syracuse-based, East Coast mall developer, its buildings and parking lots stretch for almost a mile along the shore of Lake Onondaga. Perhaps because the lake is heavily polluted from receiving a century's worth of industrial waste and raw sewage, the mall does not take advantage of its lakeside setting. Instead, it walls itself off from the lake. Visitors to the mall can spend all day there without knowing there is a large lake right next door. Nor does the mall open up to the city; nothing but two miles of empty, scrub-filled lots fills the space between Carousel and the center of the city to the south. The nearest neighborhood, to the east, is separated from the mall not only by extensive parking lots, but also a major interstate highway. Carousel Center is, and was designed to be, fully self-contained. It is a separate city, comprising five main anchor stores, several restaurants, a large multi-screen cinema, and the Sky Deck, designed for community uses.

Carousel Center is massive (Figure 4.2). The interior hallways stretch for almost a kilometer, although the sightlines are broken by pushcart vendors, gleaming glass elevator banks, and advertising kiosks (Figure 4.3). The food court and seating areas are always crowded, as the

---

* A *civitas* is a community or union of citizens. It is usually discussed more as a feeling or sense of civicness than as a collection of people governed by a particular state.

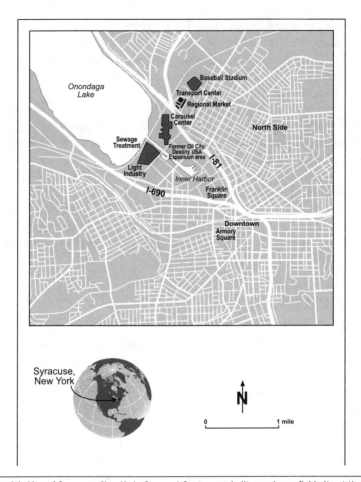

Figure 4.1 Map of Syracuse, New York. Carousel Center was built on a brownfield site at the edge of Lake Onondaga, a couple of miles from downtown, and separated from it and the Northside by elevated expressways. Syracuse University is just off the map in the southeast corner. (Cartography by Joe Stoll, Syracuse University Cartography Laboratory.)

mall has become the premier gathering place in the region. The mall management sponsors Christmas concerts, blood drives, non-profit fund-raisers, and other community events. In short, in a city like Syracuse, where snowfall averages almost three meters per year, where thirty years of deindustrialization have taken a deep toll on downtown and its surrounding neighborhoods, and where suburban sprawl is occurring at some of the most rapid rates in the country, Carousel Center has become the new—indoor—city center.

In fact, the earliest plans for the mall called for it to be even more of a center. The plans included construction of some 2,000 new residential

Figure 4.2 Carousel Center Mall, Syracuse, New York. The former community rooms, now converted into space for planning Destiny USA, are in the upper floors of the central tower. Photograph by Don Mitchell.

Figure 4.3 The interior of Carousel Center Mall. The photograph is taken from the center of the atrium looking north, and the anchoring Macy's department store is about a half a kilometer ahead, Lord and Taylor's about the same distance behind. The glass elevators ascend past the multiplex cinema to the former community rooms. Photograph by Don Mitchell.

units nearby, a hotel, other shopping centers, and a marina in Lake Onondaga (which is under an Environmental Protection Agency mandate to be cleaned up) (Short et al. 1993, 217). To finance all this, the Pyramid Companies secured a 25-year payment in lieu of taxes (PILOT) agreement that freed it from ordinary property taxes. It also secured significant public financing for environmental remediation, lakefront development, access roads, and so forth. As a declining industrial city,

Syracuse eagerly supported the Carousel development as one of the city's last best hopes for economic revitalization (Roberts and Schein 1993; Short et al. 1993).

In the more than a decade the mall has been open, none of the amenities called for in the plans have been built, but the mall has nonetheless thrived. One would be hard-pressed to find a Syracuse resident who does not spend at least some time there every year. By contrast, it is not difficult to find area residents who never go downtown. Carousel Center is truly the new gathering place for central New York. And it is poised—perhaps—to become an even more important new urban center. In 2000, the Pyramid Companies announced plans to transform Carousel Center into a massive, retail-entertainment "destination resort" called Destiny USA, expanding the mall by millions of square feet of commercial space, developing numerous hotels, and creating a massive, glass-enclosed park, portions of which will be designed to look like a Tuscan village, others a bucolic upstate New York glade. In short, Pyramid Companies hope to create a resort that would be "the world's largest enclosed and integrated structure . . . [o]perating with a unique single-owner model [where] all of Destiny USA's dining, shopping, entertainment, hospitality, and recreation venues are physically and virtually connected, providing guests with a matchless combination of experience and convenience."* To that end, Pyramid Companies has obtained (after much wrangling and a lawsuit) a new PILOT agreement, hired numerous planners and others, engaged in a concerted public relations campaign to win the support of a skeptical public, and over the years released several revised plans for the expansion. What links all the plans is a desire to literally *internalize* public life, and to create an all new community setting governed by a unique single-owner model.

REGULATING THE COMMUNITY AND CREATING THE PUBLIC IN THE MALL

As owners of private property, mall management utilizes many of the same tools to regulate spaces as do public property owners. Mall managers, however, do not have to pay attention to the same sorts of political niceties as do managers of publicly-owned property—niceties such as speech rights, obligations to constituents, or legal obligations to accommodate homeless people. To continue the language from Chapter 2, they do not have the obligations of the sovereign, only of the landlord.

---

* "An experience like nothing else": www.destinyusa.com/mainSite.html (accessed 28 May 2006).

The regulation of space in the mall, therefore, may be much more direct and less contorted than is the regulation of public streets, plazas, and shopping areas. To the extent that mall managers are concerned with the creation and sustenance of a public, it is presumably a consuming public, rather than a democratic public. If calling a mall a "new town square" helps in that regard, so much the better. If it does not help, then mall management can shift tactics without regard to the broader political and social concerns of how—and where—a democratic public can be constituted. Obligation as a principle of democracy, after all, doesn't pay the rent.

Despite the property-based realities of mall management, malls must still attract people in order to flourish, and so a public of a sort may be formed in the mall—with or without the protections of political rights and with or without landlord consent. As we have argued in previous chapters, modes of the regulation of space lend themselves to particular kinds of publics. But is it a public of sociability in this case? Is it a public that can formulate dissent? Or is it a public concerned only with shopping in the comfort and ease of a single-owner model? What *are* the modes of regulation in the mall and how do they create a public?

Regulating the Institutions and Functions of the Mall

The first (and perhaps most obvious) mode of regulation in the spaces of the mall is in the kind of functions or institutions that are allowed into it. Consistent with the rights accorded to property owners, malls select the tenants allowed into the mall and thereby regulate the kinds of activities to be found there. Mall owners do not have complete control over this, of course, as business owners exercise their own agency, but mall owners set the parameters for the kind of institutions and functions allowed into the mall. Mall owners are clear that malls are first and foremost spaces of consumption, and so they will try to create a retail mix that will attract a particular segment of the consuming public. The flip side of this is that owners are unlikely to allow functions that will interfere with commerce or that will allow non-commercial institutions to "compete" with services available for purchase in the mall. Competition in the mall is carefully managed based on comments from tenants, consumers, and management's predictions about future retail trends. As Carousel Center's manager commented, "Our primary purpose is to make money. . . . We are constantly looking at traffic to see how we're doing from day to day, month to month, year to year, looking at sales reports to see how tenants are doing. We're getting feedback from customers to see who they would like, all those kinds of things." In this sense, the function of the mall as a gathering place or as a new kind of downtown is clearly secondary, and the mall prioritizes its primary purpose of profit over other concerns such as building community or a public sphere.

Mall owners do, however, often recognize their role in the community and allow functions into the mall that are not obviously commercial. In Knoxville, Tennessee, for instance, a newly built shopping center offers a host of civic functions, in the name of taking the services to the people (Kohn 2004). Since the population is growing at the periphery of metropolitan areas, it makes some sense to take services there. The kinds of services and community functions, however, may be tightly controlled. The manager of the Carousel Center was completely clear on this point, saying that the management can refuse to allow different users into the mall precisely because the mall is *not* downtown and is not a traditional civic center:

> We have the ability [to control functions in the mall]. It is private property. You probably get to the point where everybody thinks that it ought to be like a street corner and everybody can do what they want. But the mall is not a street corner. . . . If I look at a downtown corner in the city, I think anybody could go there and stand on the corner and do what they want. I think you have the ability to do that within reason. But the people that control that would be the police. The police would control as to when you're going overboard and things like that. I'm not sure that's something that we want. . . . There's a lot of people here. They feel that they're not shopping downtown. They're shopping here.

Furthermore, he argued that it was the responsibility of mall management to ensure that the services provided by non-profit, local government or community groups did not compete with the paying tenants in the mall. Restrictions on the community functions allowed into the mall, then, are intended to insure that they are consistent with the primary goal of consumption; access is limited and permission to use the mall may be rescinded at any time.

At the same time, the restrictions cannot be too strict, and mall owners recognize a certain symbiosis. When people use the mall for community or civic functions, they may also do some shopping, and the "generosity" of the mall in making space available for community functions can generate a loyalty to the place. Newly developed malls try to foster a sense of community and of the mall as a place of sociability; comfortable chairs clustered in "living rooms" that shoppers can use to gather and to chat are one part of this effort. Also important is making the mall available to "mall walkers" by creating walking circuits through the mall where senior citizens get cardiovascular exercise in the climate-controlled comfort and safety of the mall. And many malls, such as Carousel Center, offer community rooms that non-profit organizations can use for meetings or special events. At Carousel, these two rooms and the kitchen attached to them are known as the Sky Deck. The manager of the mall argued that these two community rooms served the public good, providing a meeting place. He neglected to say, however, that the meeting place required $300 for room rental. Furthermore, there were limitations on the way these rooms could be used.

It is not clear, for example, that the rooms were used by a wide variety of groups (as one might expect, given the relatively steep room rental). The mall manager's description of the users was vague, but what he did mention hardly seems representative of the community at large or of the range of activities that one would expect to see in a public sphere:

> It can be used for weddings. Stores use it for training, for interviewing. Proms. There was a Boy Scout dinner up there last night. We also have a private community room, which is an area for anywhere from a couple of people up to 25, 30 people, and it's a little more private. . . . I know we have crisis groups that meet there, and you know. It's a variety.

While recognizing that the manager would not be able to provide a complete list of users off the top of his head, the users he did list do not in any way span the range of public or non-profit organizations in the city; most of the functions listed are, in fact, private uses of the space. The users seem consistent with the idea that the mall is a building that is public only insofar as some members of the public are invited to it. In this sense, the community rooms are not that different from conference rooms at hotels, such as Chicago's Palmer House.

Part of the difficulty in seeing the public function of the mall may reside in the fact that the mall management did not make it known that the Sky Deck was available for community use. For example, one of the members of the Syracuse Common Council (the elected governing board for the city), who was involved in working with the mall to make it more accessible to city residents, did not know there were community rooms in the mall, as this exchange makes clear:

> *Don Mitchell:* There are already community rooms in the tower [the Sky Deck] that we'll be going in today. I don't know what all the restrictions are, the ways to get access to the community rooms.

Respondent: See, I didn't even know that. If there are rooms, they are not well advertised. . . . And I don't want to say that's on purpose, but once again, with a for-profit attitude, they're worried about tenants and people shopping, not people using it for other purposes.

Indeed, the community rooms were not mentioned anywhere on the center's website.*

A second factor limiting public use of the space may be cost. As noted, mall management charged a hefty sum for rental that would be too expensive for many community groups to pay. It also charged a 15 percent surcharge on caterers to serve food, and only six caterers had the right to provide food in the Sky Deck, thereby limiting competition amongst the caterers. In response to questions as to whether the surcharges would be passed on to non-profit organizations, mall management simply said, "I can't answer that question. I hope the caterers would not be doing anything like that." When caterers were asked whether the restrictions on who could cater events were fair, one caterer commented, "The Carousel Center can do anything they want. It's their place" (Carr 1991). Apparently, it was not the community's place. It certainly no longer *is* the community's place, either, as the Pyramid Companies decided in 2005 they would no longer allow the rooms to be used for community functions.

But was the issue of community access also about definitions of community and about the public? When Pyramid negotiated with the City for a new PILOT agreement in 2000 to create Destiny USA, the company promised they would make educational spaces available for the public. As one member of the Common Council recalled:

There was an educational aspect of the plan where they were going to have dedicated space for basically an educational initiative, where they're going to allow people to get their GED.† They're

---

* Instead, under "Community" the Carousel Center website shows pictures of an iconic building on the (private) campus of Syracuse University and the inside of Syracuse University's Carrier Dome sport arena during a basketball game. It also provides a potted history of the city, and mentions key cultural institutions such as the symphony, the M&T Jazz Fest, and the Everson Museum. It does not mention the redeveloped Amory Square entertainment district, or even the Franklin Square area not too distant from the mall, which was redeveloped by Pyramid owner Robert Congel. http://www.carouselcenter.com/content.asp?contenttype=Community (accessed 28 May 2006).

† The GED (General Educational Development) credential is for people who leave secondary education before completing degree requirements. To obtain the GED, people must pass a test certifying they have the equivalent knowledge of someone who has passed the standard course work. People often take classes to obtain that knowledge before taking the test.

going to allow schooling to go on inside the Carousel Mall. So that was something that was able to be worked in. Although, it is not in the PILOT agreement, it is once again "trust me," a leap of faith. We have a commitment that the developers are going to allow that.

In another interview a few hours later, however, we learned that the mall management had a different idea of what that educational initiative would involve. The "learning center" would involve the Syracuse library and some of the higher education institutions in the region, but would focus on job training and adult education for construction and retail workers as part of the proposed expansion of the mall. This is rather different than a place to obtain general education or a high school equivalency degree; it is education in support of the commercial function of the mall or of the mall as private property. Other quasi-educational institutions proposed for the mall expansion, such as an aquarium and a reconstructed Erie Canal village museum, would be commercial establishments. Commerce, after all, is the primary function of the mall, and putatively public goods would be supported insofar as they supported that function. By regulating the kinds of institutions—even ostensibly public institutions—present in the privately-owned space of the mall, mall owners attempt to shape the community in ways that are consistent with commerce, which is not necessarily consistent with an inclusive public sphere.

Regulating Inclusion

Malls require traffic—people—in order to survive. Thus mall owners emphasize the ways in which malls serve as a gathering place; as noted previously, however, it is a gathering place of a particular sort, in which people are invited to come and to conform to particular norms of civility. It is in the process of inviting—and uninviting—people that the kind of public gathering is shaped.

Most mall owners would undoubtedly argue that they have the right to exclude people from the mall. They would focus on the fact that the mall is private property and argue that forcing them to allow everyone onto the property would be a "taking" of their rights. Courts in the United States approach the issue somewhat differently, questioning whether the malls actually function as a public space, and therefore weigh the relative importance of property rights and individual liberties, such as freedoms of assembly and speech (Freeman 1998; Kohn 2004). Their conclusion has been that malls do play a role in providing a public setting, and that property rights of owners do not automatically supersede the rights to speech; rather, court rulings have left the question of the balance between individual liberties and property rights somewhat open, in part to reflect the constitutional protections of speech and assembly that individual states might enact. While we develop this point later in the chapter, for now it is important to note that courts have recognized the rights of property owners, including mall owners, to limit access to their property.

There are a host of ways that mall owners can effectively "uninvite" certain elements of the public. The placement of malls in suburban areas or areas without adequate public transit is one way that access can be limited. In the case of Carousel Center, the Pyramid Companies' expansion plans call for a multipurpose, destination entertainment shopping center that remains disconnected from the rest of the city of Syracuse and from other redevelopment efforts. One design proposal, for example, surrounded much of the mall with four-story parking decks, requiring a long trek through the parking structures and across a highway if someone were to come to the mall using public transportation. One member of the Common Council commented that Pyramid was more interested in building a moat around the redeveloped center than in building connections with the rest of the city. While the mall manager agreed that it would be nice to have a connection with the city, he said it would be up to some other entity to design and build it.

Other strategies to limit access include codes of conduct and the use of surveillance and security teams to make people who do not "belong" feel uncomfortable or in some cases, to remove them (Goss 1993; Hopkins 1991; Kohn 2004; Shields 1989). From the perspective of mall owners, this makes sense in terms of the kind of market niche they want to attract and in order to provide a feeling of safety and comfort for their targeted consumers. Many people do avoid the downtown centers of cities precisely because they feel uncomfortable being confronted with people who are different from them or who seem threatening, thereby limiting the kind of public that is created there (Allen 1994; Ellickson 1996; Teir 1993). But whereas this limitation arises through the choices of members of the public to remove themselves from public space, malls try to limit access to the private space of the malls as a way of attracting a very specific kind of public—a consuming public that is not threatening to other consumers. As the manager of Carousel put it, "One of my objectives is to maintain a safe, clean environment so that, no matter what time of the day or what time of the week anybody wants to come here, they would expect to find a place where they don't feel threatened." The effort to create a non-threatening, non-challenging environment has led many malls to exclude or to severely limit access to the mall for one segment of the public: youth.

Teenagers and young adults occupy an ambiguous position within the public, with some rights accorded to them, but other rights withheld. What does seem unambiguous, however, is the wariness that many older adults feel around youth, and in particular, young males or young people of color (Collins and Kearns 2001; Pain 2001). By their very presence, youth can be challenging and threatening, disrupting the feeling of safety that many expect in the mall. But malls cannot simply exclude youth, since youth are also an important part of the consuming public the mall needs to attract for survival. One national study in 2003, for example, found that nearly 75 percent of youth between the ages of 13 and 18 either had jobs or hoped to find jobs during the school year, and that over 50 percent of them spent their earnings on clothing and entertainment, including music, movies, and video games (Auer 2003). In American malls, clothing stores that cater to youth and music and video stores are important tenants. Youth not only purchase goods in the mall, they also buy food and are an important part of the fast-food customer base. But youth do not just buy their clothes and a hamburger and then leave. They often hang out and socialize in the mall, using it as the gathering place that malls promote themselves as providing. Their presence in malls is obvious on weekend evenings, as the mall has become a place where youth can socialize indoors without the direct supervision of parents; in places with uncomfortably cold or hot climates, malls are important social spaces.*

The success of malls in attracting young customers, however, increasingly seems to be at odds with the demands of other customers, and so malls around the country have begun to implement curfews for teens. The Mall of America, the largest mall in the United States, may have been one of the first to implement a curfew. Mall management there estimated that over 10,000 unsupervised teens would gather in the mall on Friday and Saturday evenings, and would sometimes engage in raucous behavior, shouting, laughing, and running. Even when gathering quietly, some older customers complained that the youth dressed in gang colors. After a shooting at the mall, a "parental escort policy" for youth under age sixteen was implemented. While some mall users were

---

* It should also be noted that for all the heavy-handedness of policing youth feel inside malls, it is often worse outside. In many cities (including Syracuse) youth, and particularly youth of color, are questioned, moved along, or otherwise hassled by police whenever they appear in public, often on the pretext of protecting neighborhoods against gangs. As a result, many parents would prefer their teenage children to hang out in the mall because of the perception that it is necessarily safer than the streets.

comforted by this, others argued the policy was racist, as most of the youth were African American, whereas most of the people complaining about youth presence were Caucasian (Freeman 1998).

The Carousel Center management had been reluctant to implement a curfew, but ultimately imposed one in 2003. The policy states:

> Carousel Center has instituted a Parental Escort Policy on Fridays and Saturdays between the hours of 4:00 p.m. and closing.

> Anyone under the age of 18 visiting Carousel Center must be accompanied by a parent or guardian 21 years of age or older. One parent or guardian (21 years of age or older) is permitted to supervise up to five teens. Teens must remain within the company of their parent or guardian. Acceptable proof of age is a driver's license, state/provincial non-driver ID, military or college ID, passport or visa.

> This policy does not apply to the cinemas or stores with exterior entrances.*

The policy was implemented after adult patrons complained that groups of youth were just hanging out on Fridays and Saturdays, "running around, making noise, and fighting" (Doran and Errington 2003). In implementing the curfew, Pyramid hired "greeters" to check identification and to ask teens to leave. A new "community room" was established to hold teens violating the curfew until a ride could come to pick them up. Teens, of course, complained, as did some older adults who wrote letters to the editor. No one has seemed capable of mounting a defense of youth in the spaces of the mall, however, and the curfew remains in place. Youth are apparently part of the public when consuming, but not when socializing—or at least not on Friday or Saturday evening.

What does it mean for ideas about "the public" to implement restrictions like this, particularly when the behavior of some people means that other members of the public avoid a place? Democratic theorists have failed to take on the significance of the spaces in which the public can gather, and by extension, the problems when privatized spaces, which legally can restrict access, become the primary gathering place for the public. As Kohn (2004, 80) writes in a word play on the "malling" of America:

---

* See the Carousel Center website, http://www.carouselcenter.com/content.asp?ContentId=53 1&inside_ mall=Yes (accessed 28 May 2006).

In this mauling of public space, democratic theorists have confronted extremely sophisticated marketing experts, and the democratic theorists have been the losers. The political theorists who are most concerned with democracy have failed to offer a convincing rationale to challenge the privatization of public space.

As a result, the publicly private spaces of the mall are cleansed of those people whom "legitimate" members of the public find offensive or worrying, or more specifically, the mall is cleansed of those people who may challenge social norms and expectations related to civility (and perhaps to consumption). Accordingly, the importance of responsibility to the community seems to have trumped the importance of an inclusive, democratic public sphere.

Regulating Activities

The trumping of publicity is perhaps most clear in the regulation of activities in shopping malls, for it is through the regulation of activities that the full implications of the regulation of institutions and of the terms of inclusion can be seen. As we demonstrate in the following paragraphs, the regulation of activities in malls is justified in terms of the responsibility of people invited into the mall to not upset or disrupt other members of the community who are using the space for consumption and for accepted forms of sociability and civility.

One can think of the teen curfews as an example of regulating activity (e.g., hanging out) by regulating inclusion. In this case, the activities of some teens were deemed disruptive to other community members, justifying the exclusion of an entire class of people—at least at certain times or unless accompanied by a "responsible" community member. Another example—and one perhaps more obviously related to our concern for the ways in which the regulation of property transforms the public in, and mutes the democratic potential of, the new town squares in malls—is the regulation of political activities.

If malls are to function as the new town square or a new civic space, then the political activities allowed in public space should be allowed in malls. If they are not, then allowing only certain kinds of community functions and certain community members into the mall makes it possible for these members to be shielded from dialogue, confrontation with competing ideas, and dissent—confrontations that are the hallmarks of the spaces in which a democratically constituted public can operate. The effect, according to Kohn (2004), would be as though civic functions and conversations were surrounded by a moat, disconnected from the people who actually live in the city. Yet that is precisely what malls attempt to do.

While mall management often does allow certain civic and community functions into the mall, they also rely on the status of the mall as private property to limit speech and assembly. These limits have been upheld by the U.S. Supreme Court under certain circumstances, and whether the mall presents itself as a public space is key to interpreting these circumstances. In 1980, the Court ruled in *Pruneyard Shopping Center v. Robins* that while mall owners could not claim complete supremacy of property rights, mall owners could limit speech and assembly as long as the regulations were not "unreasonable, arbitrary, or capricious and the means selected shall have a real and substantial relation to the objective sought" (quoted in Kohn 2004, 73; see also Mitchell 2003a). In this regard, representations of the mall as a public space by mall owners become important, as malls that sell themselves as public spaces may be required to meet a higher standard for protecting speech and assembly (Freeman 1998). The Court also allowed that states could set a higher bar and protect more political speech in malls, but only five states do; New York is not one of those states. Furthermore, the political will to challenge speech rights in malls through constitutional or legislative means is often lacking, given the ideological dominance of property rights in the contemporary United States and that many people prefer to shop in malls precisely to avoid political confrontation and dissent (Kohn 2004).

Carousel Center and the Pyramid Companies have responded to the rules set forth in *Pruneyard* by steadfastly maintaining that their primary goal in opening private property to the public is to provide a space for consumption, not politics. Restrictions on political activities, therefore, have a real and substantial relation to their goals. Furthermore, they point out, the restrictions do not limit all political activities or assembly, but simply attempt to manage them so that the activities do not interfere with the flow of traffic in the mall, do not create a safety hazard, and do not compete with the commercial functioning of the space. And they argue that they have to provide a balance in political perspectives. So for example, in 2000, the mall hosted debates between Republican and Democratic congressional candidates in what the organizers called an "Old Fashioned Political Rally." In addition to debates between congressional candidates, the rally included sessions where citizens could speak atop a real soapbox (Breidenbach 2000). The positioning of the rally as "old-fashioned," and the use of a soapbox were hardly accidental. Rather, they were designed, through the use of nostalgia, to conjure up an older sense of community and to explicitly position political debate in the past, rather than the contentious present. For Carousel Center, politics were an *invocation* of a simpler past, a simulacra of political community, and in that sense not at all contrary to its usual prohibition on politics in the mall. The public it sought to conjure up remained the narrow public of community.*

It is no surprise, then, that the mall is much more restrictive when contemporary community groups, such as political organizations seeking to transform the contentious present rather than affirm the past, want to put up a booth or distribute information. An organizer for the Accountability Project, a local organization trying to force greater public access to the mall, claims that the Project was denied permission to set up a booth for voter registration—an activity that most commentators would see as enhancing democratic governance and as consistent with activities in the town square. Mall management counters that there are clear guidelines regulating the conditions under which booths can be set up, and that community organizations can use the main spaces of the mall; groups are only denied access when they fail to comply with the rules or when too many groups want to use the mall at one time. These conditions include restrictions on the size of tables and booths, restrictions on selling merchandise that would compete with what is already sold in the mall, staffing of the booths, times for setup, and a $1 million insurance policy. As the mall management argued, the mall is a busy place and they have to regulate the space to allow people to do their shopping. All uses of the mall by nonprofit organizations had to be compatible with the mall's primary purpose: shopping (Brieaddy 2000).

Conflict over restrictions on use of the mall for speech activities came to a head during the lead-up to the second Iraq war in 2003. As noted in the beginning of the chapter, mall management refused to allow peace groups to use the mall for distributing information and raising awareness. Peace groups attempted to change their materials in order to comply with Carousel Center rules, but the company refused access, nonetheless. Despite an outcry from the press and from many community members, Pyramid stuck to its policy. The central New York chapter of the American Civil Liberties Union reluctantly decided that Pyramid was within its rights and would probably win in court (Gadoua 2003). This restriction on distributing political information is telling in that it represents the triumph of ideals related to private

---

* To the extent they conjured a historical political community, it was from the turn of the twentieth century at the latest, and thus it was one that did not include women, only partially incorporated African American men, and, tellingly for a mall with a curfew, excluded 18- to 21-year-olds altogether.

property and the responsibility of individuals to the norms set by a private corporation over a commitment to open, public, civil debate.

It is hard to imagine that the ACLU, the residents of Syracuse, or members of the Common Council would have acceded to a similar restriction on political activities in downtown Syracuse. While cities place a number of restrictions on the "time, place and manner" of protests (see Chapter 1), and while some city officials might like to ban political activity on their streets, a blanket restriction on political activity on publicly-owned, publicly-accessible property is impossible. The Carousel Center's actions are only understandable in the context of the de facto (but not de jure) public space of the mall. As owners of the private property, the mall owners could justify their actions in terms of its need to regulate activities in the mall in order to accommodate the community of consumers. What is remarkable, perhaps, is not the action of the mall owners, so much as the acquiescence of the broader public to this regulation of this space of publicity.

USA'S DESTINY?

The plans for Destiny USA are nothing short of spectacular. The opening sequence at the Destiny USA website shows a city of soaring skyscraper hotels and apartment buildings webbed together by a lattice work of glassed-in winter gardens and glassed-over glades and waterfalls.* Surrounding the development is a lush urban forest where now only small industrial buildings and toxic scrub brush exist. No parking facilities are visible. This is to be a fully internalized, and completely separate, city.†

As residents of Syracuse know, the plans for Destiny are ever changing. Aquariums have come and gone; Tuscan villages seem to remain; plans for a third-floor re-creation of the Erie Canal are still reported in the press, but no sign of them can be found on the Destiny website.

---

* See Destiny USA website, http://www.destinyusa.com/mainSite.html (accessed 28 May 2006).

† The photomontage on the Destiny website is as telling as it is spectacular. The view is apparently from somewhere over Lake Onondaga and looks to the south. The near wall of Destiny completely blocks access to the lake. To the south, beyond the towers, the city of Syracuse has been obliterated. Where the current downtown now stands is a forest of trees and lakes (the photographs used to cover over where the city should be appear to be from just north of Lake Onondaga and show Cross Lake and a portion of the Seneca River valley). Syracuse University, the iconic representative of community on the Carousel Center website, should be visible at the top of the image, but it too is wiped away, replaced by a hazy view of suburban tract homes—perhaps homes meant for the thousands of workers at the new resort?

Figure 4.4 Two piles of steel were brought to Syracuse, amid great fanfare and much television coverage, as part of Destiny USA's campaign for special tax breaks from the city and county. As of January 1, 2007, the steel still stood untouched, despite a series of backroom deals and court cases that seem to have cleared the way for construction. Photograph by Don Mitchell.

And as residents of Syracuse also know, while ground for the big project has been broken several times, while a number of new employees have been hired (and then fired, when it turned out there was nothing for them to do), and while a concerted television public relations campaign about the development has been unveiled, no construction had begun six years after the expansion of Carousel Center was announced (Figure 4.4).*

In mid-2005, Pyramid closed the Sky Deck to create a technology command center for the expansion, severing its even tenuous commitment to provide "community space" at the mall. Even earlier, Pyramid refused to permit the Syracuse Common Council and Onondaga County Legislature to write provisions for community and political access to the mall as part of the new PILOT and bond financing agreements. Both legislative bodies acceded to Pyramid's refusal, despite the

---

* The city of Syracuse for several years argued that the highly scaled back plans for the expansion of Carousel Center that the Pyramid Companies actually filed (as opposed to those announced in the press and on its website for the full-scale development of Destiny) were not enough to trigger the PILOT deal. Pyramid sued, and early in 2006 a judge ruled in Pyramid's favor, finding that an 800,000-square-foot retail expansion of the mall was enough to trigger the PILOT and that Pyramid could use the payments in lieu of taxes to construct access roads, parking garages, and other mall infrastructure. Subsequently the city and county struck an agreement as to how new sales tax revenue would be split, and Pyramid Companies owner Robert Congel announced that construction on the expansion would begin sometime during summer 2006. It did not.

fact that hundreds of millions of dollars of public money will be devoted to the expansion. Pyramid truly seeks to internalize all urban functions—except the political. And in doing so it is providing a glimpse of not only what the new American city, but also what the new American civic community might come to be.

A PUBLICLY PRIVATE *CIVITAS*?

Throughout this chapter, we have followed the lead of Pyramid Companies management in using the term "community" to stand for "public." *We* are interested in the creation of publicity, but of a particular kind—a democratic, inclusive form of publicity. But the management of Carousel Center has made it clear that is not *their* objective. Instead, their goal is to create a place for public gathering in which shopping and consumption are the primary functions. As such, they are clear about their intensions to create a particular kind of gathering, with particular kinds of people. In doing this, Carousel management has attempted at various times to foster a sense of community, rather than of publicity.

"Community" is a slippery term; indeed, in the mid-1980's Larry Lyon (1987) had counted well over one hundred definitions in the sociological literature alone. While many definitions cocoon community members in feelings of belonging, protection, and mutuality, most definitions also recognize the role of community in excluding nonmembers and the obligation of community members to conform to communal norms. Community, in other words, may be a tool to discipline people in their relations with other people and institutions. From the perspective of a community, it may be acceptable, then, to set a norm of civil behavior, and to exclude people who do not conform to that behavior by panhandling, by being boisterous, or by making other community members feel uncomfortable. If the rules regarding community norms and behaviors are set in an undemocratic fashion, one could reasonably expect that community could be the basis of exclusion in a way that limits the potential for a democratic public to form. Political communities, no less than other communities, are shaped by these same processes of disciplining, inclusion, and exclusion. The result, Gerald Delanty (2003, 90) argues, is that the public, or the *civitas* created in and through community, is likely to emphasize "less the entitled citizen than the dutiful citizen."

Property rights are fundamental to the kinds of community fostered in the new town square of the shopping mall. Relying on the rights attendant on private property—even property built with substantial public subsidies—the owners of malls can use ideas of community to create a particular kind of *civitas*. The community of shoppers may not fit the ideals (or our romanticized reconstruction of the ideals) of ancient Greece with its agora, but it may be a community that conforms to the expectations for the space. Importantly, speech rights and other civil rights may play a role in this community that is secondary to the obligations of conformity and obedience in the new town square.

This is not the end of the story, however, as property rights always exist in *relation* to other rights and are given meaning through a host of processes and struggles. Teenagers still come to the mall on Friday and Saturday evenings and protesters still try to spread their message in the mall—where the people are. Sometimes, as will be demonstrated in the next chapter, the meanings of property rights are contested. And sometimes, the people—the public—seem to gain a foothold in their efforts to grow a different kind of *civitas* beyond the one in the new town square.

5

PUBLICIZING PUBLIC PROPERTY?

The Struggle for the Public in
*New York's Community Gardens**

If it is not hard to be skeptical about the kind of community—and the kind of public—fostered on the publicly-accessible spaces of the mall, it is nonetheless important to remember that community remains a contested concept and sometimes can be deployed in ways quite at odds with the manufactured sense of belonging found in places such as Carousel Center. In New York's community gardens, for example, community may remain exclusionary, as any public is. The relations of community in the gardens, however, are structured in very different ways than they are at Carousel, in Horton Plaza shopping center, or even on the pseudo-private property that is Horton Plaza Park and the streets of San Diego's Gaslamp Quarter. Community gardens in New York, we will argue in this chapter, serve as a new kind of *publicized* property that fosters a certain kind of community, and thus has its own effects on how the public is structured and who is included in it. For, in some senses, the creation of community gardens might seem to be a taking or expropriation of land, which is often a process of privatization. We argue, however, that gardens were in reality constructed through a process of remaking the publicity accorded to publicly-owned property. As such, the struggles over community gardens put into conflict two sets of rights: the right to property as it is spelled out in deeds and

* This chapter is revised from: Lynn A. Staeheli, Don Mitchell, and Kristina Gibson, "Conflicting Rights to the City in New York City's Community Gardens" *GeoJournal* 58 (2002), 197-205. With kind permission of Springer Science and Business Media.

Figure 5.1 Early spring work in a community garden in the Bronx. Gardens provide green space, fresh fruit, vegetables, and flowers, and community organizing or socializing space. Photograph by Lynn Staeheli.

understood through the ownership model, and the right to space as a foundation for the creation of a public and a community.

The community gardens of New York are located on plots of land owned by the City.* In most instances, the City granted rights of use to particular community groups who wished to create community gardens (Figure 5.1). For the oldest gardens (started in the 1970s) use-rights were granted to gardeners who had simply taken and transformed what appeared to be abandoned land; newer gardens were often "seeded" by the City government's Green Thumb program after community interest had been indicated and a certain amount of "sweat equity" was invested. Founded in 1978, Green Thumb was created to "foster civic participation and encourage neighborhood revitalization while preserving open space."† It regularized the process of securing use rights, provided gardening advice and supplies, and served as a forum for community gardeners. Green Thumb is also responsible for ensuring that rules of public access to the gardens are enforced.

Gardens have been developed in all parts of the city, but are particularly associated with neighborhoods ravaged by 1970s disinvestment and deindustrialization where the City assumed ownership of property in tax arrears (see Harvey 2005 on this period in New York). In some neighborhoods, the gardens have been a significant asset for gentrifiers, even as they have often been a site for organizing community

---

* In this chapter we will use "City" (upper case) to refer to the government and "city" (lower case) to refer to the geographical area.

† See http://www.greenthumbnyc.org/mission.html (accessed 28 May 2006).

opposition to gentrification. Gardens have different personalities in different neighborhoods, with many of those in the Lower East Side closely associated with radical and progressive politics, those in Harlem with its second renaissance, and those in the Bronx with the fierce struggle against neighborhood decay. In all neighborhoods, the gardens typically invoke the idea of a refuge or oasis of green in parts of the city with few, and often underfunded, parks and open spaces; they sport names such as "The Creative Little Garden," "The Garden of Happiness," or "Green Oasis." The gardens are quite varied. Some are carefully planned, horticultural gardens with a unified landscape theme. Others have individual plots for gardeners to do as they wish—whether growing flowers, or food, or building sculptures. Still others are tightly linked to local food or youth empowerment programs. Many provide space for meditation, community events, educational programs, or just sitting in the sun. Some gardens have small casitas on them, and it is not uncommon to hear complaints that these casita gardens are the domain of a single family or a small clique of residents. And some gardens seem well past their prime, as their founders have lost energy, moved away, aged or died, and no one has kept the garden from falling into disrepair.

The gardeners themselves are as varied as the gardens. In some areas, they are a racially and economically mixed group of people who have come together to make a community space, but in other areas, the gardening groups are more homogenous in racial and economic terms. To some extent, the gardeners reflect the neighborhoods in which they live. In general, the gardens represent an effort on the part of neighborhood residents to make a claim on a part of the city and turn it into something that suits their needs. They are, in this sense, an important place for the formation of a community and a public.

It is this latter characteristic of the gardens and gardeners that have put them frequently in conflict with the City—the owners of the land that most gardens are on, and an owner that in the 1990s developed new ideas about the best use of the plots. The sale of garden plots began under the Dinkins administration, but picked up steam in 1994 when newly-elected Mayor Rudolph Giuliani asked the City's Department of Housing Preservation and Development (HPD) to identify "abandoned" lots that could be auctioned to developers, both to help balance the City's books and to create new housing. As it happened, many of the lots identified by HPD hosted community gardens. In the next few years, dozens of gardens were destroyed by the City, despite vehement and creative protests by the gardening community, and the land sold to developers. Giuliani's second inauguration in 1998 saw large-scale protests by gardening activists, continuing the tradition of street theater that defined the community gardens struggle in so many people's minds. Indeed, it sometimes seemed as if Giuliani had perversely engaged in a struggle to the end with a motley crew of giant butterflies, frogs, flowers, and fairies—or at least a crew of protestors in those costumes—who had taken to the streets to preserve the gardens (Figure 5.2).

Unmoved by the parade of insects, plant life, and mythical beings, the administration removed 741 gardens from Green Thumb and gave them to HPD to be auctioned as vacant land so they could be developed as "affordable housing"; this was done despite city records showing there were more than 11,000 vacant plots in the city that did not host gardens. In January 1999, declaring that "this is a free market economy; the era of communism is over," Giuliani announced the auction of 112 of the transferred plots. Massive protests ensued, and eventually a garden preservation deal was brokered with the Trust for Public Lands and the New York Restoration Project, which saved many, but not all, of the threatened gardens. After filing a suit in 1999 to prevent any more auctions, in 2002 New York Attorney General Elliot Spitzer struck a deal with the new mayor, Michael Bloomberg, to transfer some 500 Green Thumb gardens out of HPD and to the City's Parks Department and thus to save them from the auction block.*

CONTESTED NARRATIVES OF NEW YORK'S COMMUNITY GARDENS

The contemporary community gardens of New York, according to gardeners, City officials, and historians of the subject alike, is rooted in the fiscal crisis of the 1970s when thousands of housing units throughout the city were abandoned by their owners (if not always their tenants) and fell into disrepair (Gibson 2002; Schmelzkopf 1995, 2002; Wilson and Weinberg 1999). As they fell into tax arrears, the City confiscated the property. Without City investment, however, buildings decayed and many were destroyed by arson or by City demolition crews, leaving holes—from a single lot to whole city blocks—in the urban fabric. Some 11,000 vacant lots in tax arrears were transferred from private owners to public ownership. Bankrupt itself, the City could not afford to replace abandoned or destroyed housing. The lots were placed under the control of the Department of General Services, where they languished.

---

* An excellent timeline of the gardens controversy can be found at the Not Bored website, http://www.notbored.org/gardens.html (accessed 29 May 2006).

Figure 5.2 The Rites of Spring Parade, New York. The parade was not only a significant community event, but also central to organizing opposition to Mayor Giuliani's plans to reclaim the gardens. Photograph by Kristina Gibson; used by permission.

Throughout the city, local residents began taking over the land—squatting it, really—and building gardens, often without official permission. Gardeners created much needed green space by painstakingly clearing out tons of debris, trucking in soil, and building fences, pathways, raised beds, and sculptures, and placing benches along walkways or tables and chairs in the shade of newly planted trees. Gardens provided safe spaces for children, served as focal points for grassroots community revitalization, and became a source of fresh vegetables and fresh cut flowers. Gardening advocates and City officials alike agree that in some cases community gardens were instrumental in halting and reversing community decline. Recognizing this, the City began to legitimize and legally validate the gardens through its Green Thumb program. Green Thumb offered leases for many of the gardens, and gardeners often thought they had staked a permanent right to the land.

City officials thought differently. According to a representative of the HPD in the Giuliani Administration (1994–2002), much of the gardening land was always intended to be redeveloped for housing:

Most of the community garden sites were at one point in time housing sites. . . . I definitely use the word "City-owned" when I think about them. I definitely think about them as "City-owned, designated for housing."

No one doubts that housing was, and is, desperately needed through-out New York City. The questions—and the flashpoint for much of the struggle over the gardens during the Giuliani years—were what kind of housing was needed, how the need for housing should be met, and especially *where* the housing should be located.

HPD claimed that the Giuliani administration had built or rehabili-tated approximately 68,500 units of housing citywide, with most of the housing intended for low- and moderate-income families; additional housing was built for special needs populations, such as people with HIV/AIDS or with disabilities. In 2001, a representative of the City argued that as the City developed new housing, only a small number of gardens had to be destroyed:

> So what has happened over time is we've built on all the other available City-owned land first. You always take the path of least resistance and build on the places with the least encumbrances first, so now we're getting to the point where there are very few clusters of City-owned vacant land that don't include a garden. We build in clusters. We do that, not only for economies of scale, but in order to truly redevelop a community. We need to do more than one building. If we put up an odd house in a sea of a dis-tressed community, that house is not going to stay nice for a par-ticularly long time. So we build in clusters and try to do a block at a time or scattered sites in a concise geographic area at a time.

HPD has exerted considerable effort in trying to get that message across, including a large display in the lobby of their building (Figure 5.3). Their message is that the gardens were always an interim use for City-owned land, and that the land itself was always slated for housing development to meet a greater public good. People who tried to halt the sale of prop-erty to developers were presented as holding the residents of the city hostage and as blocking their rights to adequate housing.

The issue of "public" and "public good" was critical in the City's framing of the issue. The City was at pains to counteract the image of the gardens as public, community space by reminding people that the gardens were often not really public space. As a representative of HPD asserted:

> The best of the community gardens are truly accessible to the community; the worst of the gardens are weeds. In some cases, chicken and rooster coops are locked up in the purview of the few, and the vast majority of the public does not have a key to the gar-den. . . . [E]ach garden group signed an agreement saying this is an interim land use, and there will come a point in time when the

Figure 5.3 Display in the lobby of the New York City Department of Housing Preservation and Development. Photograph by Lynn Staeheli.

City will develop this land and, in the interim, you are welcome to garden there.

By contrast, this official argued that the need for housing was overwhelming. She noted that in one offering of 96 units in the East Village, over 6,000 people from the neighborhood applied for the units. Following the old Housing and Urban Development Real Estate filtering model, she argued that even though not all the housing was affordable for low- and middle-income households, the new units created a housing ladder whereby upper-income residents of the neighborhood vacated units that then become affordable to middle-income residents, which in turn opened up units for lower-income people. She argued that housing was the most pressing need facing the public.

More than a need, creating housing was a responsibility of the City, she argued. In making this argument, which was a common refrain of HPD and the Giuliani administration during the gardens controversies, the City reversed its position of 30 years and once again promoted housing as a basic right for residents of New York.* But for whom—for which public—did these rights seem to apply? The housing built on City-auctioned sites, including former gardens in low-income neighborhoods, was overwhelmingly market rate, with only 20 percent of the

---

* The Giuliani Administration did not seem to hold this position very deeply, but rather deployed it strategically in the battle against gardeners. In fact, the City was, at the same time, in contempt of court for failing to provide adequate shelter for homeless families, families who would not even come close to having the wherewithal to purchase or rent the housing made available by the sale of the gardens.

units designated for moderate-income households. According to HPD, moderate-income units had to be owner occupied, and households in 2001 had to have an income between $32,000 and $70,950.

HPD argued that designating housing for upper- and moderate-income households was strategic, since an influx of wealthier homeowners would help "save" neighborhoods from further decline in a way that renters could not or would not. The representative of HPD, for instance, claimed:

> Homeowners in a distressed neighborhood, in good times and bad, will rally for sanitation, they'll rally for schools, and they'll rally for crime reduction. They'll rally for housing needs in ways that renters, who are not necessarily invested in their neighborhood, won't do.

While some gardeners supported this idea in principle (see Gibson 2002), they noted that the City's invocation of claims about housing rights and improvements to neighborhoods was disingenuous. When the Giuliani administration first sold a block of 113 gardens, for example, there were no restrictions on the uses of the lots; there were no housing requirements at all. The gardening community mobilized in response, taking to the streets in colorful displays and with a high degree of militancy, gaining a great degree of favorable publicity. Following this, a second proposed sale of over 400 gardens included stipulations that at least some of the land needed to be dedicated to "civic functions" such as affordable housing or economic development. According to one of the lawyers we interviewed who was involved in litigation against the city's garden seizures, the City added this stipulation to dampen the public outcry against the auction of the gardens. It also removed the basis for further legal action based on civil rights claims that the seized gardens were disproportionately located in neighborhoods with large minority populations. So while the City recognized the importance of civic functions, the right to housing was not explicitly recognized and was not stipulated in the restrictions on how the land was to be used; the further question of who constituted the new "public" remained unaddressed.

By contrast, the constitution of the civic (the *civitas* of the last chapter) and the public were key to the narratives of the garden advocates, and they tell a somewhat different story from that of the City. While acknowledging the real need for housing—a need that many gardeners experienced personally—the gardeners and garden advocates disputed both the motives of the Giuliani administration and the City's property rights (the deeded "ownership" of the gardens that gave the City the right to dispose of them as it pleased). In so doing, the gardeners advanced a conceptualization of property and of rights that included a basic right to public space; these were rights that were not held exclusively by individuals (as the ownership model would have it) but by communities or publics, and especially by those who had invested sweat and money in improving the land. This conceptualization of property rights was the basis for forming a broader public than that served by the construction of high- and moderate-income housing units; individuals who did not hold deed to land were still members of this public.

The greening community, as many called themselves, largely dismissed the argument that the sale of the gardens was intended to address the need for housing for the public at large. Rather, they argued that the Giuliani administration was cultivating a narrow public comprised of the white middle and upper classes, as well as of real estate developers and potential and past campaign donors. One activist in the environmental justice movement made this argument directly:

> If you look at a map of where [Giuliani] got contributions from, there's a very direct relationship I feel between who ultimately was getting the bids [and bought the land occupied by the gardens]. Who controls land use issues in the city drives what happened to the land, and how big the buildings are, and what gets bulldozed. And those are indeed the same people that funded Mayor Giuliani and a number of prominent politicians in the city.

Other activists echoed the feeling that the public Giuliani was interested in promoting was that of the middle class, and that the administration was concerned that the gardens were proving *too* effective as sites of (alternative) community building. One gardener, for example, explained:

> Well, don't ask me what's in Mayor Giuliani's head, but I think personally it has to be some sort of payback that he gave to the developers that contributed to his political war chest. All of a sudden, he said, "Well, hmm, these community gardens look so nice. Let's see if I can get my developers to come in and start doing some development."

An aide to a City Council member who did not support the sale of the gardens was even more direct, saying that Giuliani was threatened by the gardens as sites of mobilization and empowerment for people opposed to his policies. And other gardeners argued that the issue of the gardens could not be understood outside the context of race relations in the city.

Ironically, the Giuliani administration's strategy of reclaiming the gardens may have backfired, as one of the gardeners noted in 2001 that "the cork is out of the bottle now." Whereas before the gardeners worked individually,

> we have now become a collective force throughout the five bor-
> oughs. We're networking. There are people, young kids, who
> through nothing more than gardening, are now becoming com-
> munity activists, are standing up for a right. Because of the fact
> that if it's a community garden today, it's your apartment tomor-
> row [that is threatened]. It's your school the next day. So it all
> interrelates. And as a community, you must take a stand. You
> must take a stand for control of how your community is run. And
> that's the most important thing that I think we're learning from
> the work that we're doing on community gardens. And we're try-
> ing to let people in New York City know about that. It's not that
> community gardens are "anti" anything. We're community work-
> ers. We're just trying to make the city and our community a little
> bit better.

The sentiment that the "cork was out of the bottle" was repeated over and over by gardening advocates. There was a sense that the threat to the gardens was really a threat to communities and to the ability of the gardeners to claim a space to construct a public sphere, or as two gardeners put it in separate interviews, to create "a space of democracy, with a little 'd.'"

The gardeners imagined the gardens as places where people could work together—even while recognizing and valuing difference in class, race, age, gender, and citizenship—in the building of an inclusive com-munity and in developing a voice that could be heard in the city as a whole. Equally, there was a sense that people were waking up to the scope of the threat, and that they were in danger of losing their right to even be in the city. The cork was out of the bottle in the sense that they were not going to let the Giuliani administration confine the conflict to issues of housing or to use housing as a means to demonize garden-ing advocates and their claims to a place in the city. What was critical to the rights claims of the gardening community was that the gardens were spaces that the residents of marginalized and abandoned areas had actively made, and people across New York were beginning to real-ize how important they had been to the survival and revival of the city in the wake of the fiscal crises of the 1970s. The common refrain was that the gardens may have been *owned* by the City in a narrow legal sense, but they had been *made* by the residents themselves; it was not until the gardens became spaces for political mobilization that the City began to take a real interest in them—to assert its ownership rights. The gardeners argued that as residents of the neighborhoods and as people who had devoted countless hours transforming the lots from junk piles into green spaces for work, play, and gathering, they had a fundamental right to the land and a fundamental right to the city they had made.

Indeed, it was precisely because the gardens were successful in mobilizing their communities and working outside a legal framework (using the gardens as bases from which to organize parades and demonstrations, community festivals and agitation at city council meetings, auctions, and mayoral press conferences) that legal defense groups picked up their cause. They were eventually successful in persuading Attorney General Elliot Spitzer to bring a lawsuit seeking to block the sale of the gardens. There was a value, they argued, in the gardens as a space in which communities could organize; as a space to organize, the gardens served a need that was equal to housing. As one lawyer working on a lawsuit based on civil rights claims put it:

> The genius of community gardens was that they were sort of grass-roots, indigenous, native, whatever you want to call it, institutions within a neighborhood putting public space to use for that community. A natural outgrowth of empty space sitting there, and the community deciding to put it to use. Here you had the extra element of a community or members of it deciding to create it, in essence. And so not only people benefit by whatever public use comes out of these public spaces, but [there is] also the engenderment of a sense of community created by people working together to create community gardens. . . . Civil rights litigation has evolved where the days of thinking we are going to get great new advances in judicial decisions in civil rights have come and gone, because the courts have become much more conservative. In contrast to say the '60s, where you might get courts in an aggressive way helping in these issues, that's less true today. That's why we think the idea of working with communities and not being totally dependent on the success of litigation, and yet where litigation will play a beneficial role, is the way to go these days.

As the lawyer noted, the ability to press these legal claims depended on prior acts by the gardening communities, and these prior acts depended on having a space of organization—the gardens themselves. In these terms the gardens are far more than just gardens, and certainly far more than just sites for future market-rate and moderate-income housing.

As such, it is too simple to tell the story of the struggle over the gardens as a struggle over property rights (the ownership rights of the City, the use rights and sweat equity of the gardeners), for the struggle is also over rights to the city, rights to form and to be part of the public. They are struggles over just what a *people's* property is.

RIGHTS OF THE CITY (OF NEW YORK) AND RIGHTS *TO* THE CITY

Rights, as the foregoing makes clear, are not fixed, universal, and abstract; rather, they are a product of continuous struggle (see Mitchell 2003b). As such, it is helpful to think of rights as being a strategy deployed in the ongoing process of trying to build a radically democratic society (Rasmussen and Brown 2002). Rights, then, are part of a larger, continuous process in which groups seek empowerment, not an endpoint of a goal that is won through rights claims. It is probably less helpful, therefore, to talk of the rights of the public (or of community) than of deploying rights to *make* the public (or community). Rights claims (such as gardeners' claims to the gardens because of the sweat they put into them) remain important, but such claims must be understood within the context of larger struggles, in which the legal status of a right becomes a tool that is more or less useful at different points and with regard to different issues (Williams 1991). But more than this, there are qualitatively different kinds of rights. As can be seen in the struggle over the gardens, differences in the kinds of rights and their deployment shape not only the nature of political conflict, but also the kinds of publics and even the kinds of cities that are created in and through conflict.

In the gardens conflict, the City invoked its right as a property owner to do with its land as it saw best. In this case, the City felt it was best to sell the land to developers who in turn would sell housing to individuals. The rights claims invoked here were ownership rights of property held by individual entities, regardless of whether those individuals were human or corporate. This vision of rights as being held by individuals is enshrined in the U.S. Constitution. As many political theorists have argued, this construction of rights, rights holders, and political subjects rests on an assumption of autonomous individuals and citizens whose power and personal characteristics are universal (cf. Pateman 1989; Young 1990). Its understanding of how the "public" is constituted is one that works particularly well with capitalism, even as it limits the kinds of rights claims that are allowable—or perhaps interpretable—within the liberal polity (see Chapter 1).* In asserting this view of rights and of property rights in particular, the City engaged in a view of the public

---

* This point is developed, if in different ways, by Glendon (1991), Isin (2002), Laclau and Mouffe (1985), and Sandel (1996).

as constructed by abstract *individuals* who could claim property rights absolutely and who had an entitlement to the monopoly use of property (Singer 2000). In this view of the relationship between property and publicity, rights in property are as clear as the deed upon which they are written, and the public is thus structured as an aggregation of abstract political subjects.

The claims made by the gardening community, however, invoked a different set of rights and rights holders and a different conceptualization of the public. Like many of those in Santa Fe who sought access to the Plaza, and like anti-capitalist protesters in Washington, DC (or immigrant rights protesters in Chicago), the gardening movement claimed a right to spaces within the city in which a public—or in the terms of many of our informants, a community—could be formed, mobilized, and empowered. The holders of rights from this perspective are not so much individuals as they are communal entities marginalized through capitalist and racist power relations within society—communal entities that came into being in part by taking public *property* and making it public *space*. This point is significant, as the gardeners claimed a right to public space for communities that were otherwise deprived of the resources of the city. They did not, for example, make the same sorts of claims about the necessity of gardens for the wealthiest areas of the city. Rather, their claim was that as marginalized communities, they had a particular communal right to the space in which they could organize, mobilize, and seek empowerment. Yet this is a view of rights barely recognized in modern U.S. Constitutional jurisprudence.* The entire issue of group rights (to say nothing of rights to space as different from rights to property) is uneasily incorporated into most liberal constitutional systems.† Just as the ownership model of property tends to prevail, so too does the notion of rights as being held by autonomous, "atomic" individuals.

Being weakly defended by the courts, activist groups sought to assert and protect communal rights in other venues. Groups like More Gardens!, Reclaim the Streets, and Green Guerrillas pressed their claims in support of the gardens and communal rights in the streets, the media, and community board meetings—in what can be called the "public sphere." Other groups, largely composed of gardeners, organized watches and a system of alerts that was mobilized when gardens were

---

* Though as Akhil Reed Amar (1998) has shown, much of the debate over the writing and ratification of the Bill of Rights was concerned with what he calls "public" rights—the rights of the people as "a people" rather than as individuals.
† They are better incorporated into European than North American constitutional systems, but still weaker than individual rights (Glendon 1991).

threatened by bulldozers. It was in these settings, and through these actions, that the rights claims of the gardening community were made interpretable for the broader public in New York City. Even more than making their causes and claims understandable to a broader public, however, these groups came to recognize themselves as what Nancy Fraser (1990) would call "subaltern counterpublics"—groups that could speak from a position of marginality to make powerful claims in and on the public sphere. The gardens provided a setting to advance a new set of claims by groups that had traditionally been marginalized. They did not necessarily make universal claims for an abstract public (e.g., for the right to speak for all), but claims on behalf of specific groups for whom access to public space is constitutive (cf. Bondi and Domosh 1998; Podmore 2001; Ryan 1990; Young 1990). They argued that the gardens were critical in the organizing efforts of groups who sought to be included in the polity, even as their particularity and their differences as citizens had to be recognized. That is, while the gardens may often have started simply as gardens, they became a site of struggle in which public property was made into public space and hence a space for organizing. But since gardens were *community* spaces, and since *difference* was so critical to the formation of community, these public spaces were created through acts of exclusion to create safe places in which it was possible to conceive of different kinds of publicity; they were thus the domains of particular counterpublics that operated from a position of marginality. What is crucial here, is that the relations of exclusion were (and are) radically different from the relations of exclusion in, say, Syracuse's Carousel Center or San Diego's Horton Plaza Park after the development of the Clean and Safe program. In the gardens, visions of publicity *incorporated* difference and nonconformance into dominant views of acceptability—views that some gardeners argued are tainted by racial and class-based biases and prejudices. Rather than excluding people from the public through the exercise of individually held property rights, the gardeners claimed the property to create alternative visions of publicity that are potentially open to all people; while they relied on a form of exclusion, they argued that it was to create radically open democratic possibilities, rather than to discriminate.

While some in the City tried to use the fact that community gardening necessarily entailed exclusion as a tool in the fight to reclaim the gardens, the sorts of claims gardening groups made proved to have deep resonance, even with those constituents to whom the Giuliani administration was putatively appealing. After the first garden destructions in 1994, gardeners began a long campaign that included everything from letter-writing campaigns to annual garden tours to spring festivals to street protests. Their struggles reached a climax in 1999 with the negotiated garden purchase by the Trust for Public Land and the New York Restoration Project, and another climax in 2002 when new Mayor Michael Bloomberg reached a settlement with Attorney General Elliot Spitzer to save a number of gardens and to still build some 2,000 City-sponsored low-income housing units (Steinhauer 2002).

The resolution of the conflict, however, should not necessarily be read as a victory for communal rights or for the standing of collective counterpublics against the individualism of a rights-based legal system or the ownership model. The ways in which the various lawsuits against the City were settled—that is, through sales to the land trusts and through negotiated settlement—did not recognize the *legal* claims made on behalf of gardening groups, and in many ways, property rights as read through an ownership model remain relatively unscathed. While the public's right to garden in some already-established gardens has been affirmed by the land trusts, they have been affirmed because the land trusts now *own* the gardens. The implications of this shift of ownership are worth examining in some detail.

PRIVATE RIGHTS TO THE CITY?

Land trusts operate in the murky region between public and private. They own land as private entities, yet they claim to do so in the public interest. In this way, the land trusts apparently take a view of the regulation of property and space in ways that are similar to the management of the Carousel Center Mall. We should not minimize the differences between malls, which define the public interest in terms of consumption and capital accumulation and land trusts, which do not, but neither should the similarities be ignored. If Destiny USA is planned to privately produce all the social functions of the city in a "single-ownership model," how different is that from the ways in which land trust management of public parks in New York City (such as with the Central Park Conservancy) create a kind of "private production of nature" (Katz 1998; 2001; 2006)? Those private productions often conflict with the ideal of public space as a space for autonomous, collective action developed from the grassroots. No less than private developer ownership of the "new town square" transforms the kinds of rights that can be claimed and publics that can form, land trust ownership of the gardens sets a new stage for public struggles. If community gardens created on abandoned property were in some deep sense a people's property, will they remain the people's property now that they are held "in trust" for the people?

When the two land trusts—the New York Restoration Project and the Trust for Public Land—took ownership of the garden lots, they ensured the survival of the gardens as spaces with public access. When asked what the biggest challenge facing the gardens was, almost everyone we talked to in New York in the spring of 2001* gave the same answer: survival. So the importance of the purchase of the land in the public interest is clear: it saved a significant number of gardens.† But it remains unclear whether—or how—the role of the gardens as spaces of empowerment and mobilization will be transformed under the new property regime.

It must be remembered that one of the things that made the gardens sources of power, and significant sites for the formation of counterpublics, was that they were in some sense *taken* land. This taking of property was crucial to the gardens' meaning and function, representing as it did for many of our interviewees, a claim about the rights of people to decide for themselves what was best for their neighborhoods. With the land trusts, however, control may be shifted, along with legal ownership, to more distant, more bureaucratic organizations. The meaning and function of the gardens is likely to change, therefore, and with that change will come a change in the meaning of the right to the city as it is produced through and in the gardens. Lefebvre (1996) argued that the hallmark of a progressive, collective right to the city was the construction of the city as an *oeuvre*—a work. But through this agreement, control of the *means* of production—the means for creating the *oeuvre*—is being shifted.

The land trusts are private organizations that hold ownership of the land "in trust" for the gardening groups. As with the streets and parks that comprise the traditional public forum, and which governments hold in trust for the people, there is no guarantee that this trusteeship will be interpreted broadly. Just as people have continually had to

---

* We conducted our interviews after the first big purchase of gardens by the land trusts, but before rules for their regulation were well established and before the City's settlement with the attorney general.

† Not all gardens were saved by the purchases and the settlement. Some significant community spaces, such as the Esparanza Garden, were destroyed before the settlement. See Hays (2002). Others, such as the Liz Christy Garden, originally built by and named in honor of the Green Guerilla's founder, remained threatened until a separate settlement was reached in 2005 after a long struggle. See: http://www.greenguerillas.org/speakup. asp?id=204 (accessed 1 June 2006).

retake the streets that are held in trust to make them a space for public protest, gardeners may likewise have to continually retake the very gardens that they themselves have made. So far the land trusts have proven trustworthy, and the gardeners we interviewed seemed largely relieved that their gardens have been spared the bulldozer.

For their part, representatives of the trusts aver that much of the day-to-day management of the gardens will remain the responsibility of the gardeners, but at the same time, the land trusts want to ensure that the gardens are actually maintained and kept open for public use. As such, they have initiated projects to teach gardeners management skills, and have set out guidelines for maintaining the properties that have to be followed. Gardens will be monitored by the trusts to ensure that access requirements are met. And the trusts have retained the right to remove the management or governing structure of gardens that the trusts feel do not meet their obligations as public stewards. The near-term goal of the trusts is to engender stable, and in their terms, "responsible," operating rules for the gardens.* As one representative of a trust commented:

> We want to change the dynamic, the model for how community gardens are operating and running in the city. . . . And the best way we think we can do that is to make sure that there's some accountability. We feel that if some entity has responsibility, not just for a couple of years, but for 25, 30, 50 years down the road, the entity will take the responsibility to ensure that these gardens are going to be maintained as gardens, as beautiful open spaces for community use, for public use. . . . This is not going to happen overnight, obviously. We've set up [the trust] to add some accountability, to ensure that the gardens are public, that the gardens are open, that the gardens are beginning to be community tools so that different aspects of the community can use them. . . . That's one of the main reasons why [the trust] was established, was to have accountability. We'll monitor and we'll encourage and we'll work towards opening up or including more residents and more members of the community in the garden. But again, it might take years to do that. But we're willing to wait and to work on it.

While the language of accountability and responsibility are explicit in the trust representative's comments, just as important is what is implicit:

---

* The language of responsibility, and the land trust policies more broadly, resonate well with the neo-liberal ideologies of governance, and reflect what has been called the "NGOization" (nongovernmental organization) of social movements—their professionalization and move toward accountability by funding agencies, both of which can blunt their radical potential.

that the gardens are meant to function as beautiful open spaces, more than as political or mobilization spaces. Their value is in their greenness, and openness is geared toward enhancing that, rather than an abstract "public" or "community," and far less for the sorts of intentional, political counterpublics that many of the gardens had fostered.

To be sure, in working with the gardening groups, some of the land trust representatives recognize that it may be difficult to build the accountability they desire and also to retain the gardens as sites for autonomous community building. They worry that externally imposed notions of accountability and responsibility may be viewed with suspicion by the gardeners and thus be counterproductive. As one representative commented:

> If the trusts get too heavy-handed, it's a disaster because these are spaces that are created by people in their neighborhoods. And despite your best intentions, if you wield a big stick in trying to make it public, you're exercising a level of control that in some ways is inappropriate for the grassroots space.

The gardeners also worry about this issue, and some are a bit resentful that an outside organization has assumed more control over the gardens. Some of the groups that have built leadership and management from within their neighborhoods—groups that have been proactive in using the gardens for neighborhood mobilization—are somewhat suspicious of what the new owners expect; they are also resentful of the implicit message that the gardeners have not already built accountability structures and that they are incapable of working in solidarity with other gardens to teach them how to build those structures. Furthermore, the issue is overlain with the politics of race in the city, according to two gardeners we interviewed, with oversight focused most heavily on gardening groups in minority neighborhoods.

At root, some of the gardening groups are concerned that the land trusts may exert too much control and will channel the activism promoted in the gardens into particular ways of operating and being. In short, the possibility exists that the land trusts will change the operation of the gardens in ways that limit the radical potential of the mobilizations that occur within those spaces. As the lawyer quoted earlier noted, the genius of the gardens is that they are "indigenous" sites of mobilization. Some of the gardeners worry that this genius will be constrained by the new regulations and oversight.

While no one raised this issue with us specifically, it should be noted that the civil rights issues raised by gardeners in their earlier suits against the city are transformed with the transfer of ownership. The land trusts now manage the land in "public trust." Since they are publicly *private,* however, they are not as stringently constrained by legal or moral obligations to the "public" as are government agencies. And it remains unclear just which abstract—or actual—public or community the land trusts seek to serve when they promise that they will guarantee the gardens will be opened to public and community use. As Mulder (2003) argues in a somewhat different context, it may be the public that lives next to the gardens, it may be the people who can access the scenic and environmental benefits of the gardens, or it may be the city as a whole. Since the formation of a public—or a public space—*necessarily* entails exclusion, the relationships of exclusion that will be put into effect are no more clear than are the beneficiaries of those exclusions.

The land trusts are under no obligation—again, legally or morally— to construct the public as those who use the space for mobilization, or for those who use the space as an indispensable foundation for the formation of a subaltern counterpublic; indeed, the land trusts may well argue that political mobilization in the gardens is contrary to the public interest, for which they hold the land in trust. One of the advantages of land trusts is precisely that they can do things that governments cannot do. In this situation, they may be able to limit the political potential of the gardens in a way that the Giuliani administration could not do. Or to put that in terms laid out earlier, precisely because land trusts are private, they can operate more freely as landlords, with fewer of the kinds of *public* obligations that constrain a sovereign. As publicly private entities, they might prove to be a more formidable barrier to taking and making public space out of (formerly) public property.

CONCLUSION

There was no indication from any of the people we interviewed in April 2001 that the land trusts had done, or were planning to do, anything to limit the ability of gardeners to organize their communities. And, in fact, in 2004 the Trust for Public Lands announced that it would transfer ownership of many of its gardens to smaller, locally based land trusts, which it set up in city neighborhoods, and to which it promised a high degree of self-governance (Mooney 2004). Yet there was an undercurrent of worry expressed by many of the gardeners and greening advocates with whom we spoke. The issue from their perspective was that land trusts have become a new and powerful agent in the struggle for the right to the city—powerful precisely because they are owners of property, and private ones at that. The resolution of one conflict is usually the basis for the next struggle. The struggle for the right to public space, and for the ability to form a public in the city, is always ongoing, and conflict over and between *different* rights to the city never ceases.

Law, and the U.S. constitution, have a lot to say about property and other kinds of rights. But they do not have much to say at all about giant butterflies, frogs, flowers, fairies, and community gardens. Nonetheless the *nature* of property and of rights cannot be understood without these creatures and what they represent. The Giuliani administration's insistence that its property rights gave it the further right to determine the shape of development on previously abandoned, but now productive and beautiful lots led to a broad mobilization of opposition across the city. The threat to the gardens united a variety of counterpublics, many of which had been nurtured in the gardens themselves. The gardens were a locus of counterpublic formation, the place where they could develop and even flourish. The streets, parks, and city council chambers where rallies were held became the places where these counterpublics became visible to the larger public as a whole. Parades of butterflies, frogs, flowers, fairies, and outraged gardeners—to say nothing of the similarly mobilized armies of lawyers, spokespeople, and behind-the-scenes workers in organizations like Green Guerillas and More Gardens!—sought to reclaim the property. In so doing, they hoped to redefine what constituted its "highest and best use" (see Blomley 2004b) and to plant, in the marginal spaces of the city, a vision of how urban development ought to proceed. In the process they also created a different kind of public. The spaces of the gardens and of this new public, however, are not constructed only by the gardeners, but also through the "publicly private" actions of the land trusts. As such, these sites may not be fully secure, but instead are sites for continual struggle. In these struggles, different rights claims and visions of "the public" will continue to be put forward. Is it an accountable public? A responsible one? A militant one? What are its *properties*?

6

PLACING THE PUBLIC
Discourses of Publicity and Practices of Property

The phrase "public space" does not appear on the official website of Chicago's Millennium Park,* yet few would doubt that it is nonetheless a public space. It is heavily used by the public—for sitting and strolling, ice-skating, listening to concerts, enjoying art work. Features such as the Crown Fountain, which sports larger-than-life faces of ordinary Chicagoans, and which invites children and adults alike to play in its spray, assure that the park is a lively gathering place. The new Boeing Galleries, an outdoor exhibition area, aims "to be a democratic and compelling destination for modern and contemporary art, where the public can directly experience the work and ideas of living artists, providing a high quality historical, social and cultural context of the art and architecture of our time."† And make no mistake about it: the park *works*. On a nice day, winter or summer, it is crowded with a population of the young and old, representative of the city's diverse ethnic and racial mixture. Yet as noted in the Preface, Millennium Park is also the product of a great deal of private and foundation capital, is heavily policed, and whole portions can be rented out by private parties. Given that portions of the park (the ice rink, the Boeing Galleries, the Chase Promenade) are frequently closed for private parties and that concerts usually require a ticket, the only rules for the park listed under "Rules and Safety" on the park's website are cryptic, to say the least: "While in

---

* http://www.millenniumpark.org/ (accessed 2 June 2006).
† http://www.millenniumpark.org/artandarchitecture/boeing_galleries.html (accessed 2 June 2006).

the park, please respect the rights of others by allowing free and open access to all areas of the park at all times."* It is, it seems, the responsibility of the people using the park to ensure that rights of access are respected "at all times." What, however, does this mean when a concert is in progress at the Pritzker Pavilion? What does it mean when the skating rink has been rented for a corporate party? What does it mean for a homeless person resting on a bench on the Chase Promenade? What does it mean for the park as a public space?

Public space, as the case studies we have examined begin to make clear, is not the same as public property. Indeed, the *quality* of publicness—the publicness of space—seems to consist of the relationships established between property (as both a thing and a set of relationships and rules) and the people who inhabit, use, and create property. A key issue with regard to the publicness of a space is the quality of access, which in turn is established in part through property relationships. Access in this sense, however, is not a simple matter of a space being open or closed at a given time, as a park or a shopping mall might be. It is also a matter of *how* one enters a space, even if not physically barred from it. In this sense, access is conditioned by feelings of receptivity, of welcome, of comfort (or by the lack of all these feelings). Access also encompasses the kinds of actions and behaviors that can be taken in a space or that are acceptable within it. Furthermore, access to one space may set the conditions for access to other, perhaps metaphorical spaces, as when access to the streets for immigrant protestors conditions access to the public sphere of American society and governance. The relationships among public space, property, and publicity, however, has not always been examined in these terms in geography or urban theory. In this chapter, then, we address the questions: What is public space? What is the relationship between people and property? In so doing, we step back from our case studies to more carefully and directly outline our conceptualization of the relationships among people, property, and public space; in the following chapter, we then discuss what this means for the kind of public and public sphere that is constituted in public space.

WHAT IS PUBLIC SPACE?

What *is* public space, after all? We have invoked several examples that we argue are public spaces, but are they *really* public? Are the parks,

---

* http://www.millenniumpark.org/generalinformation/rules_safety.html (accessed 2 June 2006).

gardens, streets, and malls all public? Are they public in the same way? Do they function the same way? At first blush, these seem as though they should be obvious questions—or to paraphrase one of our respondents, they seem like they should have obvious answers. But the case studies have demonstrated that "public space" is a slippery, complicated, and shifting kind of space.

The complicated nature of public space means that it has been the focus of a great deal of work in geography and urban theory. In part, this fascination reflects an ideal of public space as a crucible for democracy and sociability, but a crucible of a particular type that seems amenable to the kinds of questions that geographers in particular have asked. If a central concern in geography is the mutual interactions between spatial relationships and social relationships, public space is a compelling and important example that connects geography with questions that speak to the heart and soul of a society.

The earliest work on the geographic qualities of public space (e.g., Jackson 1957) explored the importance of physically open space to the experience of visitors to cities; it was focused on *spatial morphology*. Some of this early work, including James Duncan's (1979) examination of tramps' (homeless men's) use of public spaces as part of their survival strategies, focused on the importance of publicly-accessible space including derelict or abandoned spaces for marginalized people. To some extent, public space in this kind of work was conceptualized as the space between (and sometimes within) buildings that was accessible to the public at large. The quality of public space is conceptualized as a function of the built form.*

There is no doubt that built form—the actual shape and physical structure of public space—is deeply important. Writing about Millennium Park, Chicago journalist Jonathan Black (2005, 7) says, "To step off Michigan Avenue and onto its pathways and promenades is a thrilling experience." He goes on to quote architect Richard Hitchcock: "Overall the space is magnificent. It hangs well together. The people are distributed throughout. . . . It sucks you right in" (7). Conversely, many have shown that the corporate plazas and open spaces built during the 1960s and 1970s in exchange for added building height or other zoning exceptions are frequently nothing but dead public spaces, made unwelcoming and even foreboding by accident or design (Ford 1994; Sennett

---

* This was the abiding concern of J. B. Jackson and his *Landscape* magazine and it remains an important strand of research. See, for example, Bunge (1971), Bunge and Bordessa (1975), Curtis (1993), Domosh (1996), Foote (1983), Ford (1994; 2003), Francaviglia (1996), Hebbert (2005), Herzog (1993), Riley (1994), and Van Deusen (2002).

Figure 6.1 A corporate plaza in Chicago. Photograph by Don Mitchell.

1994). Often such corporate plazas are separated from the street by elevation (presenting, for example, a smooth granite wall at street level), plantings, or architectural features that make the space appear more private than open to the public (Figure 6.1).*

The point of analyzing the spatial morphology of public space is not to understand what kind of public can form in it; rather, the focus remains squarely on the space itself and the kind of public space that is formed in a particular setting. The questions asked in this literature include questions about the patterns of interaction and sense of place that the morphology enables. Does it allow for the kind of "place ballet"—the attractive, relatively unscripted interaction of users that resembles an intricate, ever changing (but still structured) dance—such as that described by Jane Jacobs (1961) in her classic account of Greenwich Village life, or that analyzed by William Whyte (1988) in his path-breaking studies on the social uses of small urban spaces (and now carried forward by New York's influential Project for Public Spaces†)? Or is it the kind of defensible space that keeps out unwanted people and allows for community oversight, as promoted by Oscar Newman (1973, 1996)? Or is the space, through the failure of good design, one that seems unused, unwanted, and unloved?

---

* For an analysis of the form, function, and success of publicly-accessible (but privately-owned) spaces created through New York's zoning program, see Kayden (2000). See also Miller (forthcoming).

† See http://www.pps.org/ (accessed 4 June 2006).

As J. B. Jackson knew, however, spaces that are apparently unused or unwanted often perform a vital function in urban areas, providing space for excluded groups in society; they may, in other words, still be *spaces of sociability*. Spaces such as street corners, empty lots, or neglected river or creek banks often provide a stage for vital economic, social, and even political activities (Duneier 1999; Whyte 1993), ranging from hanging out to courting to sleeping to sex to drug dealing to other informal economic activities. Public spaces in this sense are in the first instance *social* spaces—spaces of and for sociability. Consequently, much urban theory has focused on the ways in which the physical arrangement and location of public spaces influence experiences, uses, and perceptions, and how they control meaning and social interaction.* Much of the research has examined how, through social actions, space is *made* public. In this sense public space is *produced*; it never pre-exists social action. As Lefebvre (1991) argued, space is produced out of a struggle between designers, planners, engineers, or other powerful actors who seek to create a space of order and control, and users of the space who necessarily perceive space differently and thus act in it in ways not necessarily anticipated by their designers. Following this, many scholars seek to understand what specific social forces make a space more or less public, more or less open.† In this telling, public space and the social relations that it hosts are co-produced. The relationships involved in these productions can be highly exclusionary, and so there is much debate on what makes a space "truly" public.

One argument is that public space is only ever an ideal, something to be struggled toward. As such, the substance of those ideals—what is being struggled for—is political. For example, ideals of openness and inclusion or ideals of relatively unmediated interaction may not be shared by everyone—by all people, by all government agencies, by all businesses—in a community. Indeed, to some extent, these ideals stand in opposition to an ideal of an orderly, controlled public space that may be structured more as a retreat or a space of comfort (Mitchell 1995; Kohn 2004; Staeheli and Mitchell 2006). Furthermore, some scholars have argued that the goal of an unmediated space is itself exclusionary (Domosh 1998; Lees 1998, 2001), such that ideals of inclusion can only be achieved through the regulation of space. These scholars argue that highly designed and controlled spaces like the mall or festival market-

---

* See, for example, Boyer (1992), Bunge (1971), Findlay (1993), Fyfe and Bannister (1996), Seamon and Nordin (1980), Sibley (1981), and Miller (forthcoming).

† See, for example, Domosh (1998), Light and Smith (1998), Low (2000), and Mitchell (1996).

place may be more inclusive in some ways (Goss 1996), and that people often use publicly-accessible spaces in ways that their designers do not intend (Goss 1999; Hopkins 1990, 1991). From this perspective, the ideal form for public space is one that allows for a range of activities and for the appearance of a range of identities, but the way in which this is managed is left open or unresolved.

Yet such an argument tends to underplay how public spaces are often "taken" spaces—places that are appropriated from other "owners" and made into qualitatively different kinds of spaces than the previous owners may have intended. Berkeley's People's Park (Mitchell 1995), Vancouver's CRAB Park (Blomley 2004b, chapter 2), or any number of homeless people's encampments (Wright 1997), for example, exist because they were actively taken, transformed, and then defended as open, public spaces. In the process of taking, and despite the fact that such takings are hardly democratic in any straightforward sense, a new space for democratic sociability can be created, and a space for a new kind of public sphere is possible.*

The public and private spaces that form the foundation for public and private spheres are often conceived of as existing along a continuum from private to public. Some spaces are seen as more public (parks, squares, the traditional public forums of Chapter 1), others less so (malls, places of work), others partially private (stoops, front yards), and others completely private (the interior of homes, back gardens). In this schema, the kinds of public spaces we have been discussing in this book can all be located on a continuum: traditional public forums far toward the public end, community gardens somewhere toward the center, the inside of the Rachel's Center homeless shelter for women in San Diego closer to the most private end. Similarly *actions*—engaging in political discourse, undertaking economic activities, attending to bodily needs, caring for family—are also often arrayed along a public-private continuum, and the easy assumption is made that public space is the place for public activities, private space for private activities. And yet this is an assumption that does not really hold (Staeheli 1996). If public space is the space for public actions—engaging in politics, for example—then how do we account for all the political organizing that takes place around the kitchen table or in front of a computer screen? And how do we account for the fact that some private actions—carry-

---

* The public sphere, as we discuss more fully in Chapter 7, is a realm in which discourse and politics occur. In some conceptualizations, it is a realm socially and spatially apart from the private sphere. In this view, the public sphere is where ideas can be debated as to the public good, and is where an identity or sense of publicness can be fostered.

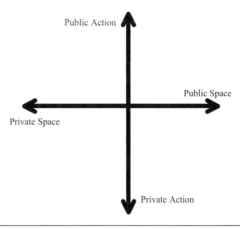

Figure 6.2 Conceptualizing public and private spaces and activities. Redrawn from Staeheli (1996).

ing on a private conversation on a cell phone, say—are now considered relatively acceptable in public space? One way to begin to address these questions is to understand that the two public-private continua are not necessarily parallel, but are orthogonal (Figure 6.2). Conceptually, at least, making this move allows for new questions about public (and private) space and about the nature of publicity (Staeheli 1996; Anderson and Jacobs 1999; Fincher and Panelli 2001). Most importantly, it allows us to raise new questions about *struggles* over public and private. These questions include: how is it that some activities are scripted as private ("women's" activities, for example) and others ("men's") as public? How is this the result of various struggles? How does differential access to public spaces come to be and how do people contest it? How is some space taken and made *more* public, as with the community gardens? How are some spaces privatized, as with San Diego's Horton Plaza Park, and what political goals are achieved through privatization? And how are behaviors scripted, in part through the quite purposeful transgression of norms, but also through the prohibition of certain activities? These are all struggles over public space and particularly over public space in relation to changing relations of gender, race, ability, and sexuality in public and private spheres.* They are struggles over what public space *is*—and what it *can be*. They are struggles over the social production of public space. Even more, these are struggles that call into question who or what "the public" is—about how it is constituted and

---

* See Bell et al. (1994), Bell and Valentine (1995), Brown (1997), Jackson and Penrose (1993), Little et al. (1988), McDowell (1983), Schein (2006), and Tyner (2006).

about the qualities and conditions that make an aggregation of people in some sense a public.

WHAT IS THE PUBLIC?

The answer to "what is the public?" seems as though it should be obvious, as we have invoked the public with great regularity. But thinking a bit more carefully about it, the answer seems far from clear. For instance, are the immigrants who protested in Chicago in March of 2006 part of the public? Are the people in Washington, DC who conducted acts of civil disobedience—who violated norms of community behavior and who violated laws—nevertheless members of the public? How about homeless people in San Diego, or youth in Santa Fe and Syracuse—people, that is, who seem to scare away others who may wish to use publicly-accessible space? Or are they only part of the public at certain times and places? Who or what is the public served by economic development? While the time, place, and manner restrictions we discussed in Chapter 1 may have referred to protests, do they apply in other circumstances? That is, is a person part of the public at only certain times (e.g., not on Friday or Saturday evening), or in certain places (e.g., not in public parks and plazas), or when comporting themselves in a certain manner (e.g., when not panhandling or playing hacky-sack)?

It may, however, be a mistake to think about an abstraction such as "the public" by only considering real people, with very particular characteristics. Certainly, the scholars who have considered the spatial morphology of public space are not thinking in those terms. They frequently write in reference to abstract bodies of people; women, the homeless, middle-class residents appear as "types" (if indeed they appear at all) rather than as real, embodied individuals. Similarly, some of the scholars who write about the sociability of public spaces sometimes frame their arguments in terms of being present *in* public, but leave open the question of belonging *to* the public. In light of this work, it might seem better to approach the question of publicity using abstract or normative ideas (e.g., "the public interest," "the body politic") or institutions (e.g., the state, civil society, political community, economic development community).

As we will demonstrate, there is a pervasive tension between conceptualizations of the public as comprised of an aggregation of real individuals, as compared to a public comprised of an aggregation of abstracted, disembodied subjects, and as compared to the public as a normative vision without a necessary material or physical form. But even if one were to resolve that particular tension, it would only be a partial resolution: the question of who or what comprises the public encompasses many more issues, as our case studies make clear. In order to try to make our way through the discordant discussion of publicity (and hence of public space) in the case studies, a categorization developed by Jeffrey Weintraub (1995) is particularly helpful.*

Weintraub sorted through an extensive literature (primarily in political theory and philosophy) and identified four primary ways in which publicity and privacy are discussed. In the first perspective identified by Weintraub, the public is located in the *state,* or perhaps government. The state, standing as the sovereign (see Chapter 2), embodies the public interest or the accumulation of interests as expressed by the people it governs. From this perspective, public space should be used to further the aims of the public expressed in the state and its ability to function. So when the government attempts to use space and the property it controls in order to make dissent manageable and capable of being incorporated into governance, the government can be seen as acting in the public interest and as a legitimate representative of the public. This is a definition of publicity that is consistent with much liberal democratic theory. The second definition of publicity identified by Weintraub also considers the state, but is rooted in analyses of political economy and locates publicity in the realm of *state and economy.* Most of the theorists working from this perspective see little distinction between the state and economy, so the public is located in the realm created by the joint operations of institutions (e.g., government agencies, firms, public-private economic ventures) within them. What is not directly incorporated in those realms—for example, household and social reproduction—is implicitly located in the private sphere. This is why governments will often argue that it is in the public interest to promote an economy in which firms can flourish, even if it means cutting public funding for schools or medical care or if the actions depress wages; in these cases, they are locating the public within the realm created through the operations of the political economy. This perspective on publicity is often associated—and associated through critique—with Marxist and feminist conceptualizations of publicity.† Moving away from the state and economy, Weintraub's third conceptualization of publicity identifies the public as a *collective, but non-governmental entity,* variously described as a political community, civil society, or the *civitas* (Chapter

---

* This discussion draws from Staeheli and Mitchell (forthcoming).

† Interestingly, Weintraub and the theorists he summarizes do not identify a perspective on publicity associated with economics. Whether this is due to the relatively poorly developed nature of public economics or whether economic theorists simply do not consider the issue is not clear.

4). The literature discussing this form of publicity is often concerned with how communities come to define themselves collectively, the rules or practices of inclusion and exclusion, and the norms of behavior, obligation, and responsibility to the community exhibited by members—at least in the ideal. In democracy theory, the public discussed under this rubric is often associated with republicanism and communitarianism (cf. Etzioni 1993; Putnam 2000). Finally, there is a fourth perspective on publicity that defines it in terms of *sociability* and *display*. Here, public is defined in terms of symbolic display and representation; the hallmarks of publicity are visibility and the intentional performance of certain attitudes, behaviors, and identities so that they can be seen and be accounted. This is a view often associated with some strands of feminism, cultural studies, and sociology.*

We heard each of these perspectives on publicity from the people we interviewed for our case studies. When, for example, government agencies in Washington, DC seemed to repress dissent, representatives of these agencies justified their actions on the basis of claims that some protests challenged public order and the ability of the government to maintain smooth operations and functioning for the public at large. Minimizing traffic disruptions and ensuring the safety of the president were important to the government's ability to function and to meet public needs. Protesters themselves often spoke of the importance of protest in terms confronting government with their objections in the hopes of changing government policy. While this meaning of publicity is easily and perhaps glibly offered, it does still leave unresolved the issue of what a public need is and who is incorporated; those issues, one could say, are matters of politics, and should be debated openly amongst the people being governed, and people who are presumably incorporated in the sovereign. If that is the case, then attempts to stifle protests and to harass protestors should not have been allowed. But still, police commanders and other governmental agents attempted to repress dissent and protest as not being in the public—often meaning the sovereign's—interest.

---

* Weintraub was most interested in political aspects of publicity and privacy, but here the *social* importance of spaces for sociability should also be stressed. While display and representation are crucial to the formation of a political public, they are also crucial in and of themselves as a means of making a group claim to the right simply to be in public space; the value of hanging out should not be discounted even if it often is in law (the U.S. Supreme Court, for example, is quite explicit in delineating rights to public space for "speech," but is reticent even to the point of dismissive of the right simply to hang about in public space).

More often in our interviews, however, publicity was discussed in terms of the operations of the political economy; the public, in this perspective, was comprised of the interests of the commercial and governmental sectors. It was clear in San Diego and Santa Fe, for example, that the efforts to redevelop the central areas of the city—the Gaslamp District and the Plaza—were intended to foster economic development in the cities; officials argued that this met a public good in that it was necessary to provide a healthy tax base to support other needs and in order to provide a safe and interesting place for the public to gather. From many of the people engaged in the redevelopment, we heard that these new spaces were open to everyone, tourists and the general public alike. Homeless people, however, were uneasily incorporated in this public, if indeed they were included at all. Similarly, in Syracuse, the Pyramid Corporation intended to build a place "to which the public is invited," but management "disinvited" youth. And in New York City, the Giuliani administration operated with a model of public good or public interest that, according to most gardeners, empowered property developers and Giuliani's upper-income campaign supporters at the expense of the spaces of democracy that had grown in the gardens.

What seems so obviously public to the people in the Chambers of Commerce, to the economic development corporations, and to some city officials in our study sites, however, did not always seem to be representative of the ways that other people understood publicity. Many people were more concerned with the changes to the spaces of the city that affected the ability of people to gather and to participate in public. Political activists and some members of the Common Council in Syracuse, for example, worried that the new town square would be devoid of even the most basic activities through which a public could be constituted. If voter registration was too political, what, they wondered, would be allowed into the premier gathering place in the area? When teenagers were excluded from the mall and from the Plaza in Santa Fe, some activists and planners wondered what it would mean for the ability to incorporate future generations into the public—by which they meant a public defined by something other than the political economy.

It must be said, however, that many people who worried about exclusionary actions very much agreed with the changes that were supported by economic development and city officials. So, for example, while some people worried that the changes in the Plaza limited the public accessibility and utility of the Plaza for locals or for "real" Santa Feans, other people noted that public drunkenness, unruly behavior, the presence of people with mental illnesses, or even just the presence of people who seemed threatening by virtue of their differences also demeaned the quality of publicity in downtown spaces. As Father Joe Carroll in San Diego (who runs one of the largest service centers for homeless and destitute people in the United States) commented without any sense of irony, it was necessary to have the ability to exclude people from public space if one wanted to make a place that was really useable by a wide variety of people.

Father Joe notwithstanding, many of the people we interviewed worried that more and more places *in* the city were not accessible to the people *of* the city; they were worried, in other words, about a different kind of public than that of the state or the political economy. In New York, for example, the gardeners were worried that without a place to gather, to work—cultivating both flowers and political solidarity—they would be pushed even further to the margins of the city. Many of the gardeners were immigrants, and the gardens provided a place where they could participate in public life; some of the gardens went so far as to encourage this by offering English as a Second Language and citizenship classes. In promoting these activities, many of the gardening advocates claimed they were building a more expansive and active citizenry—one capable of participating in governance despite gardeners' marginal status, often as people of color, as immigrants, as low-income families, and as people without previously cultivated political skills or organizations. These were not just spaces of democracy, they were spaces in which republican virtue was fostered and a collective sense of identity as citizens was encouraged. The *civitas* constructed in the spaces of the gardens, however, was politicized in ways that differed from the *civitas* created in the controlled spaces of Carousel Center.

To the struggles of the gardeners, but also to the locals in Santa Fe, visibility or public sociability was very important. Efforts to be part of the political community or *civitas* in some senses depended on visibility, on making their presence known. That was one reason why the locals and teenagers who were pushed off the Plaza (either by city ordinance or by the path that economic development followed) felt they were excluded from the public. Similarly, parades and protests make visible the ways in which certain people or ideas may be excluded from the collective public. Whether it is Rolling Thunder, a motorcycle parade of thousands of Vietnam veterans to draw attention to the MIAs (missing in action) from that war, or opponents of George Bush's election, visibility and public display have been important means of expanding a sense of who is present in a society and, therefore, of highlighting the issues that should be of public concern.

Yet in some cases, sociability can be turned against prospective members of the public, and ideas of community can be used to enforce exclusion, rather than to build a sense of inclusiveness. Such is the case in San Diego where the unruly—indeed, socially unacceptable—behavior of homeless people is the basis of their exclusion. The very visibility of homeless people makes them targets of policing by the "ambassadors" of the Downtown Partnership. Homeless people are tolerated, only insofar as they are not visible, are not present in the sanitized spaces of the redeveloped Horton Plaza and Gaslamp District.

Obviously, these definitions of publicity—related to the state, political economy, polity, and sociability—can be related, both in the academic literature and in the ways we experience the public spaces of the city. So, for example, third-wave feminism often brought issues and relationships of social reproduction and their unrecognized role in the political economy—the unpaid labor of women, the ways in which gender roles are "functional" for economic production and maintaining a reserve army of labor—into public streets, thereby engaging in public sociability in order to make their point. While academics and theorists often talk about this in terms of transgressing space (e.g., Cresswell 1996), taking issues from the private realm into the public can also be thought of as a form of transgressing theoretical perspectives in that this movement highlights the ways in which different senses of "public" are interlinked. And by engaging in acts that are unexpected, and to some degree unexplainable using standard approaches, they may advance a particular political agenda (cf. Anderson and Jacobs 1999; Cope 2004; Fincher and Panelli 2001; Staeheli 1996; Wilson 1991).

Indeed, we found that these perspectives were frequently interwoven in the controversies we have examined. Enhancing the ability of the state to govern seems much easier when it is also consistent with economic development initiatives of local growth coalitions; by contrast, protests that challenge globalization or the acts of international corporations are often seen as threats to governing or to security. As we argued previously, attempts to gain visibility and to expand the understanding of who is a part of the *civitas*—the public—often also involves efforts to change the conceptualization of public interest, which is the basis of state policy, if not necessarily economic growth.

Sometimes, however, the interweaving of ideas of the public becomes confused or blurred, and seems incapable of achieving resolution. In those situations—and indeed, probably in *most* situations—different ideas about the public and publicity are at odds, as perhaps that lonely "rule" for Millennium Park (the one that requires users to "respect the rights of others by allowing free and open access to all areas of the park at all times") seems to indicate. These are conflicts in the psychological sense; they are "psychic struggles, often subconscious, resulting from the opposition or simultaneous functioning of mutually exclusive impulses, desires, or tendencies."* In these situations, as we argue in all of our case studies, it becomes important to understand not just the definitions of publicity that various agents employ, but also the tools, resources—the power—that they are able to mobilize in their struggles. Here, the role of property is central to the ways that public space is used, to who can use it, and is thereby fundamental to the public that emerges through struggle.

PROPERTY, PUBLIC SPACE, AND THE PUBLIC

We have purposely been using the term "public space" rather than public (or publicly-accessible) property in the previous sections of this chapter, in large part because public space is how both the academic literature and common language refer to the open spaces of the city. But as the five case studies reported here show, property is a crucial part of the equation that creates public space and forms the public in its many configurations. It is both a tool of power and a result of the exercise of power. What could be called the "practice of property"—the relations, regimes, and struggles over what property is and how it is deployed—is one of the means by which the different meanings of, and therefore, the different activities that define the four categories of publicity and privacy are sorted.

The first definition of property is "something owned, a possession."† Property *rights* define the nature of ownership and how, by dint of that ownership, others may be excluded from its use. This is the basic definition of property we have been working with throughout this book: property as the "right to exclude." By extension, ownership entitles an owner to dispose of a thing as he or she wishes: property is *alienable*. It is separable from other things (the obelisk from the Plaza in Santa Fe, perhaps), and it is fungible (it can be exchanged) (Blomley 2004a; Olwig 2005). The process of alienation (and also of exchange) thus entails a *loss* of rights in the property, and their assumption by someone else. Because ownership in land, in real property, usually entails not only legal entitlement but also affective belonging, the loss of rights in property through alienation "is also psychologically alienating" (Olwig

---

* This definition is from *The American Heritage Dictionary of the English Language*, 3rd ed. (Boston: Houghton Mifflin, 1992).
† *American Heritage Dictionary*, "Property: 1."

2005, 20). In capitalism, where ownership of and title to land is so deeply engrained, and where the ownership of property is often a mere expedient for exchange, such psychological alienation is experienced as part of the psychic struggle noted above.

Yet, as should be clear, ownership—the rights of use and exclusion—is rarely simple. It is often occluded by the claims of others with legal, social, or cultural rights to the thing. Partially in recognition of this:

> The Anglo-American legal tradition has recognized essentially three kinds of property rights. Private property is the right of individuals to exclude others from the benefits of resources. . . . Public property, owned by governments, gives state officials the right to determine who has access to resources held on behalf of a wider constituency. Common property is an individual's right not to be excluded from the uses or benefits of resources (Blackmar 2006, 51, drawing on Macpherson 1978).

What is most intriguing about struggles over public space in the United States—whether psychic, cultural, social, or legal—is how little a role is played by notions of common property, and thus by the right *not* to be excluded. It is hard, if not impossible, to conceive of public space as a species of common property, unless we likewise understand, as in San Diego, that the near-exclusive community of interest with a right not to be excluded from "the uses and benefits of resources" is the community of nearby private property interests.* The alienability of land as property, Olwig (2005, 30) argues, entails "the loss of rights which effectively makes one alien, or a foreigner, in the land." As alien, one necessarily possesses fewer psychic, cultural, social, or legal rights. Between private and public property there is little space—literally—for those who have been alienated, for those who have lost their entitlement and their rights of use.

Many contemporary claims to community, to belonging in the *civitas*, to being a citizen, are thus couched as efforts to reclaim the commons—to revivify the notion of common property.† As Elizabeth Blackmar (2006, 57–58) details:

---

* Robert Ellickson (1996) argues that such an community of propertied interest should be understood as a normative good more than an exclusionary practice since owners of surrounding property have a vested interest in assuring the common property between them is maintained, orderly, and inviting (for desirable classes of people). Blackmar (2006) subjects libertarian and neoliberal arguments about the commons (which subject them to the rule of private property) to close scrutiny.

† See, for example, the People's Park poster reprinted in Blomley (2004b, 26).

Public space was repoliticized in the postwar era through demands of access to the uses and benefits of resources that, whether publicly- or privately-owned, presented themselves as public spaces. Ending Jim Crow required making visible the relation between discriminatory public policies and private profit. . . . Although historians have contrasted the politics of the civil rights movement to an older (class) politics of property, it was against the backdrop of democratization and redistribution implied by equal protection of the law that the discourse of property rights was not only reanimated but expanded to reintroduce the concept of common property rights.

In the popular environmental discourse of the 1960s and 1970s, according to Blackmar (2006, 60), "'Common' and 'public' stood in ambiguous, almost interchangeable relation to one another." In urban space, however, this relation is more contradictory than ambiguous. *Public*, as often as not in urban practice, is interpreted as the realm of the state, *common* as the realm of the people (the polity). And yet "common" as it relates to property remains so much weaker in law, in part because the ownership model holds such sway. "Common" can be, and often is, quite different from public. For Carol Rose (1998, 132), "limited common property"—"property held as a commons among the members of a group, but exclusively vis-à-vis the outside world" (quoted in Blomley 2004b, 17)—names a form of ownership somewhere between public and private. But the salient point remains: even limited common property is alienable. People can be, and are, made strangers to it. Common property is not common in quite the sense it was when it was a commons under English (and other European) common law (Olwig 1996, 2005). Common property, limited or otherwise, is not necessarily the same thing, that is, as public space.

Although New York's community gardens often functioned as neighborhood commons, they were owned and were alienable by the City of New York. Many are now owned by the Trust for Public Lands, the New York Restoration Project, or smaller conservancies set up by these two. They remain alienable, even if deeds restrict the conditions under which they can be alienated. They certainly remain *controlled* by specific corporate entities (the boards of the trusts), which can curtail use of them if, for example, a board feels those given use rights to the gardens are not acting accountably or responsibly. The rights of property remain. And it is these rights, set against the rights of usufruct, that set the stage for the struggles in New York. In part, the struggle was one between the public conceived of as state and market and the public conceived of as *civitas* and a place of sociability. But the conceptualization—or really the legal status—of the *property* upon and over which this struggle occurred, was far simpler. The property was "public" because it was *owned* by the state. With the transference of ownership rights to the trusts, the stage for struggle remained, even if it was rearranged and different actors came to the fore.

More than changing the stage for struggle, however, land deals like the one in New York that saved many gardens, or private tax arrangements like the one that created the Clean and Safe P-BID in San Diego, transformed the property *regime*. It is critical to remember that no property exists in isolation. One of the things that sets property-as-space (real estate) apart from other kinds of property (an owned belonging such as a car, a painting, or a toothbrush) is that it cannot be extracted from its environment.* Parcels of land necessarily exist in geographical relationship to other parcels of land. Nothing could be more obvious. But the implications for public space and publicity are important. As noted in Chapter 3, the *use value* of property is a function of the location of a property in relation to other properties and especially other uses. Relationships between uses determine the *exchange value* of property, or its worth to other owners and users. Property owners thus have a real interest in the disposition of nearby properties. The concept of a property regime helps to clarify both the nature of those interests and how they may be exercised. If the public, or the public interest, is defined in market terms, then appropriate uses are those uses that preserve or enhance the exchange value of property, and property regimes should support that. Changes to property and the provision of public space are conceived of in specific ways: they support development, or attract new residents to downtown, or allow for a pleasant shopping experience.

If, however, the public is defined as a realm of sociability, the provision of a pleasant shopping experience might remain important, but it is likely also to be supplemented by spaces designed not only to enhance exchange, but also to invite diversity and create a space "to be" (cf. Amster 2004; Waldron 1991). Property regimes that recognized the provision of public goods that were not narrowly and instrumentally

---

* This is a considerable problem for capitalism, which relies on the full exchangeability, and therefore the physical circulation, of things. On the one hand, land (parcels of space) cannot be moved. On the other hand, capital fixed in space (attached to the land in the form of soil improvements, transportation infrastructures, buildings, machinery) is a necessary precondition for the circulation of things. Capitalism addressed this problem, in part, with the invention of circulating titles in land, titles that allow real estate to circulate "ideally" (and thus for markets in land titles to form), if not in physical actuality. Harvey (1982) explores these issues and their importance for the urban built environment.

economic would have to be developed. To be sure, the intervention of the public land trusts in New York herald something of a changed property regime, based in a different sense of the public, than that envisioned by the Giuliani administration, even if this regime might bring with it a new set of struggles and contradictions. The preservation of the gardens requires the formation of new kinds of relations among properties (and their owners), relations that recognize the preeminence of collective use value to the public good. The practice of property is transformed and public space now sits on a different foundation and serves a different kind of function. If the property that supports public space remains alienable, it is now alienable in a different way, and its alienation will have different kinds of effects on surrounding properties.

On the one hand, then, relations of property, and thus the uses and functions of public space, are shaped by the relative power of different conceptualizations of "the public"—as state, market, polity, or sociable collective—as they are put into practice. On the other hand, relations of property shape the kinds of public that may form. A certain kind of sociable public gathers each evening on the streets and sidewalks (and in the bars and restaurants) of San Diego's Gaslamp, and it is a very different kind of sociable public than used to gather in Horton Plaza Park or along the "seedy" streets of downtown in the past. Similarly, Carousel Center constructs a certain kind of sociable public and seeks to implement a particular form of *civitas*, even as its main function is to create a publicly-accessible space, even a kind of "commons," in support of market functions. On the streets of Washington, DC, permit systems, which are a means of regulating the uses of publicly-owned property through a form of "soft" prior restraint, shape both what public space is and the nature of the public that forms there. Even in dissent, it is an affirmative public. But, as with New York's community gardens, people who operate with very different ideas about what the public is and what the public is for may transgress the norms of property, and in so doing significantly reshape it. "The ownership model," says Nick Blomley (2004b, 153), "does not exhaust property. . . . The city is crosscut by claims to land that are neither private nor statist. Lacking formal rights-status, these claims are nevertheless defended, articulated, and mobilized."

Even so, property remains a delineable, mappable, reified *thing*. It has borders, boundaries. "Although property, formally speaking, is concerned with relations between people, the ability to delineate a bounded property is essential. The boundary, moreover, has legal effects. Trespass, for example, often turns on whether a boundary has been crossed" (Blomley 2004a, 93). These boundaries are literal lines on the ground; they can separate—physically, geographically—places where the right to speech is (relatively) strongly guaranteed, and places where it is not (Mitchell 1992, 2003a). Maintaining boundaries is thus an important task. Fences, hedges, walls, landscaping, plaques and other markers, property maps, and surveys are all tools for staking and maintaining a claim to property. Deploying them is an essential part of shaping a property regime. One of the problems with Horton Plaza Park, at least from the perspective of the owners of Horton Plaza Mall, was that the line that separated the two was not clear. People did not know where the city's property ended and the mall's began.

And maintenance of property claims matters for another reason, too, as the history of the community gardens makes clear: it protects against common law claims of "adverse possession." Adverse possession holds that "if the owner of a piece of land ceases to use it, and someone else openly and continuously encroaches on that land, title can shift to the encroacher. . . . Gardening matters here: the cultivation of land by an encroacher, for an extended period, is seen as grounds to sustain a claim of title by adverse possession" (Blomley 2004b, 94). Maintaining borders protects against encroachment; lines on the ground make claims to territory (and thus rights to and on that territory) clear, even though property is always a relation between people.

The boundaries that delineate property are legal and physical markers, but they are also conceptual lines. For public property, they mark that point where the state transmogrifies from a sovereign to a landlord, from the embodiment of "the people" to the owner of land, from the protector of the rights of the public to the enforcer of the rights of (its own) property. Perhaps no more telling example of this is available than the old National Park Service practice of making *itself* the permittee of record for all protests, demonstrations, marches, and parades associated with presidential inaugurations, and its new one of handing the overarching permit over to the Presidential Inauguration Committee. Yet because real property is a thing, because it is bounded and those boundaries are used to control and shape the constitution of the public, trespass itself becomes a tool that throws into relief the relation between the state as sovereign and the state as landlord. The ritual of arrest at many protests in Washington is an example. Though often negotiated in advance and timed for the evening news, arrests for trespassing (or breaking similar laws) in front of the White House or in other symbolic spaces is designed precisely to challenge what the state *is* and who the state *is for* at any particular moment. Similarly, trespass was a crucial tool in the making of New York's community gardens. The gardens are, many of them, *taken* land, and this act of expropriation is foundational to their meaning and use as community, or common, spaces. And, all too frequently, homeless people trespass on both public and private property simply to create a space to be. In so doing the nature of the public, of public space, and of property is changed. Finally, the existence of many city parks, Olwig (2005) reminds us, is owed to acts of mass trespass (see also Williams 1997, 1–2). Trespass, no less than property, is a tool in the struggle to shape the public sphere.

DIFFERENTIATING PROPERTY, DIFFERENTIATING PEOPLE

Mass trespass does not necessarily create a space for "all the people," any more than does a city government setting aside land (and rounding up financial support) for a place like Millennium Park. In large part this is because "the people" itself is an impossible abstraction, as much as we might like to think otherwise. The very fact of the immigration rallies of 2006, like the one in Chicago's Federal Plaza, makes that clear. Those rallies were sparked by the immigration bills being considered in the U.S. Congress, but as we noted in the Preface, they were very much about Latino immigrants making themselves visible as part of the public, part of "the people" (Figure 6.3).

Some six weeks after that first demonstration in Chicago, and following weeks of demonstrations in cities across the United States (including massive ones in Los Angeles), African American activist Ted Hayes organized a counter, anti-immigration, forum in Leimert Park in Los Angeles's Crenshaw district (Watanabe 2006). Hayes is a well-known homeless advocate. In the 1980s he founded the Justice-

Figure 6.3 Some of those rallying in Chicago made it explicit that they were part of the American "public." Photograph by Giuseppe Alcoff; used by permission.

ville homeless encampment in Los Angeles's Skid Row—a taking and reworking of derelict property that sought to give homeless people greater control over their everyday lives in the midst of a crisis by creating a place that was at once a private and public space (cf. Rowe and Wolch 1990; Wolch et al. 1993, more generally, see Wright 1997). In the wake of the immigrant demonstrations of 2006, Hayes created the Crispus Attucks Brigade, an African American anti-immigration organization, which aligned with the white Minute Man organization that made a name for itself by "patrolling" the U.S.-Mexican border in areas where it felt the U.S. government was failing. Leimert Park is the premier site for African American public speaking and organizing, described by one commentator as "that grassy promontory in the Crenshaw district where black activists of all creeds and credibility come to say their piece or spread their word" (Kaplan 2006, B13). This time, speakers like Hayes were met by a vocal group of counter-demonstrators, both black and Latino, kept apart from each other by a yellow-tape police line. For some, "the debate is beautiful," despite the acrimonious exchanges: "These people are honestly trying to sort through all of these conflicts and contradictions" (quoted in Watanabe 2006, B3). But for others, the very fact that there *had* to be a debate was the crucial point: "That the super-patriots in Leimert even had to hold a news conference to ask for consideration [of the ways in which African Americans remain discriminated against and how large-scale immigration has exacerbated this]—this, not immigration, was the issue" (Kaplan 2006, B13). Leimert Park was, as it had long been, a site for the struggle for inclusion, even though it might have felt like just the opposite. As Erin Aubry Kaplan (2006, B13) wrote in the *Los Angeles Times*:

> By its very existence, the event made the painful point that blacks still belong least of all. The anxiety over that is justifiable. It's also different from the xenophobic anxiety of the white Minutemen who were ostensibly there to support the anti-immigrant blacks but whose own law-and-order agenda hardly embraces the interests of any ethnic minorities. Such differences were never addressed, though they were sharply in the air.

Leimert Park was a site for airing of difference; it was a site for the struggle for inclusion; it was a site where one group of people sought to say to another, "you are not one of us"; it was a site for a "beautiful" debate; it was a site where African American, Latino, and white activists in favor of immigrant rights met African American, Latino, and white activists seeking to close off the border (Watanabe 2006). It was, that is, a site where differentiations among "the people," became clear. It was all of these things because of the kind of place—the kind of property—it was.

Neither Horton Plaza, nor Carousel Center could, it seems, ever be a place like this, even though they, too, are places designed to differentiate the people, one from another. Leimert Park, like the other places we have examined, is a site of exclusion, but it is also a site for the struggle for inclusion in the polity and for the shaping of a *civitas*. People are differentiated in and through space. Yet space itself is differentiated by property. Carousel Center mall provides a space within which a certain kind of public can form, but while blacks and immigrants may both work and shop in the mall, they are unlikely to engage in debate there. Indeed, such debate is pretty much forbidden. In a different mall owned by the Pyramid Corporation, visitors wearing innocuous T-shirts urging us to "give peace a chance" were asked to leave the mall (Kohn 2004; see also Chapter 4). The processes of exclusion are quite different in a mall than they are in Leimert Park.

The exclusions and differentiations of people in Horton Plaza Park, now that it is maintained and policed by a Property-based Business Improvement District, are different yet again. If homeless people in San Diego are made less and less welcome on city streets, however, and if the streets are all but set aside for a "legitimate" public of homed residents, tourists, shoppers, and bar hoppers, it does not mean that homeless residents will somehow simply disappear. As much as they seem to be cast out from the precincts of "the people," they must sleep somewhere. Ted Hayes's solution in the 1980s in Los Angeles (where a growing majority of homeless people were African American) was to take over derelict property and create a homeless-run encampment; in so doing, he made a claim to space and a claim against the prerogatives of both public and private property. By the 1990s in San Diego, there were very few derelict spaces left on which the homeless population could camp; it is in part for this reason that Father Joe Carroll's St. Vincent de Paul campus expanded so rapidly. St. Vincent de Paul, Father Joe told us, had become one of the biggest property developers in the city, though not without opposition from other property owners in the area. Yet even with the expansion of St. Vincent de Paul Village, San Diego still hosted a homeless street population estimated to be more than 7,000 in 2001. The city was thus under a court order to provide winter shelter. The homeless population might in practice be expunged from the realm of the public, but in law they still retain some rights. Each year, however, the city of San Diego finds it harder and harder to find a site for a winter shelter. Old warehouses have been converted to "higher and better" uses; empty lots now sport new lofts. The

Figure 6.4 A "sprung shelter," erected in the middle of a dead-end street, and used to house homeless people in San Diego. Photograph by Lynn Staeheli.

city's solution has been to buy several "sprung structures"—giant tents like those used in the winter to keep road salt dry—and erect them in the middle of out-of-the-way streets on the edge of the East Village (Figure 6.4). The city erects the tents there because it still formally *owns* the streets and in its role as landlord, can dedicate them to uses other than transportation or commerce. But the main reason it locates the winter shelters in the middle of the street is that it cannot afford to use any other property. Homeless residents remain part of the public because they are literally on public property.

This is a differentiation of the people with a vengeance. But it is not the only way to think about differentiation. The construction of community gardens in New York had many functions: they provided green and open space in struggling communities; they provided fresh vegetables in neighborhoods that were often nutritional deserts; they provided a space for community development and the organization of political action; they provided a place where people could work and relax and, simply, garden. In many neighborhoods, they were a solidaristic space—a space in which people could come together as a people. But this too required a differentiation and an exclusion. As a space of collective engagement, the gardens required a recognition of those who were not part of the people: developers, gentrifiers, and so forth. As we noted in Chapter 5, community gardening was a means of transforming the public nature of public property. A different public—a different people—forms there than on the publicly-owned streets that host San Diego's sprung structures, on the still formally publicly-owned streets of the Clean and Safe district, or in the public forum that is Leimert Park, or that is the heavily policed public forum of downtown Washington, DC, or that is the publicly-accessible private property of the mall. All of these are different again from Santa Fe's Plaza. This too is publicly-owned property, and the struggles over belonging are intense. But the transformation of the city has taken it off the daily path of so many locals that it has become a largely ceremonial space for them, even as it is an everyday space for tourists. As such the property relations that govern the Plaza's use encourage a rather different kind of public—and publicity—than they had previously.

The important point is that differentiations of property are productive of differentiations within peoples. The opposite is also true. Differences within peoples—differences that may be differences of identity, of citizenship status, of political view point, or of class—are productive of, and are reflected in, differentiations of property. Power, property, and people, in other words, are inextricably bound together.

Public and publicly-accessible *space* is where differences—of people and of power—are worked through. Relations of publicly-accessible *property* structure *how* they may (and may not) be worked through. "Property," Nick Blomley (2004b, 156) argues, "can be the problem and the solution, the threat and that which is threatened. Property relations can be configured as exclusionary, violent, and marginalizing. They can also be a means by which people find meaning in the world, anchor themselves to communities, and contest dominant power relations." Property relations can be all of these things, not only because property relations provide some of the means by which the grounds for struggle are created (especially within capitalism), but also because property relations are difference-making machines (cf. Isin 2002). Understanding differences in property relations allows for a better understanding of the complexity of any space purporting to be the "people's property."

Furthermore, understanding these processes of differentiation requires an appreciation of the struggles over public space. These are struggles in which power of different types and capabilities is exercised. Power relations are never balanced, however, and are never in equilibrium. Rather, as the struggles over public space in Washington, DC, San Diego, Santa Fe, Syracuse, and New York City demonstrate, power relations set the stage for a system of social, cultural, political, economic, and property relations in which a public is—or perhaps more accurately, in which publics are—constructed. They operate, as we argue next, in a regime of publicity.

7

POWER, POLITICS, AND REGIMES OF PUBLICITY

At the heart of this book has been a question: What is publicity? What shapes the ability—for differently situated people—to be in public? What are the conditions of possibility, in particular times and places, of public-ness? We have explored the issue of publicity by focusing particularly on the changing relations of property and public space in American cities. And we have examined how various social agents have, in their everyday actions, their plans, and their struggles, continually unsettled the relationships among property, public space, and publicity so as to make them anew. That is, each of the case studies has shown that the ability to fix a definition of publicity, to shape the constitution of the public, or to control the relations of property that make space accessible or not, is an exercise of power. And because it is an exercise of power, the relations among people, property, and the public will never be fixed or settled, once and for all.

But to make that claim is *not* to say that space, property, and publicity are somehow completely fluid, amorphous, or wholly indeterminate.* While constantly subject to transformation through the exercise of power—for they are not just produced but also reproduced—space, property, and publicity are nonetheless deeply structured. They are structured precisely by the struggle to "fix" them in place, to create an order beneficial to specific interests (property developers and gentrifiers in San Diego, gardeners and community activists in New York, tourists or locals in Santa Fe), and therefore to create what could be called a specific *regime of publicity*. In Chapter 3, we defined a regime

---

* For a close examination of the indeterminacy of space and how it works both socially and philosophically, see Massey (2005).

of property as the prevailing system of laws, practices, and relations among different properties. We used the concept to show that while relations of property are continually contested and transformed, they are also systematically structured, relatively predictable, and because they work as a regime, *enforceable* in particular ways. In other words, this regime—the relatively settled and socially agreed upon rules that govern how property operates—is a crucial determinant in how power will be deployed and in whose interests. It also establishes the points at which that deployment of power, and the social relations that the regime supports, may be contested. In this chapter our goal is to show, in concluding this book, that the concept of regime, as a system of laws, practices, and relations, can be usefully extended to lay out a means to answer that central question: What is publicity?

In particular we will suggest that a regime of publicity comprises three main intersecting aspects: relations of property, social norms and community membership, and practices of legitimation. Property, we have argued throughout this book, *grounds* publicity. But we have also argued that property relations are themselves, while structured in a regime, highly contested. They are frequently unsettled. And property is complex, as we have seen: different ownership claims to the same parcel of property can be lodged simultaneously, carrying different implications for the public that is located in it or that can use that property. Property is thus a site of structuring, but also of unstructuring, social relations. It is both a means of sorting community and social norms, and of upsetting them. After all, transgression, disruptiveness, unruliness, and dissent all imply that there is something fixed—something settled—that is capable of being challenged, confronted, or rebelled against. That something is the co-joined relations of property and the *normative* public (or what is too often called "community") that appears to be the "natural" constituency of a public space or neighborhood. As such, dissent, transgression, or any disruption or breaking of rules calls into question the social legitimacy of members of the public. Understanding publicity as a regime makes it clear that relations of publicity are always simultaneously relatively structured and continually subject to challenge and revision. The relations of power embedded in property are solid, but they are not enduring, and this has critical implications for the nature of the public that is created through political struggle in and for public space. In the words we used in Chapter 1, the politics *of* public space are a crucial determinant of the politics possible *in* public space.

In this regard, it is impossible to "locate" the public once and for all (to invoke another issue raised in Chapter 1). Questions of how publics form, and where, are empirical questions, as each of the case studies

criticisms possess value, and Habermas's own ideas have been reshaped through the debates he sparked.* And yet there are two further, but related, ways in which abstraction from the space of the coffeehouse has served to mask the power relations that operated within the coffeehouse (or any other similar publicly-accessible space). The first is in the analytical separation of public from private, and the second is in the lack of attention to property.

Our focus in this book has been, almost exclusively, on the public realm: publicly-accessible properties and spaces, the formation of publics, the conditions of publicity. Yet, of course, publicity is not interpretable without understanding privacy (Cohen 1997; Squires 1994; Staeheli 1996). The theorists whose work was summarized by Weintraub, for example (see Chapter 6), rarely wrote about publicity except in relation to privacy. In liberal political theory, the relationship is conceptualized in the following manner: whereas the public sphere is where citizens, or members of a political community, can exercise their freedoms, imagine a polity, and formulate political claims on the state, the private sphere is a space in which the ability to participate in public is nurtured and sustained. The importance of the private sphere is that it is the site of physical and social reproduction. But it is more than that. The private sphere is also political in that political ideals can initially be formed there, free as it is (theorized to be) from the state or society; it is a space of negative freedoms that makes it safe as a place to try out ideas before taking them "public." Once again, the objections are numerous. Anyone tracking debates over same-sex marriage, abortion, teen pregnancy, or welfare can easily see that what goes on in the private space of the home or "closet" is subject to public scrutiny and regulation by law (cf. Brown 2000). The private sphere is far from being free of state interference, and it is, in fact, created in part by the state, the economy, and "public" social relationships. The ability to shift the boundary between public and private or to change its permeability is thus an exercise of power in which the public is made more or less inclusionary, more or less accommodating of difference. It is precisely through struggles over that boundary that the content of the private, or of the public, is determined. As was perhaps most clear in the San Diego case, but certainly evident in Syracuse and the others, putatively private interests always have a strong interest in shaping the public, just as the public continually seeks to shape that which is somehow private.

In this regard, the case studies make it clear just how important it is to focus on relations of property, a focus that is almost entirely lacking

---

* See the essays collected in Calhoun (1992); see also Goode (2005).

from debates over the constitution of public and private spheres. While it is true that many critics of *The Structural Transformation of the Public Sphere* have noted that Habermas's iconic coffeehouses were private property, the real implications of this have not been developed: that the coffeehouse, and thus debate within it, was *subject* to the relations embedded in property.* Property, we have argued throughout this book, is a synecdoche for the relations that constitute publicity. But it is also more than that. It is not just representative of or a condensation of these relationships; it is also, and especially, a key structuring node in them. Property is a literal place where such relations take on material form. Just as we argued in Chapter 3 that it was important to think of private and public properties in relation to a broader regime of property, we also need to think about how that regime of property, and those specific properties, define and lend material form to the broader set of relations that constitutes the public *in relation* to the private. In so doing, we can begin to see the differentiation of the public (the public sphere question), and of publicity, as not an all-or-nothing question of inclusion and exclusion, but rather as an ongoing struggle over the forms and means of inclusion and exclusion. That is, we need to conceptualize *regimes of publicity* that can be understood as rooted in, but as never reducible to, regimes of property.

REGIMES OF PUBLICITY

If a "regime" can be defined as a "prevailing social system or power," then it is important to examine the constituents of that system or power and how it comes to prevail.† Three constituents, or elements, are particularly salient for understanding the structuring of publicity: (1) the interrelationships between property, both as a thing and a set of relationships; (2) social norms and community membership; (3) strategies, practices, or forms of legitimation. Together these condition inclusion, exclusion, and differential access to the public realm, as well as the nature of the struggle over and in the public realm. They condition *how* the public is differentiated and the *modes* by which inclusions

---

* By contrast, and of course working out of a very different theoretical and practical context, this point about property relations was clearly grasped by the Supreme Court of *Hague v. CIO* (see the Preface and Chapter 1), when they asserted that streets and parks were made for the discussion of political questions "wherever the title may rest." The disappointment is that this recognition has rarely been carried through by subsequent Courts.

† The definition is from *The American Heritage Dictionary of the English Language*, 3rd ed. (Boston: Houghton Mifflin, 1992), "Regime," 2.

and exclusions are enacted and contested. Understanding the *interplay* among these three elements is necessary in order to answer questions about the quality, as well as the structure, of the democratic public sphere, which are precisely questions about how (and in whose interest) differentiation is achieved and how it might be challenged.

Property

Of the three elements of the regime of publicity, we have devoted most of our attention in this book to property. This has been done not because it is *a priori* the most important element, but because it is a crucial one that has not been discussed fully and directly enough in the literature on public space and publicity. Through the case studies we have shown how property regimes—the laws, practices and relations among different properties—have been tools or resources in the efforts to make spaces functional for certain kinds of publicity, for governing, for economic development, for political debate, and for sociability. *Claiming* property and exercising rights associated with ownership creates patterns of differential access to spaces within the city, sometimes intentionally, sometimes perhaps not. *Contesting* those rights is thus a strategy for challenging the nature of differentiation, and attempting to change the prevailing social system, even if only in what might seem like minor ways, such as preserving a space for homeless people to rest or for teens to hang out. Property relations are thus always an ongoing contest, as the protests, court cases, new rules and regulations, and changing designations of property we examined in each of the cases made clear. As the term "differentiation" should imply, we are only occasionally talking about outright exclusion from access to space. Rather, the nature of differentiation in and through property is contingent upon and enabled by the social norms that adhere to different kinds of property, social settings, and definitions of the normative public. Of course, as our examination of homelessness in San Diego, the social uses of the Plaza in Santa Fe, and the struggle for political access to Syracuse's Carousel Center all attest, this differentiation might be decisive in the ability of some people literally, physically, to be in and part of the public—to be part of the polity. In that regard the structuring power of property regimes, and of specific relations of property, cannot be minimized.

Social Norms and Community Membership

Community, the *civitas*, the polity: these terms all imply something about the existence of a commonality—the *res publica*—that might be the basis of a public sphere (Kemmis 1990). Though seemingly inclusive terms—the welcoming embrace of the community, the collective project of the *civitas*—they are, as we have seen throughout this book, also means by which "the public" can be narrowly or exclusively defined, real people can be excluded or marginalized, and political views and actions that challenge social norms and expectations can be quieted. There are rarely explicit laws—beyond those governing voting, perhaps, and certainly those governing immigration and citizenship—that determine membership in that amorphous collectivity we have been calling "the public." But there are innumerable rules, regulations, and expectations that position individuals and groups within the public sphere, and these often rely on notions of community and membership.

One of the striking things about the cases examined in this book is how norms and definitions of community are rarely critically examined or collectively agreed upon; more often, they are simply asserted. The ability to make those assertions and to have them take on the force of law—to be backed, that is by the explicit or implicit police power of the state—is a reflection of political and economic power (including the power of property), rather than of rational discussion in the public sphere. Between equal rights, Marx once wrote, force decides. Sometimes this force is explicit, as with the "pretextual" arrests of anticorporate globalization activists in Washington in 2001. Probably more frequently it is implicit in the social acceptance and social policing of norms. These norms include: norms of behavior as varied as those invoked by Bob McElroy of San Diego's Alpha Project, the planner in Santa Fe who objected to teens with their "little hacky-sacks" in the Plaza, or the land trusts who sought to bring more accountability to the community gardens of New York. They also include norms of community, those everyday determinations of who socially belongs in a space and who is therefore transgressive.

Among the means for structuring the collectivity or community—for determining and enforcing the norms and exclusions that allow the collectivity to come into being—is property, both as a tool and as a set of relationships. As a tool, property is double-edged, being used both in struggles to gain access as well as to condition or deny access. In differentiating the public, it is used in particular ways to enforce, as well as to allow, certain behaviors. Working in conjunction with other resources, property becomes one means by which access to the public realm and positioning within it is structured. The struggles over this positioning may lead to greater openness for a time, as was the case with the community gardeners, with homeless people who trespass on public and private property, and with protesters who challenge the government or dominant private interests. The struggles, however, may also involve attempts to exclude or marginalize people through regulations and actions that make certain people and behaviors unwelcome in "the community," as was the case in Carousel Center or the Santa Fe Plaza. This is why types or categories of property matter. Whether property is fully private (but publicly-accessible), becoming pseudo-private, some kind of public, or potentially "common," is both the result of such struggles and sets the conditions for further contestation and transformation.

The deployment of community and social norms is also significant in the ways that it rejigs the relationship between rights-bearing entities and political subjects in the public sphere. If property entails a set of specific rights, such as rights of ownership and alienation, and the ability to exclude, the invocation of social norms implies a different set of rights that attach to communities, which may or may not be in direct conflict with the rights of property. Whereas the rights of individuals (including corporate individuals) to invoke their property rights is enshrined in law, the ability of a community or a collectivity that lacks ownership to claim *space* is less clear. This right to inhabit and occupy space is clearly essential; it is an indispensable foundation for existence. And as Lefebvre (1996) makes so clear, the assertion and struggle for such a right possesses a deeply radical potential for the democratic remaking of the city. Yet the right to inhabit space is also a socially and legally weak right, and one that can often be used by owners of property themselves as they use their property to define and support a particular public interest, such as the interest of the public to shop and party in the Gaslamp undisturbed by homeless people, or the right of bureaucrats and tourists of Washington to easily move about the city undisturbed by the unruly protestations of the disenchanted. The invocation of community, and the usually unspecified norms that go with it, together with the invocation of an also unspecified public interest can divert attention from the power of individual and collective political subjects to shape community and public interest, and thereby the public itself, through the rights that adhere to property.

This is a critical point to remember when considering how a *democratic* public sphere is constructed, because it highlights the permeability of publicity and privacy. Property rights for individuals and the decisions about how to deploy them are in some senses decisions that are located in the public sphere, a sphere that some theorists argue is pre-political or that is beyond legitimate scrutiny from the public. Yet decisions made about property have been important for the kinds of collectivities that are constructed and for the socially conditioned exercise of rights in the public sphere. One might reasonably ask how decisions made in private and without regard to public interest or a concern for making space more accessible can lead to a democratic public sphere. It often seems that they do not.* Further, and as we argued in Chapter 6, ideas about common property and rights attached to it that might be used to build different kinds of public space and different norms of community have little traction in the United States; common property has, in fact, been eroded. But perhaps this is not all bad, for as the case studies have demonstrated, community values and social norms can still be exclusionary and undemocratic in important ways. The reliance on social norms and common or collective rights—just as the reliance on individual judgments and individual rights—are political and always riven with power.

Legitimation

We have argued that the ability to shape ideas of community and to work the boundary between public and private is an exercise of power. The ability to fix that exercise of power in the public sphere—to become part of the regime of publicity—however, requires a third element: relations of property and assertions of norms and community must be seen as *legitimate*. We mean legitimacy in a specific way: the normalization or taken-for-grantedness of publicness or publicity. This can be understood in three ways. First, and seemingly self-evidently, power, property, or a particular form of the public sphere is legitimate when it is consistent with social norms. So, for example, when a property owner exercises the rights of exclusion in accordance with the expectations of the surrounding community (however defined), she or he is acting *legitimately*. This form of legitimation is, in fact, easiest to see negatively; it comes into stark relief in those moments when a property owner transgresses established community norms. For much of the Jim Crow

---

* In late June 2006, the Syracuse Common Council voted 6–3 to reject the latest deal struck between the mayor and Destiny USA developer Robert Congel. This deal was meant to settle an outstanding legal appeal to a decision earlier in the year that granted Congel's Pyramid Companies the tax breaks they had been seeking. The appeal was to go forward. On July 4 (a holiday), the mayor negotiated a new deal with Congel that cut out the Common Council as a party, but still required approval from the Syracuse Industrial Development Authority (SIDA), which will issue bonds for the construction of Destiny as part of the deal. The SIDA members are all appointed by the mayor. On July 5, the SIDA met in a hastily called meeting that likely contravened New York State open meeting laws, since no notice was given to the public or the media and at least one member of SIDA who was likely to oppose the deal (the corporate council for the City of Syracuse who had to represent the interests of the Common Council as well as the executive branch) was probably not properly informed of the meeting and was in any event ordered by the mayor to take the day off. While the attorney was horseback riding, the SIDA approved the deal. Later in the day, the Onondaga County Legislature, who also had to vote on it, took up the issue as an off-agenda item in its regularly scheduled meeting and gave its approval, too. Whatever the exact legal status of the SIDA meeting, there is no doubt that the democratic process concerning the premier publicly-accessible property in the city and region was circumvented.

era, for example, there was simply nothing illegitimate about refusing entrance or service to blacks in the American South. Only when norms and laws changed—through struggle—was legitimacy thrown into question. This form of legitimacy is perhaps most clearly articulated by a geographer we once interviewed, who remarked: "I have a basic disagreement with a lot of critical geographers in that I've found that almost everyone is allowed in [public space]. . . . I'm more optimistic, I'm happier with the situation than I believe most critical geographers are. I don't see very many people being excluded. And the ones who are, very often, are the ones that I would exclude if I had the option." Acts of exclusion, according to this person, can be legitimate.

This geographer's argument also indicates a second way legitimation is a process of normalization: when the specific extant form of a public is normal in the sense of being unremarkable. Unremarkability is, in fact, an accomplishment, not a given, and so it is essential that the exercises of power through which unremarkability is created are both consistent with community norms and unostentatious. Even our colleague just quoted would likely flinch at seeing a homeless woman or man bodily dragged out of a public park, or teens blocked from entering a mall by a phalanx of armed deputies. When the police in Washington, DC became too heavy-handed, as we saw, there was a public outcry that reached quite deep.* Yet when these same police successfully restricted the ability to gather and express political positions through the permit process, it was seen as normal, as legitimate, as "well-oiled."

Finally, legitimacy through normalization requires that the outcome be consistent with existent notions of publicity, and this hinges on the ability to draw on, and to strategically deploy, the different senses of the public discussed in Chapter 6. The ability to variously and strategically point to the public interest of economic development, the ability of a community of people to gather, the ability of the state to manage dissent or disorder in the public interest, and especially the ability to move across these different definitions is a means of conferring legitimacy upon particular constructions of the public sphere. Consider the various publics and public interests invoked in Santa Fe as people sought to explain why the Plaza was so important, and especially who

---

* As we were writing the draft of this chapter we had the opportunity to have cocktails and dinner with a group of economists sharing our facilities for a conference on exchange-rate mechanisms. A few were from the World Bank, and one of them made a point of presenting us with a quite scathing critique of the policing of the protests against the bank and the IMF that we analyzed in Chapter 1. He argued, strongly, that the police were completely out of line, even though they were ostensibly protecting his (institutional) interests and (personal) safety.

the Plaza was ideally or really for. They mentioned tourists and teens, locals and people of color, the wealthy and the poor, and they identified interests ranging from community gathering to hanging out to economic development to social interaction. Existent notions of publicity must also necessarily reflect existing notions of privacy, such as the norm of keeping sexual behavior and often identity private, or of not conducting private acts necessary for survival in public areas.

Regime of Publicity

In this way, norms of property and norms of community can be made to work together to legitimate access to public space and to marginalize groups and behaviors within the public sphere—street musicians on Chicago's Magnificent Mile, teens on Santa Fe's Plaza, or radical anti-globalists in their convergence center in Washington, DC. That is, these together (norms of property, norms of community, and legitimation) constitute a *regime* of publicity—a *prevailing* social system of power. Through property, norms, and legitimation, relations of publicity become and are reinforced as relatively settled. "Relatively" is the operative term, because like any regime, a regime of publicity will necessarily be rife with contradictions and inconsistencies. No regime is ever immune from conflict, contestation, and transformation. Indeed, regimes often become the focus of such contestation and transformation, precisely because (since it is only ever prevailing and never absolute) it is a crucible for conflict. Deligitimation is always a possibility, even if the odds against it might often appear high. And other norms of inclusion and exclusion can be asserted, as in the long struggle of the community gardeners or the explosive outburst of protest that was the immigrant rights rallies of spring 2006. These other norms seek to configure public space differently, sometimes directly challenging prevailing norms of property and community, other times seeking to work within their interstices. Either way, they must confront the extant regime of publicity and understand the elements from which it is comprised. They might throw into question what was heretofore taken for granted. In doing so they may make space—and indeed property— for *other* peoples, other publics, than those for whom the current regime seems to have been constructed.

PRODUCING THE REGIME OF PUBLICITY— PRODUCING THE PEOPLE'S PROPERTY

In the interworking of property regimes, social norms, and processes of legitimation, we can see the ways in which specific regimes of publicity are produced, what effects they can have, and how they are transformed. The specific form or character of a public sphere in one place and time necessarily differs from others, as struggles for access to the public spaces of the city unfold. In this unfolding, power and the political strategies and goals of the protagonists create differentiations of property and people. In tracing the elements of regimes of publicity, as we have attempted to do in this book, we can begin to understand how a particular public sphere accommodates difference, how it includes certain kinds of people, behaviors, and values—and how it does not. We can begin to understand the ways in which particular, *actually existing*, public spheres become more—and less—democratic.*

Regimes of publicity and of the public sphere are therefore never abstract, removed from the political struggles of people, from their histories, from the histories of the places in which they are situated, from the public spaces they create, or from the public and private spaces from which they arise. This is true despite the processes of abstraction we have used to come to this conceptualization. This is true, we know, from that Friday in March 2006—an otherwise fairly typical day in early-spring Chicago—when all those immigrants and activists met downtown to demand recognition and political change. It is true that protesters were using space in a particularly spectacular way, but that does not set them too far apart from the late-afternoon tourists strolling through Millennium Park and stopping to gaze at the Cloud Gate, or from the shoppers and bar hoppers on the Magnificent Mile. For these latter groups, too, were forming a public within the confines of a regime of publicity structured by relations of property, social norms, and legitimation—and the struggle over them.

As our studies in Washington, Santa Fe, San Diego, Syracuse, and New York have shown, regimes of publicity are produced and reproduced through both everyday and more spectacular activities and struggles. Sometimes those activities and struggles occur within the precincts of the law (First Amendment law or the Santa Fe City Code), sometimes in defiance of the law (taking land for gardens, protesting without a permit), and sometimes seemingly quite removed from the world of law and formal politics (designing the space of the mall to encourage certain activities and discourage others, finding a place to sit when you are homeless and tired). All of these reproduce and sometimes change exactly what property, public space, and the politics of the

---

* Fraser (1990) argues that public sphere theory must always contend with what she calls *actually existing* democracy, not democracy as it is hoped to be. We contend, in turn, that public sphere theory also needs to contend with actually existing *spaces*, especially as they are produced through relations of property.

public really are and what they mean for the rights of different peoples to be in and part of the public.

This book has shown, we trust, that there is value in a close examination of *actually existing* public spaces, grounded in real property and specific property relations, as we seek to understand the structural constitution of public spheres—of regimes of publicity. In particular we hope it has made clear how a thorough analysis of the struggles in and over actually existing public spaces, as these are produced within and are productive of actually existing regimes of publicity, is a necessary step in figuring out just how actually existing public spaces can be transformed into—truly—the *people's property.*

POSTSCRIPT: INTERVENTIONS

We completed a draft of this book in the seemingly private space—and definitively private property—of the Villa Serbelloni, the Rockefeller Foundation's study center in Bellagio, Italy. It is not a space that is accessible to the public (indeed, it is a highly elite space), but it is one in which we engaged in a form of academic sociability, talking with a range of scholars, artists, and people involved with governmental and non-governmental organizations. In that sense, the Villa was much like the public space of the conference rooms in Chicago's Palmer House where we, with other geographers, presented our research on public space while immigrants were demonstrating just a few blocks away. In talking with people at the Villa, and in particular, in talking with people working in NGOs and governments, we were often asked whether our research was just theoretical or whether there was something practical to come out of it.

This is a question we are often asked—by students, by activists, by university administrators, by leaders of our discipline, by the funding agency that sponsored our research. It is a question that is particularly pertinent for us (and even rather perplexing, since it is not at all apparent that theory and practice are so easily separable) because the larger project from which this research is drawn concerns the politics of relevance in social research and about how—or whether—research leaves the academy and is drawn on in other parts of the social and political world. As a postscript to *The People's Property?* we want to address the kinds of interventions that readers might consider, and the problems, concerns, and politics that must be confronted in contributing to public—in all its senses—debate about the spaces of publicity.

SPACES OF INTERVENTION*

When people talk about making research relevant and about taking it outside the academy, they are often thinking about doing so by having research used by businesses or by governments; researchers, in this sense, can often seem to serve a role that is equivalent to consultants, to be little more than "hired guns." Certainly there is a great emphasis on this kind of intervention in the funding agencies that support research and by leaders of academic disciplines, such as geography. For example, the funding guidelines for the National Science Foundation require a discussion of the broader impacts of proposed research, focusing primarily on the impacts for government policy or for businesses (NSF, n.d.). Many leaders of the Association of American Geographers (AAG), the primary association for academic geographers in the United States, also emphasize making research relevant in this way, arguing that it is a waste of intellectual capital if research is not directly linked to the needs of end users such as policy makers, NGOs, or businesses. And an exchange in *The Professional Geographer,* one of the two journals sponsored by the AAG that publishes research from across the discipline, included the argument that research should be justified in terms of the "return on investment" for the same set of "public" interests (Harman 2003).

Interventions in these kinds of forums are important, as they hold the potential to be directly applicable to pressing problems related to public spaces; as we have demonstrated, property developers, planning agencies, police departments, and economic development agencies wield a great deal of power in shaping public spaces and thereby the nature of publicity in American cities. Yet as we have also argued, those agents do not operate in an apolitical fashion. Furthermore, not everyone who contributes to planning or policy making is listened to, and the outcomes may be rather different than what they had hoped. The planners we interviewed in Santa Fe, for example, were not entirely pleased with the way the Plaza was redesigned, managed, or used, noting with nostalgia that the Plaza no longer served as the "heart of the city." Thus, engagement with agencies and agents involved in the making of public space does not ensure that interventions will be to one's liking. Politics, not just people, intervene.

A second arena in which many academics hope to make a difference, to intervene, is in their teaching. As part of our larger project, we interviewed scholars who had been involved in research on public space, and we asked them how they wanted their research used and who their

---

* This discussion draws from Staeheli and Mitchell (2005).

primary audience was. Almost everyone we talked with wanted their research to be relevant to their students, and so used their research and the research of other scholars in their teaching. This is a kind of intervention that is often not discussed. On the one hand, some people argue that it is not really an intervention at all, as the research still remains in the academy, but is merely diffused to students; the implication is that what is taught in the classroom stays in the classroom, or at the most, remains relevant to the students only for the length of the academic term. On the other hand, some people are wary of being seen as attempting to politicize their students through their teaching, as campuses in the United States are under assault for being liberal "strongholds" that "brainwash" students into politically correct political postures.*

When instructors do try to demonstrate the relevance of scholarship for their students, they often try to do it in one of several ways: by exposing students to different ways of thinking about issues in public space and the complexity of the issues; by highlighting the contradictory social and political impulses shaping debates; and by drawing attention to the ways in which the problems they see "on the ground" are connected to broader processes and forces—processes and forces that they recognize students will unlikely be able to affect. According to the researchers with whom we spoke, the goal is to help students draw connections between processes that are often discussed in theoretical terms and the daily life of the cities in which they live. Through their teaching, researchers hope they can change the ways in which students understand urban problems and perhaps influence their ways of thinking in whatever careers the students ultimately choose—whether in urban planning, investment banking, government service, or policing. Tracing the influence of this kind of intervention is not easy—or perhaps even the goal.† As one of the researchers we interviewed

---

* Efforts in this regard include the American Council of Trustees and Alumni's 2005 report *Intellectual Diversity: a Time for Action*, and the efforts of David Horowitz to persuade state legislatures to pass academic bills of rights. Both efforts are intended to staunch what they claim is the overwhelmingly liberal bias in academic teaching and research. See www.goacta.org/publications/Reports/IntellectualDiversityFinal.pdf (accessed 9 June, 2006).

† It is hard, for example, to trace the role that serendipity plays. At the Association of American Geographers meeting in Chicago, for example, we met a graduate student who had read the article we wrote about our Santa Fe case study. He then sent it to his father, a relatively recent migrant to that city. The father reported to the student both that we seemed to have got it right, and that it helped him understand why the Plaza was such a contentious place—what the Plaza meant in the current and changing social structure of the city. There is nothing earth-shattering in this story, and the social effects of our article might be vanishingly small (who knows if the father will act in any particular way, or have any effect), but the point remains: an academic study, read by a student, "traveled" outside the university through wholly unpredictable means and was "picked up"—found to be relevant—by someone else.

commented, her goal was to give students a framework for understanding their experiences so that they could connect their experiences with those of others. Faculty often "helped" students do this by including service learning components in their classes, by teaching in interdisciplinary programs that forced those sorts of connections, and by helping students enter careers in which they would become more directly involved in shaping the spaces of the city.

A final way in which researchers talked about their interventions was through activism, either by direct activism or by working with activists to provide information that they needed. This form of intervention may seem to be the most directly appealing, particularly for those people who are sympathetic to radical, liberal or community-based action critical of both the government and economic development sectors. Yet there is remarkably little support for this kind of relevance in most universities. Many of the researchers with whom we spoke noted that their universities did not support that kind of work, only paying lip service to "outreach" activities, and then only to conventional activities directed to either governments or local businesses. Pre-tenured faculty, in particular, lamented the fact that publication directed at non-academic audiences had no real value when it came to their personnel evaluations, and some assistant professors worried that it would even count against them, as they would be seen as not being "serious" scholars. As we argued in Chapter 7, norms, rules, and processes of legitimation can be powerful forces shaping a regime of publicity, and thus public discourses. This is as true in the academy as it is outside of it.

DILEMMAS OF INTERVENTION

In thinking about relevance, about interventions, about using one's research to make social changes outside the academy, however, it is important to remember the ineluctably political nature of public space and interventions in it. Implicit in many people's desire to be relevant is a desire to be relevant to the "right" group or side of an issue. Those who want to intervene in public debate enter a regime of publicity, the prevailing system of social power that shapes public and private interests, public and private property, and positioning within the public sphere. "Successful" intervention and the costs associated with intervention, therefore, are conditioned by how "normal" a political position or intervention might be. Does it make sense in a given constellation of ideas, practices, and interests? What kind of effort does it take to get a message across in a given setting? And finally, in whose interest—from what position relative to other people in the public realm—do scholar/

activists intervene? These questions cannot be answered a priori, and efforts to address them may seem either like navel gazing or an excuse to *not* intervene.

As we began the fieldwork on the case studies, we were committed to making our research useful to, or relevant for, the people we interviewed. Quite quickly, and perhaps because the first case was in San Diego where we talked with a number of people whom we did *not* want to help, we began to reflect on what intervention meant and how we could provide not just something useful, but something useful to the "right" side.

A common strategy amongst researchers who want to conduct research that is useful for participants in various struggles, whether over public space or over other issues, is to create metaphorical spaces in which knowledge is co-produced (Nagar 2002; Pain 2004). This often means that researchers change their research project to fit with the goals of the people with whom they are working and that much of the research is conceptualized and conducted by those people. There are exemplary cases of this kind of committed research in geography, including the work of Richa Nagar (2000) and Linda Peake and Alisa Trotz (1999). These researchers have engaged long-term projects in which members of community or activist organizations are involved in the development of theory, research methodology, and the political practice that is part of the research. We were not able to emulate their strategies in our own work, and we believe we are not alone in not being able to do that. We also understand that such co-production creates specific kinds of knowledge, and that other kinds of knowledge, designed for other purposes, may require other strategies. Co-production may not always be the best strategy.

As a result, we want to discuss some of the dilemmas we faced as a way of raising broader issues about interventions in and through research. If research is or should sometimes be a radically democratic space,* then it is important to understand some of the dilemmas in traversing that space.

Logistics of Research

One of the immediate issues we confronted reflected the practicalities of attempting to engage the struggles of the people in the controversies we examined. The process of developing a project that meets the needs

---

* We say *sometimes* because, just as in some of our cases seemingly "undemocratic" means—squatting on derelict land to create community gardens, for example—created what were in fact more democratic spaces, "undemocratic" (e.g., solitary) research can sometimes be important to democratizing analyses (see Mitchell 2004).

of community members requires significant commitments of time and co-presence at critical points. The time commitment is in competition with other demands from our jobs and from other people to whom we have commitments, such as our families. In this instance, the time commitment was complicated by distance: how could we seriously engage the needs and interests of community members when we did not live in the cities in which we were conducting fieldwork?* It may be possible to do this at certain stages of a career, but the task becomes daunting over the long run. Yet it is important for us as a community of geographers to work with people and issues beyond those in our backyards. Some researchers have dealt with these time and location issues in creative ways. For example, Cindi Katz (2004), who is employed by the Graduate Center at the City University of New York, committed several years to her work with children in Sudan. But the distance—in absolute and metaphorical terms—prevented the intensity of involvement that she craved, so she developed a project looking at similar issues in Harlem. Ultimately, she was able to link the two projects, but it took a long time, which may not always be an option as academics attempt to manage career and life paths. And co-productions of knowledge require time commitments on the part of more than just the researchers; it takes a big commitment from the communities a researcher might want to help. The communities themselves may not be able to engage in the kind of interactions that would lead to mutually beneficial exchanges or to building their own capacities to conduct research in the future (Leitner and Sheppard 2003). In short, there may be times when one simply cannot fully engage with (live among, join struggles with, get to deeply know) the people with whom one works.

Furthermore, academic research is often more drawn out than the controversies that academics study. Time and again, people we interviewed for the case studies told us that academics did some interesting research, but that the moment for action had passed by the time the academics collected their data, analyzed it, and felt comfortable sharing it with other people. As one man said to us, "I get my research off the Internet. I don't know what takes you guys so long. What do you do with your time?" The rhythm and process of research are often incompatible with the needs of activists or of others involved in specific controversies.† It was an issue raised over and over again by

---

* While Don lived in Syracuse during the fieldwork, Lynn did not. Neither of us lived in the other four cities.

† This book is a case in point. Interviews were conducted in the first six months of 2001. No articles were produced until 2003, and this book will appear in 2007. A lot changes in six years, just as a lot changed in the six months following 9/11.

people who really did seek the information two critical geographers could provide.

Politics of Research

In any given project, one is likely to come across people with whom one disagrees, but those people are still important to talk with and to engage. The difficulty is that they will often ask for—and sometimes expect—assistance with *their* political missions. In other instances, people are not so interested in mutuality in the research process and the democratization of knowledge production so much as they are in having their story told on their terms. For example, a respondent in one of our case studies worked for the local government, and she told us precisely what we were to report. Were we obliged to do this when we believed she was seriously distorting the situation? When we were not interested in helping the city government justify its actions? In most projects, it is helpful and important to consider the arguments of people with whom one does not agree, to study the "opposition," as it were. If we have an obligation to the people we study, however, it is not clear what the nature of that obligation is and whether it differs according to the degree of agreement with the political position a respondent takes. In the case mentioned above, we simply treated the interview as one of many that were subject to critical analysis and did not overtly align ourselves with any group. But there were also times when people with whom we were sympathetic made requests, and they were requests we could not or would not meet. For instance, if we were going to have provided something useful to the community gardeners in New York, the people in that controversy for whom we had the most sympathy, we would have built a geographic information system of the gardens and the neighborhoods in which they were located. Many people asked us for that information, but it was probably the last thing we were interested in or capable of doing. Like anyone who tries to think about how to use our research (our skills and our specific projects) to make a difference in the controversies, issues, and lives we study, we had to negotiate *their* politics and *our* politics in order to make the research relevant to the portion of the public that we supported. We ultimately have not been successful in providing the kind of information that the participants in the controversies found most compelling, even when sympathetic to their needs and to their politics.

But that might not be the point. We often forget that academic researchers work within a set of divisions of labor. While we all seem (often too easily) to take for granted the divisions of labor that structure our workplace—what we do as scholars is very different from what administrative assistants, janitors, or admissions officers do, and our institutions could not function, and we could not work, without them—we rarely consider the divisions of labor within intellectual, activist, policy, or other arenas. These divisions are both local (as researchers focus on different topics with different ends) and societal. What policy formulators at the American Enterprise Institute or the Progressive Policy Institute *do* is very different than what professors at research universities do, which is different again from what workers at New York's Center for Environmental Justice, the Washington branch of the ACLU, Syracuse's Accountability Project, or homeless advocates in San Diego do. We have different social roles to play and we produce different kinds of things. What is important is the nature of the traffic between these things and the people who produce them. One of the things that academic researchers do—that they are in fact charged by society to do (contentious as this process may be)—is produce theory: systematic, structured, ways of seeing and knowing a problem.

Theory

Even so, the theoretical orientation of much academic research is often argued to be incompatible with making research useful for effective intervention. Certainly, many of the researchers we interviewed said that it was difficult to convey complex theoretical arguments in a way that was interesting or useful to some of the people they studied. And the respondents in the case studies often complained about the abstract, esoteric research they imagined would be written on the basis of the interviews. Many researchers are drawn to a topic because they see something important and intriguing in controversies or in particular issues; they see the *pertinence* of the topic. But it may well be that what academics see as pertinent is different than what the participants see. To the extent this is true, academics may well be asking different questions about a topic than do participants, and they may draw on different theoretical frameworks or different ways of understanding how things work the way they do. But the argument that activists and participants in public space controversies necessarily hold theoretical perspectives also misses the point. As activists have told us, it is not necessarily that they do not work with theory; it is that they do not have the time to *focus* on it. It is academics, they have told us, who have the time to debate the fine points of theory and concepts; activists have work to do. While we might respond that it is important to understand the competing definitions of publicity that circulate in discussions about parades, or homelessness, or feelings of marginalization, activists may be more focused on the immediate goal of gaining access to space. The important issue, given the divisions of social (and activist) labor, is that debate over concepts and theories, reformulation of ideas and practices, and the activist work of taking and transforming space need not be incompatible. They can and should be highly (if always imperfectly) complementary.

BUT YET . . .

These are all important issues that speak to the difficulties of fashioning research to meet the needs of different audiences, different people, and different political goals. In some ways and at some times, they may well be irresolvable. This is not a bad thing. It may not be possible, and especially it might not be *desirable*, to conduct research that simultaneously meets the interests we hold as researchers, the demands of evaluation committees, the questions our students have, and the needs of the communities we study or work with and that still allows us to meet our obligations to our families or the people we love. Yet interventions in public debate are important for academics to undertake. Following from the examples in this book, the constructions of publicity that shape the spaces of the city—the private spaces of the city, as well as the public spaces—reinforce normative views of how we should live and of how we can participate in public life. And the shape of the city—its relations of property, differentiation, and social struggle—shape who that "we" is in the first place. Researchers face the pressures of negotiating the practicalities of research, the theoretical constructions of research subjects, and the politics—including politics of commitment—that surround and shape the topics we study.

If one goal of critical human geographical research is to actively intervene in social issues, then it is worth remembering what "intervene" means. It means, most pertinently, to come between, to get in the way, especially with the goal of altering or hindering an action or state of affairs. To intervene means to interfere.* The critical issue for research on the properties of the public is to carefully consider the several ways it is possible to intervene in—to interfere with—regimes of publicity, and what the varying effects of doing so might be. The goal of this book has been to make just such an intervention. By focusing on a close analysis of controversies over property and public space, and less so on surveys of literature or abstract theoretical development, we have sought to change—to interfere with—how other researchers, teachers,

---

* Definitions from *The American Heritage Dictionary of the English Language*, 3rd ed. (Boston: Houghton Mifflin, 1992), "Intervene", definitions 4a and 4b.

students, and we hope, participants in struggles over and in publicly-accessible properties understand what the public is, who the people are and can be, how power functions in shaping public space, and why property matters so much to the regimes of publicity that currently exist—and that might be made to exist in the future.

METHODOLOGICAL APPENDIX

Over the years we have worked on this project, we have often been asked how we conducted the research. Sometimes the question has been framed in narrow methodological terms, but more often the questions have to do with the *process* of our research—the nature of collaboration, how we come up with our ideas, how we work together, and what the relationship is between our empirical work and theoretical ideas. In this appendix, we want to try to answer these questions, focusing not just on the method of our research, but also on what might be thought of as the method to our madness, or how we have conceptualized and operationalized both the process and product of the research. At the risk of seeming self-absorbed, we offer this discussion in an attempt to demystify the research process and to show students, in particular, that research can be carefully planned, but also sensitive to the opportunities and barriers that inevitably arise over the course of long-term research collaboration.

BACKGROUND TO THE STUDY

This project was initiated while we were colleagues at the University of Colorado. Working together, it became apparent that we shared many research interests, but that we approached research in very different ways. At a theoretical level, Don operated from a radical, materialist perspective largely influenced by Marxist and other critical theories. Lynn, by contrast, approached questions from the perspective of democracy theory (including theories of radical democracy) and feminism. At an empirical level, Don was interested in the relationships that structured access to public space and how one could be in it, including law and the relations of property. Lynn was interested in how a public came to be constituted in public space, in the kinds of publics that were formed, and in how people from different locations belonged—or did not belong—in the public. Methodologically, Don had relied on archival work and newspaper accounts, whereas Lynn relied primarily on interviews and surveys. None of these perspectives are necessarily in opposition, and in fact, it was clear from the beginning that we had more agreements than we did differences. But these perspectives mean that our research had different inflections and that we needed to be cognizant of what each perspective brings to an analysis. The result is, we think, a different kind of research than what either of us would have produced on our own. Working through our differences, though, has also meant that we have had to clarify our assumptions and our beliefs. It has also meant that we have learned a great deal from each other.

The project itself was funded by the National Science Foundation (NSF grant number BCS-9819828), and asked a range of questions that were primarily focused on the ways in which knowledge is constructed through research and how that knowledge does, and does not, leave the academy. As part of the research, we asked the people involved in conflicts over public space—that is, the people in our case studies—whether they ever used the research conducted by academics. As we noted in the Postscript, very few of the people we interviewed did. While we have reported on this element of the research in other publications, we have also used the case studies to make arguments about public space and the nature of the public that operates within it that are separate from the questions of relevance that were at the core of the larger project. Each of the case studies has been published, with the intent that they could be used in teaching—a way that research can leave the academy that is not often considered in academic debates about relevance (see Staeheli and Mitchell, 2005). This book considers the set of case studies as a whole in the hopes of highlighting the broader regime of publicity in which public space plays such an important role.

The background to the project is important to understand, as it shaped the way we conducted the research and the selection of what is more commonly thought of as the "research methodology." Those methods are, of course, important, but they cannot be separated from the broader purposes, goals, and contexts of research.

SELECTION OF CASES

The first questions asked of a student proposing a case-based methodology are always how the cases were selected and the kinds of biases that are introduced through the selection process. For us, the question was particularly difficult at the proposal stage, as we did not identify the specific cases we were going to examine. Rather, we proposed to identify our case studies by asking researchers what they felt were the most important topics or examples of public space research in which geographers could make a contribution; this strategy was linked to our overall concern with the ways in which geographic research might become relevant. Some of the reviewers at the NSF were wary of this strategy, but we argued that it would allow us to identify cases on the basis of their theoretical significance, rather than on the basis of convenience (e.g., the conflict was local) or because we wanted to do some research in a particular place.

After compiling the list of suggested controversies for in-depth study, we selected our five case studies on the following basis:

- The cases, as a set, needed to address issues surrounding the privatization of space.
- The cases, as a set, needed to highlight the ways that different marginalized and ostracized groups experience space and belonging to a public.
- The cases needed to cover a range of legal arrangements surrounding property and civil rights.
- The cases, as a set, needed to speak to questions of belonging in political, cultural, economic, and social senses.
- The cases needed to all be within the United States, but should not be in the same city.

DATA COLLECTION AND ANALYSIS

If the first questions students are asked about their proposed research have to do with the selection of cases, the second and third sets of questions usually have to do with how they will collect and analyze information in order to answer their research questions. In particular, students are asked about the role of theory and empirical evidence in shaping the kinds of arguments that are put forward. For example, will they rely on theoretical perspectives to interpret respondents' answers, thereby perhaps crafting research that supports theoretical arguments that were specified a priori? Or will the researcher describe the interview responses letting, as Peter Gould famously argued (1981), "the data speak for themselves?" Or will respondents be treated as theorists and pundits? Or will the responses be used to test theories and hypotheses?

Our analysis was based on several different kinds of information, or in the methodological parlance, was based on several different types of data. We conducted a systematic survey of the local newspapers, government agencies, web materials, and so forth for each of the cases. This information was used to help us understand some of the basic issues in each controversy and to provide an initial set of names of people to interview in each city. In a few cases (e.g., Santa Fe) there was also a scholarly literature on the topic upon which we were able to draw.

This secondary information was supplemented with semi-structured interviews with participants in the controversies, identified either through the analysis of documents or by snowball sampling techniques. These interviews were taped and then transcribed.* Both of us attended most interviews, except in cases where there was a scheduling conflict. One person generally ran the interview, with the other person taking notes, watching the interactions, and attempting to clarify issues and questions as they arose. The questions we asked addressed the nature of the controversy over public space, respondents' definitions of public space and its importance, and the sources of information the respondents used in their work; the latter reflected our concerns with issues of relevancy and whether or how research leaves the academy. The interviews all followed the same general structure, but were modified in each city to get at the specifics of the case under consideration; a copy of the interview questions for Santa Fe is included in Table A.1. Interviews generally lasted 1 to 1.5 hours. They were conducted in the winter and spring of 2001. During the interviews, additional secondary information was often collected. The number of formal interviews for each case study ranged from 6 in Syracuse to 17 in both New York and San Diego; a total of 63 formal interviews were conducted. As the latter comments imply, we also had a number of more informal conversations with people, but were not able to ask the full range of questions.

Finally, we spent as much time as we could simply hanging out in the public spaces we studied. This sort of participant observation was most important in the case studies involving the community gardens in New York and the Plaza in Santa Fe.

Our analytical strategy is one that begins with theoretical arguments, using those arguments to formulate questions to respondents (e.g., how does public space shape the public?). While we relied on respondents to answer those questions, we also used our theoretical frameworks to interpret theoretical arguments, to critique them, and to propose new arguments based on our respondents' understanding of the situation. Theory is implicated in every step, even though we do not include a section called "Theoretical Perspectives" in our chapters.

---

* After editing, we sent the transcripts to our interviewees and invited them to amend or clarify their arguments, delete anything they might have second thoughts about, and so forth. Very few respondents took advantage of this opportunity.

Written out of the chapters, however, is the process we followed in making those new arguments. In each case study, we had a set of issues we wished to address and a set of questions drawn from the theoretical literature; as we noted, these questions raised a set of possible scenarios that framed our expectations for what we should find in the news accounts if a given scenario or theoretical unfolding seemed to describe the situation. Our criterion for "seemed to describe the situation" is unabashedly qualitative and was based on an assessment of "practical adequacy" (Sayer 1984). And our method for conveying the "answers" to our questions was to tell an empirically supported, theoretically informed story.* We sought always to create a narrative that made a plausible, or preferably compelling, argument out of the news accounts, interviews, secondary literature, and other sources of information. Our test of "practical adequacy" was whether our narrative arc outlined an explanation of the controversies we were interested in that would be convincing, while always being true to what we had learned from our informants, our analysis of the cities and spaces we were interested in, and the theoretical literatures upon which we drew. The disagreements we had over whether a story provided a plausible explanation do not appear on the written page (although people who worked in adjacent offices can attest to the fact that we often disagreed!). In fact, arguing over the argument we were making was an essential part of the research and writing process. We found it crucial to constantly test ideas on each other: if simply hanging out in public spaces was vital to our understanding of them and thus for our research, so too were all those hours spent over coffee, a glass of wine, or on the phone, discussing points, pushing ideas, and making arguments critical to the final result—to the book we have written. This aspect of the research and writing process is often forgotten, and certainly rarely reported to funding agencies or others to whom researchers may be accountable.

Nor are researchers often explicit about the actual writing process. During most of the duration of this project, we lived thousands of miles from each other. Therefore, we most often adopted a strategy of having one or the other of us write a (near) complete draft of a paper or chapter. The other would read, comment, and often rewrite sections of the article before sending it back. The original author would rewrite again, until we were relatively satisfied by the result. Following journal reviews, the original author would usually take the lead in addressing reviewer and editor comments and preparing a revised version for publication.

---

* For critical discussions of the role of storytelling, narrative, and the politics of writing in geography, see Henderson (1998), Sayer (1989), and J. Smith (1996).

Sometimes, especially when significant revisions were called for, the other author would take the lead because she or he had a greater "distance" from the original article and found it easier to cut, reorganize, and develop arguments.

At Bellagio, where we were afforded a month to work closely together, we maintained this system of one or the other author taking the lead in developing the new chapters or rewriting the previously published ones. But there we were able to consult more frequently, discuss ideas more informally, and argue with each other more constantly, as we wrote and rewrote each of the chapters of this book. Though we did produce some "new" work at Bellagio, what the fellowship really allowed us was concentrated time to undertake the essential task of *re*writing. This too is something not discussed enough in primers on academic work and methodology. Rewriting is essential. There is not a chapter in this book that has not undergone dozens of revisions, large and small. We find it impossible (as we suspect most other people do too) to somehow just write up our research. Rather we write a draft, take it apart, write another, think things through, and rewrite yet again. Rarely do the "data" begin to "speak for themselves" before the third or fourth draft—and even then, they are sometimes not nearly as clear as they could or should be.

Our strategy for conducting research and for presenting "results" may not work in every setting, as different research questions and different audiences for research will require different standards of "evidence," "proof," and "rigor." As we noted in the Postscript, however, our goal was to intervene in debates over public space in particular settings, including the academy and the classroom. We hope that the stories we have told make sense, are practically adequate, and that as stories, they make sense to the people who have been involved in these controversies. Along the way, we hope to contribute to a theoretical, as well as political debate about how the public is constituted, sustained, and disciplined through strategies that involve property and the relationships that make property. In short, we hope that we have helped people to better understand the people's property.

Table A1 Interview Questions for Santa Fe

We would like to know more about the use of the Plaza as a public space. We are particularly interested in the ways the different uses of the Plaza either work together or are in conflict. We are also interested in how decisions regarding uses of the Plaza are made.

1. Can you please tell us a little bit about your organization in terms of the development, redevelopment and/or use of the Plaza? We have some background information from news articles, talking with other people, and so forth, but we'd like to have you briefly describe what you do.

2. What role does the Plaza play in the success of downtown Santa Fe? For the city as a whole?

3. Do you think of the Plaza as a public space? If so, why? If not, why not? How do you define public space?

4. What kinds of activities do you think are most appropriate for the Plaza? Is it important to have a variety of different uses of the Plaza? Why?

5. Who uses the Plaza? Is it important to have a diversity of groups and people using the Plaza at the same time?

6. Are there some uses and/or groups that are excluded from the Plaza? That should be excluded?

7. What are the main issues related to the Plaza as a public space?

8. What input do you have or role in addressing these issues?

9. Clearly, you are very knowledgeable about these issues. How did you get involved with this? Did your education play a role?

10. Sources of information
    a. How do you get information about this issue? If only name one: Are there other sources?
    b. Do you use information about other examples of plazas?
    c. What sources of information do you find most useful?

11. To your knowledge, have people from universities been involved in discussions or decisions related to the Plaza? Involved with your organization? Any of them geographers?

12. There are many geographers who have written on these topics. Are you aware of any of their work? If yes, do you find it useful in any way?

REFERENCES

ACLU (American Civil Liberties Union). 1982. *Demonstrating in the District of Columbia*. Washington, DC: American Civil Liberties Union of the National Capital Area.

Acuña, A. 1988. Convention Center is raising hopes for downtown vitality. *Los Angeles Times*, June 26, 2.1.

———. 1989. Port commissioner assails presence of "crazies" downtown. *Los Angeles Times*, November 3, B2.

———. 1990. Redevelopment looks at all of downtown. *Los Angeles Times*, October 1, B1.

Aigen, M. 1998. The D.C. Circuit review—August 1996–July 1997: Chapter: Constitutional law. *George Washington Law Review* 66:857–864.

Albuquerque Journal. 2002. Editorial: Rules for Plaza vendors get overdue update. *Albuquerque Journal*, August 21, 4.

———. 2003. Editorial: A pavilion to take pride in. *Albuquerque Journal*, January 12, 4.

———. 2003. *Journal* Staff Reports. Gazebo approved. *Albuquerque Journal*, December 11, 1.

Allen, C. 1994. The ACLU against the cities. *City Journal* 4 (2):40–47.

Amar, A. R. 1998. *The Bill of Rights: Creation and reconstruction*. New Haven, CT: Yale University Press.

Amster, R. 2004. *Street people and the contested realms of public space*. New York: LFB Books.

Anderson, K., and J. Jacobs. 1999. Geographies of publicity and privacy: Residential activism in Sydney in the 1970s. *Environment and Planning A* 31:1017–1030.

Archibold, R. 2004. Anarchists emerge as the convention's wild card. *New York Times*, August 20, A1.

Auer, H. 2003. A calmer Galleria: A year later, teen curfew has ended most disruptions. *Post-Standard* (Syracuse, NY), September 6, A1.

Barker, K., and D. Montgomery. 2001. Protesters and police say they succeed: Both sides take credit for inaugural peace. *Washington Post*, January 22, B1.

Bell, D., J. Binnie, J. Cream, and G. Valentine. 1994. All hyped up and no place to go. *Gender, Place and Culture* 1 (1):31–47.

Bell, D., and G. Valentine, eds. 1995. *Mapping desire: Geographies of sexualities*. London: Routledge.

Betsky, A. 1991. Westside Pavilion: Old-style mall turned into an assault on the senses. *Los Angeles Times*, November 21, J2.

Black, J. 2005. Civics lessons: Chicago's new Millennium Park is ambitious, expensive—and popular. *Planning* 71 (2):4–9.

Blackmar, E. 2006. Appropriating "The Commons": The tragedy of property rights discourse. In *The politics of public space*, ed. S. Low and N. Smith, 49–80. New York: Routledge.

Blomley, N. 1998. Landscapes of property. *Law and Society Review* 32:567–612.

———. 2000a. "Acts," "deeds," and the violences of property. *Historical Geography* 28:86–107.

———. 2000b. Law, geography of. In *The dictionary of human geography*, ed. R. J. Johnston, D. Gregory, G. Pratt, and M. Watts, 435–438. Oxford: Blackwell.

———. 2003. Law, property, and the geography of violence: The frontier, the survey, and the grid. *Annals of the Association of American Geographers* 93 (1):86–107.

———. 2004a. The boundaries of property: Lessons from Beatrix Potter. *Canadian Geographer/Le Géographe Canadien* 48:91–100.

———. 2004b. *Unsettling the city: Urban land and the politics of property*. New York: Routledge.

Blomley, N., and G. Clark. 1990. Law, theory, and geography. *Urban Geography* 11:443–446.

Blomley, N., D. Delaney, and R. Ford, eds. 2001. *The legal geographies reader*. Oxford: Blackwell.

Bondi, L., and M. Domosh. 1998. On the contours of public space: A tale of three women. *Antipode* 30:270–289.

Boyer, B. 1990. *The regulation school: A critical introduction*. New York: Columbia University Press.

Boyer, C. 1992. Cities for sale: Merchandising history at South Street Seaport. In *Variations on a theme park: The new American city and the end of public space*, ed. M. Sorkin, 181–204. New York: Hill and Wang.

Breidenbach, M. 2000. Candidates square off in WCNY event. *Post-Standard* (Syracuse, NY), October 15, B1.

Brieaddy, F. 2000. Activists petition city on mall plan. *Post Standard* (Syracuse, NY), September 10, B1.

Brown, M. 1997. *RePlacing citizenship: AIDS activism and radical democracy*. New York: Guilford.

———. 2000. *Closet space: Geographies of metaphor from the body to the globe*. New York: Routledge.

Bunge, W. 1971. *Fitzgerald: Geography of a revolution*. Cambridge, MA: Schenkman Publishing Company.

Bunge, W., and R. Bordessa. 1975. *The Canadian alternative: Survival, expeditions and urban change.* Toronto: York University, Atkinson College.

Calhoun, Craig, ed. 1992. *Habermas and the public sphere.* Cambridge, MA: MIT Press.

Carr, B. 1991. Carousel skydeck still rent-free but caters will pay surcharge. *Post-Standard* (Syracuse, NY), June 8, A1.

Code of Federal Regulations. n.d. 36 CFR 7.96

Cohen, J. 1997. Rethinking privacy: Autonomy, identity, and the abortion controversy. In *Public and private in thought and practice: Perspectives on a grand dichotomy,* ed. J. Weintraub and K. Kumar, 133–165. Chicago: University of Chicago Press.

Cole, D., and J. Dempsey. 2002. *Terrorism and the Constitution: Sacrificing civil liberties in the name of national security.* New York: The New Press.

Collins, D., and R. Kearns. 2001. Under curfew and under siege? Legal geographies of young people. *Geoforum* 32:389–403.

Cooley, K. 1985. Bums out, shoppers in: Downtown's Horton Plaza Park gets a shiny new face. *Los Angeles Times,* September 6, 2.1.

Cope, M. 2004. Placing gendered political acts. In *Mapping women, making politics: Feminist perspectives on political geography,* ed. L. Staeheli, E. Kofman and L. Peake, 71–86. New York: Routledge.

Cresswell, T. 1996. *In place/Out of place.* Minneapolis: University of Minnesota Press.

Crilley, D. 1993. Megastructures and urban change: Aesthetics, ideology and design. In *The Restless Urban Landscape,* ed. P. Knox, 127–134. Englewood Cliffs, NJ: Prentice Hall.

Curtis, J. 1993. Havana's Parque Coppelia: Public space traditions in socialist Cuba. *Places* 8:62–67.

D'Arcus, B. 2005. *Boundaries of dissent: Protest and state power in the media age.* New York: Routledge.

Davis, P. 1997. Protesters give parade watchers a stark eyeful. *Washington Post,* January 21, B1.

Delanty, G. 2003. *Community.* London: Routledge.

Domosh, M. 1996. *Invented cities: The creation of landscape in 19th-century New York and Boston.* New Haven, CT: Yale University Press.

———. 1998. Those "gorgeous incongruities": Polite politics and public space on the streets of the nineteenth-century New York City. *Annals of the Association of American Geographers* 88 (2):209–226.

Doran, E., and S. Errington. 2003. Grumbling marks start of Carousel Mall curfew. *Post-Standard* (Syracuse, NY), June 7, A1.

Duncan, J. 1979. Men without property: The tramp's classification and use of public space. *Antipode* 1 (1):24–34.

Duneier, M. 1999. *Sidewalk.* New York: Farrar, Straus and Giroux.

Dvorak, P. 2002. Like protesters, chief hit the Streets of D.C.: Being close to action was key, Ramsey says. *Washington Post,* April 24, B1.

Ellickson, R. 1996. Controlling chronic misconduct in city spaces: Of pan-handlers, skid rows, and public-space zoning. *Yale Law Journal* 105:1165–1249.

Enge, M. 1985. Hahn puts up $1 million to house San Diego's poor. *Los Angeles Times*, June 11, 2.3.

Etzioni, A. 1993. *The spirit of community.* New York: Touchstone.

Fernandez, M., and P. Dvorak. 2002. Protest organizers object to route: Detour avoids corporate offices. *Washington Post*, April 18, B4.

Fernandez, M., and D. Farenthold. 2002a. All sides prepare for protests: D.C. police plan IMF cordon, urge commuters not to drive. *Washington Post*, September 26, B1.

———. 2002b. Police arrest hundreds in protests: Anti-capitalism events cause few disruptions. *Washington Post*, September 28, A1.

Fillieule, O., and F. Jobard. 1998. The policing of protest in France: Toward a model of protest policing. In *Policing protest: The control of mass demonstrations in western democracies*, ed. D. Della Porta and H. Reiter, 70–90. Minneapolis: University of Minnesota Press.

Fincher, R., and R. Panelli. 2001. Making space: Women's urban and rural activism and the Australian state. *Gender, Place and Culture* 8 (2):129–148.

Findlay, L. 1993. Paths: The nature of linear public space. *Places* 8:72–75.

Flusty, S. 2001. The banality of interdiction: Surveillance, control and the displacement of diversity. *International Journal of Urban and Regional Research* 25:658–664.

Foote, K. 1983. *Color in public spaces: Toward a communication-based theory of the built environment.* Chicago: University of Chicago, Department of Geography.

Ford, L. 1994. *Cities and buildings: Skyscrapers, skid rows and suburbs.* Baltimore, MD: Johns Hopkins University Press.

———. 2003. *America's new downtowns: Revitalization or reinvention?* Baltimore, MD: Johns Hopkins University Press.

Frammolino, R. 1985. Residential hotels win panel's favor. *Los Angeles Times*, November 21, 2.1.

———. 1986. Council passes strict zoning, building rules for eastern downtown. *Los Angeles Times*, September 24, 2.3.

Francaviglia, R. 1996. *Main Street revisited: Time, space and image building in small town America.* Iowa City: University of Iowa Press.

Fraser, Nancy. 1990. Rethinking the public sphere: A contribution to actually existing democracy. *Social Text* 25/26:56–79.

Freeman, A. 1998. Go to the mall with my parents? A constitutional analysis of the Mall of America's juvenile curfew. *Dickinson Law Review* 102 (winter):481–539.

Fyfe, N., and J. Bannister. 1996. City watching: Closed circuit television surveillance in public spaces. *Area* 28:37–46.

Gadoua, R. 2003. Council works to spread message. *Post-Standard* (Syracuse, NY), March 13, B5.

Gibson, K. 2002. "11,000 vacant lots, why take our garden plots?" Community garden preservation strategy in New York City's gentrified Lower East Side. Master's thesis, Department of Geography, Pennsylvania State University.

Glendon, M. A. 1991. *Rights talk: The impoverishment of political discourse.* New York: Free Press.

Goldstein, A., and A. Santana. 2000. Peaceful protest belies rising tension: A victory cheered: Police accused of harassment. *Washington Post,* April 14, B1.

Goode, L. 2005. *Jürgen Habermas: Democracy and the public sphere.* London: Pluto.

Goss, J. 1993. The "magic of the mall": An analysis of form, function and meaning in the retail built environment. *Annals of the Association of American Geographers* 83 (1):18–47.

———. 1996. Disquiet on the waterfront: Reflections on nostalgia and utopia in the urban archetypes of festival marketplaces. *Urban Geography* 17:221–247.

———. 1999. Once-upon-a-time in the commodity world: An unofficial guide to Mall of America. *Annals of the Association of American Geographers* 89 (1):45–78.

Gould, P. 1981. Letting the data speak for themselves. *Annals of the Association of American Geographers* 71:166–176.

Gramsci, A. 1971. *The prison notebooks.* London: Lawrence and Wishart.

Granberry, M. 1991. Face-lift crew deposes park vagrants. *Los Angeles Times,* June 21, B1.

Habermas, J. 1989. *The structural transformation of the public sphere.* Cambridge, MA: The MIT Press.

Hamilton, P. 1994. The metamorphosis of downtown San Diego: How Centre City Development Corporation has guided downtown from a quiet, office only area into a vibrant urban center. *Urban Land* 53 (4):32–38.

Harman, Jay. 2003. Whither geography? *Professional Geographer* 55 (4):415–521.

Harris, R. C. 2003. *Making native space.* Vancouver, BC: University of British Columbia Press.

Harris, S. 1985. Far from the dusty lot and dilapidated downtown of only 3 years ago . . .: Horton becomes a happening on opening day. *Los Angeles Times,* August 10, 2.1.

Harvey, D. 1982. *Limits to capital.* Chicago: University of Chicago Press.

———. 1989. *The condition of postmodernity.* Oxford: Blackwell.

———. 2005. *A brief history of neoliberalism.* Oxford: Oxford University Press.

Hays, E. 2002. Garden deal hits hard in Brownsville. *New York Daily News,* September 29, 3.

Hebbert, M. 2005. The street as locus of collective memory. *Environment and Planning D: Society and Space* 23:581–596.

Henderson, G. 1998. Close encounters: On the significance of geography to the new western history. *Ecumene* 5:30–52.

Hendren, J. 2000. Street smarts: D.C. police muscle muffles demonstrations. *Seattle Times*, April 18, A3.

Herter, S. 2002. My view: Plaza needs new stage; fund has been started. *Santa Fe New Mexican*, November 3, F7.

Herzog, L. 1993. Between cultures: Public space in Tijuana. *Places* 8:54–61.

Hoebel, E. A. 1966. *Anthropology: The study of man.* New York: McGraw-Hill.

Hopkins, J. 1990. West Edmonton Mall: Landscape of myth and elsewhereness. *Canadian Geographer/Le Géographe Canadien* 34 (1):2–17.

———. 1991. West Edmonton Mall as a centre for social interaction. *Canadian Geographer/Le Géographe Canadien* 35:268–279.

Horstman, B. 1990. City OKs removal of grass, benches at Horton Plaza. *Los Angeles Times*, October 9, B3.

Hsu, S. 2002. D.C. police offer rules for video surveillance: Council member calls proposal too vague, says legislation is needed. *Washington Post*, April 10, B1.

Huard, R. 2000. Council backs private patrols downtown: City labor union raises objection. *San Diego Union-Tribune*, February 2, B3.

Hubbard, P., and T. Hall, eds. 1998. *The entrepreneurial city: Geographies of politics, regimes, and representation.* New York: Wiley.

Huddy, J. 2003. Plaza gazebo action urged. *Albuquerque Journal*, November 13, 1.

Hummels, M. 1998. Dispute develops over Plaza paving. *Santa Fe New Mexican*, December 2, B1.

———. 1999a. Committee: Hacky sack OK on Plaza, Santa Fe. *Santa Fe New Mexican*, October 19, B1.

———. 1999b. Plaza deemed safe for hacky sackers. *Santa Fe New Mexican*, October 28, A1.

Isin, E. 2002. *Being political: Genealogies of citizenship.* Minneapolis: University of Minnesota Press.

Jackson, J. B. 1957. A stranger's path. *Landscape* 7 (1):11–15.

Jackson, P., and J. Penrose, eds. 1993. *Constructions of race, place and nation.* Minneapolis: University of Minnesota Press.

Jacobs, J. 1961. *The death and life of great American cities.* New York: Random House.

Janiszewski, J. 2002. Silence enforced through speech: Philadelphia and the 2000 Republican National Convention. *Temple Political and Civil Rights Law Review* 12:121–140.

Johnson, G. 1990. City yanks benches from under undesirables downtown: Council adopts plan to replace grass with flowers, remove benches in an effort to rout criminals and drunks at Horton Plaza. *Los Angeles Times*, July 3, B2.

Jones, L. 1985. Lack of toilets downtown a problem: Council gets lesson on restrooms. *Los Angeles Times*, March 14, 2.3.

Kaplan, E. A. 2006. Hoisting the flag in anger: A protest in Liemert Park was messy, surreal, saddening—and understandable. *Los Angeles Times*, April 26, B13.

Katz, C. 1998. Whose nature, whose culture? Private production of space and the "preservation of nature." In *Remaking reality: Nature and the millennium*, ed. B. Braun and N. Castree, 46–63. New York: Routledge.

———. 2001. Hiding the target: Social reproduction in the privatized urban environment. In *Postmodern Geography: Theory and praxis*, ed. C. Minca, 94–110. Oxford: Blackwell.

———. 2004. *Growing up global: Economic restructuring and children's everyday lives*. Minneapolis: University of Minnesota Press.

———. 2006. Power, space, and terror: Social reproduction and the public environment. In *The politics of public space*, ed. S. Low and N. Smith, 105–122. New York: Routledge.

Kayden, J. 2000. *Privately-owned public space: The New York City experience*. New York: Municipal Art Society of New York.

Keen, J. 2006. Noise restrictions in Chicago muzzle makeshift musicians. *USA Today*, February 9, A6.

Kemmis, D. 1990. *Place and the politics of community*. Norman, OK: University of Oklahoma Press.

Kifner, J. 2000. Police move against trade demonstrators. *New York Times*, April 16, 1.6.

Kifner, J., and D. Sanger. 2000. Financial leaders meet as protests clog Washington. *New York Times*, April 17, A1.

King, J. 1993. Old-fashioned crackdown: San Diego goes after "panhasslers." *San Francisco Chronicle*, January 16, A1.

Knox, P., ed. 1993. *The restless urban landscape*. Englewood Cliffs, NJ: Prentice Hall.

Kohn, Margaret. 2004. *Brave new neighborhoods: The privatization of public space*. New York: Routledge.

Kornblut, A. 2000. Hundreds are arrested on eve of big D.C. rally. *Boston Globe*, April 16, A31.

Krueckeberg, D. 1995. The difficult character of property: To whom do things belong? *Journal of the American Planning Association* 61:301–309.

Laclau, E., and C. Mouffe. 1985. *Hegemony and socialist strategy*. London: Verso.

Lees, L. 1998. Urban renaissance and the street: Spaces of control and contestation. In *Images of the street: Planning, identity, and control in public space*, ed. N. Fyfe, 236–253. London: Routledge.

———. 2001. Towards a critical geography of architecture: The case of an Ersatz Colosseum. *Ecumene* 8:51–86.

Lefebvre, H. 1991. *The production of space*. Trans. D. Nicholson-Smith. Oxford, UK: Blackwell.

Lefebvre, H. 1996. *Writings on cities*. Trans. E. Kofman and E. Lebas, ed. E. Kofman and E. Lebas. Oxford: Blackwell.

Leitner, H., J. Peck, and Sheppard, E., ed. 2006. *Contesting neoliberalism: Urban frontiers*. New York: Guilford.

Leitner, H., and E. Sheppard. 2003. Unbounding critical geographic research in cities: The 1990s and beyond. *Urban Geography* 24:510–528.

Light, A., and J. Smith, eds. 1998. *The production of public space*. Lanham, MD: Rowman and Littlefield.

Little, J., L. Peake, and P. Richardson, eds. 1988. *Women in cities: Gender and the urban environment*. New York: New York University Press.

Los Angeles Times. 1985. Horton Plaza exudes life. *Los Angeles Times*, August 18, 2.2.

———. 1990. The homeless lose more ground: Actions by council, shelter agency leave indigent in the cold. *Los Angeles Times*, July 8, B2.

Low, S. 2000. *On the Plaza: The politics of public space and culture*. Austin, TX: University of Texas Press.

Lyon, L. 1987. *The community in urban society*. Philadelphia, PA: Temple University Press.

MacDonald, J. 2001. Plaza vendors permit program under fire. *Santa Fe New Mexican*, February 22, A1.

MacLeod, G. 2002. From urban entrepreneurialism to a "revanchist city?" On the spatial injustices of Glasgow's renaissance. *Antipode* 34:602–624.

Macpherson, C. B. 1978. *Property: Mainstream and critical positions*. Toronto: University of Toronto Press.

Magnet, M., ed. 2000. *The millennial city: A new urban paradigm for 21st century America*. Chicago: Ivan R. Dee.

Marx, G. 1988. *Undercover: Police surveillance in America*. Berkeley: University of California Press.

———. 1998. Afterword: Some reflections on the democratic policing of demonstrations. In *Policing protest: The control of mass demonstrations in western democracies*, ed. D. Della Porta and H. Reiter, 253–268. Minneapolis: University of Minnesota Press.

Massey, D. 2005. *For space*. London: Sage.

McCarthy, J., C. McPhail, and J. Smith. 1996. Images of protest: Dimensions of selection bias in media coverage of Washington demonstrations, 1982 and 1991. *American Sociological Review* 61:478–499.

McDowell, L. 1983. Towards an understanding of the gender division of urban space. *Environment and Planning D: Society and Space* 1 (1):59–72.

McKenzie, E. 1994. *Privatopia*. New Haven: Yale University Press.

McPhail, C., D. Schweingruber, and J. McCarthy. 1998. Policing protest in the United States: 1960–1995. In *Policing protest: The control of mass demonstrations in western democracies*, ed. D. Della Porta and H. Reiter, 49–69. Minneapolis: University of Minnesota Press.

Mendoza, M. 2003. Scrutiny the price of security? Police surveillance increases in face of terror threat. *Syracuse Post Standard*, April 6, A10.

Miller, K. forthcoming. *Designing the public: Money, access and expression in New York City's public spaces.* Minneapolis: University of Minnesota Press.

Miller, M. 1985. Homeless get help—but it's too little. *Los Angeles Times*, February 11, 2.1.

Millican, A. 2000. Ambassadors to work for a clean, safe downtown. *San Diego Union-Tribune*, July 28, B2.

Milloy, C. 2003. Arrests put civil rights in perspective. *Washington Post*, March 3, B1.

Mitchell, D. 1992. Iconography and locational conflict from the underside: Free speech, People's Park, and the politics of homelessness in Berkeley, California. *Political Geography* 11:152–169.

———. 1995. The end of public space? People's Park, definitions of the public, and democracy. *Annals of the Association of American Geographers* 85:108–133.

———. 1996. Public space and the city: Special issue. *Urban Geography* 17 (1–2).

———. 1998. Anti-homeless laws and public space: I. Begging and the First Amendment. *Urban Geography* 19:6–11.

———. 2003a. The liberalization of free speech: Or, how protest in public space is silenced. *Stanford Agora*: Now at: http://www.maxwell.syr.edu/geo/faculty/old_files/Liberalization%20of%20Free%20Speech.doc (accessed 13 May 2007).

———. 2003b. *The right to the city: Social justice and the fight for public space.* New York: Guilford.

———. 2004. Radical scholarship: A polemic on making a difference outside the academy. In *Radical theory/Critical praxis: Making a difference beyond the academy*, ed. D. Fuller and R. Kitchen, 21–31. Vancouver, BC: Praxis E-Books.

———. 2005a. Property rights, the First Amendment, and judicial anti-urbanism: The strange case of *Hicks v. Virginia. Urban Geography* 26:565–586.

———. 2005b. The S.U.V. model of citizenship: Floating bubbles, buffer zones, and the rise of the "purely atomic" individual. *Political Geography* 24:77–100.

Monbiot, G. 2004. A threat to democracy: Basic freedoms to protest are being systematically undermined by anti-terror legislation. *The Guardian*, August 3.

Montgomery, D. 2001. Lawyers allege abuse by inaugural security. *Washington Post*, March 16, A8.

Montgomery, D., and A. Santana. 2000a. Election intensifies inaugural protests: Several groups have planned demonstrations. *Washington Post*, December 21, A10.

———. 2000b. Rally web site also interests the uninvited: D.C. police monitoring information posted online. *Washington Post*, April 2, A14.

Mooney, J. 2004. For those patches of green, home rule draws near. *New York Times*, March 21, 14.5.

Morello, C., and M. Fernandez. 2002. Day of demonstrations is wet, not wild: No arrests are made: D.C. traffic delays are possible today. *Washington Post*, April 22, B1.

Mulder, A. 2003. Privately public: An exploration of the "public" in private land conservation in New York's Hudson Valley. PhD dissertation, Department of Geography, University of Colorado, Boulder.

Nagar, R. 2000. *Mujhe Jawab Do!* (answer me!): Women's grassroots activism and social spaces in Chitrakoot (India). *Gender Place and Culture* 7:341–362.

———. 2002. Footloose researchers, "traveling" theories, and the politics of transnational feminist praxis. *Gender, Place and Culture* 9 (2):179–186.

National Lawyer's Guild (NLG). n.d. Exercising your rights of political protest in Washington, DC. Washington, D.C.: National Lawyer's Guild.

National Science Foundation. n.d. Merit review broader impacts criterion: Representative activities. http://www.nsf.gov/pubs/gpg/broaderimpacts.pdf Accessed 4 March 2006.

Navrot, M. 2000. NAACP head targets obelisk. *Albuquerque Journal*, August 21.

Neary, B. 1994. Plaza wars. *Santa Fe New Mexican*, December 11, A1.

Newman, O. 1973. *Defensible space: Crime prevention through urban design*. New York: Macmillan.

———. 1996. *Creating defensible space*. Washington, DC: Department of Housing and Urban Development.

NLCHP (National Law Center on Homelessness and Poverty). 1996. *Mean sweeps: A report on anti-homeless laws, litigation, and alternatives in 50 United States cities*. Washington, DC: National Law Center on Homelessness and Poverty.

Olwig, K. 1996. Recovering the substantive nature of landscape. *Annals of the Association of American Geographers* 86:630–653.

———. 2003. *Landscape, nature, and the body politic*. Madison, WI: University of Wisconsin Press.

———. 2005. Representation and alienation in the political land-*scape*. *Cultural Geographies* 12:19–40.

Ouroussoff, N. 2000. Architecture: Fantasies of a city high on a hill; Commentary: The expansion of Citywalk embraces the myth of mall culture that shies away from the grittier realities of urban life. *Los Angeles Times*, April 9, Calendar 4.

Pain, R. 1991. Space, sexual violence, and social control: Integrating geographical and feminist analyses of women's fear of crime. *Progress in Human Geography* 15:415–432.

———. 1997. Social geographies of women's fear of crime. *Transactions of the Institute of British Geographers* 22:231–244.

———. 2000. Place, social relations and the fear of crime: A review. *Progress in Human Geography* 24:365–387.

———. 2001. Gender, race, age and fear in the city. *Urban Studies* 38 (5):899–913.

———. 2004. Social geography: Participatory research. *Progress in Human Geography* 28 (5):652–663.

Pateman, C. 1989. *The disorder of women: Democracy, feminism, and political theory.* Palo Alto, CA: Stanford University Press.

Peake, L., and A. Trotz. 1999. *Gender, ethnicity and place: Women and identities in Guyana.* New York: Routledge.

Perry, A. 1989. San Diego at large: Shop till you drop, but don't expect a bench. *Los Angeles Times*, January 13, 2.1.

Perry, T. 1993. No alms for the "panhasslers": Cities: San Diego cracks down on aggressive beggars who block paths and use threatening language. *Los Angeles Times*, January 12, A3.

Phillips, M., and Y. Trofimov. 2001. Trading places: Police go undercover to thwart protesters against globalization—meetings of IMF and NATO renew fears of violence from radical groups—"D.C. is not going to burn." *Wall Street Journal*, September 11, A1.

Podmore, J. 2001. Lesbians in the crowd: Gender, sexuality, and visibility along Montreal's Boulevard St.-Laurent. *Gender, Place and Culture* 8:333–355.

Post-Standard (Syracuse, NY). 2003. No muzzles here: Respect the American values soldiers will fight for. *Post-Standard*, March 19, A16.

Powell, M. 2002. Domestic spying pressed: Big-city police seek to ease limits imposed after abuses decades ago. *Washington Post*, November 29, A1.

Preston, W. 1963. *Aliens and dissenters: Federal suppression of radicals, 1903–1933.* New York: Harper and Row.

Putnam, R. 2000. *Bowling alone: The collapse and revival of American community.* New York: Simon and Schuster.

Rasmussen, C., and M. Brown. 2002. Radical democratic citizenship: Amidst political theory and geography. In *Handbook of citizenship studies*, ed. B. Turner and E. Isin, 294–397. Thousand Oaks: Sage.

———. 2005. The body politic as spatial metaphor. *Citizenship Studies* 9:469–484.

Redden, J. *Police spying 101.* Utne Reader Online 2000. http://www.utne.com/webwatch/2001 33/news/1860-1.html Accessed 13 May 2007.

Riley, R. 1994. Speculations on the new American landscapes. In *Re-reading cultural geography,* ed. K. Foote, P. Hugill, K. Mathewson, and J. Smith, 139–155. Austin, TX: University of Texas Press.

Roberts, S., and R. Schein. 1993. The entrepreneurial city: Fabricating urban development in Syracuse, New York. *Professional Geographer* 45:21–33.

Rose, C. 1998. The several futures of property: Of cyberspace and folktales, emissions trades and ecosystems. *Minnesota Law Review* 83:129–182.

Rosenbaum, D. 2001. The inauguration: The demonstrations: Protesters in the thousands sound off in the capital. *New York Times,* January 21, 1.17.

Rowe, S., and J. Wolch. 1990. Social networks in time and space: Homeless women in skid row, Los Angeles. *Annals of the Association of American Geographers* 80:184–204.

Ryan, M. 1990. *Women in public: Between banners and ballots.* Baltimore, MD: Johns Hopkins University Press.

Sandel, M. 1996. *Democracy's discontent: America in search of a public philosophy.* Cambridge, MA: Belknap Press.

Santa Fe City Code. n.d. Santa Fe City Code, Section 23-25.

Santa Fe Economic Development Division. 2005. *The Santa Fe economic development plan: A report to the community: The first year accomplishments.* Santa Fe, NM: Santa Fe Economic Development Division.

Santa Fe New Mexican. 2002. Editorial: No more Plaza vendors? Now there's a notion . . . *Santa Fe New Mexican,* August 20, A7.

———. 2003a. Editorial: A fresh new stage for a fine old plaza. *Santa Fe New Mexican,* May 12, A5.

———. 2003b. Plans for Plaza are a good start. *Santa Fe New Mexican,* September 14, F6.

Santana, A. 2000. Area police brace for inaugural protests: Agencies teaming up to prepare for security. *Washington Post,* December 28, B1.

———. 2001. Security tightened for Inauguration Day: More officers on parade route. *Washington Post,* January 12, B1.

Sayer, A. 1984. *Method in social science: A realist approach.* London: Routledge.

———. 1989. The "new" regional geography and problems of narrative. *Environment and Planning D: Society and Space* 7:253–267.

Schacter, J. 1985. Gaslamp card rooms face switch in city's efforts to oust them. *Los Angeles Times,* August 20, 2.2.

Schein, R., ed. 2006. *Landscape and race in the United States.* New York: Routledge.

Schemo, D. 2002. Mideast turmoil: Demonstrations: Thousands hold rally in capital to back Israel. *New York Times,* April 16, A18.

Schmelzkopf, K. 1995. Urban community gardens and contested spaces. *Geographical Review* 85:364–381.

———. 2002. Incommensurability, land use, and the right to space: Community gardens in New York. *Urban Geography* 23:323–343.

Schraeger, S. 1994. A low-rent housing alternative. *Urban Land* 53 (4):40–43.

Schwartz, R. 1985. Downtown hotel residents losing their meager homes. *Los Angeles Times*, September 13, 2.1.

Seamon, D., and C. Nordin. 1980. Marketplace as place ballet: A Swedish example. *Landscape* 24 (3):35–48.

Sennett, R. 1994. *Flesh and stone: The body and the city in western civilization.* New York: W.W. Norton.

Serrano, R. 1988. Downtown's troublesome pocket of crime: Pimps, panderers and pushers makes this stretch of 7th Avenue home turf. *Los Angeles Times*, August 22, 2.1.

Shapin, S., and S. Schaefer. 1985. *Leviathan and the air pump.* Princeton, NJ: Princeton University Press.

Sharpe, T. 1996. Vendor dispute goes to court. *Albuquerque Journal*, December 31.

———. 1997. SF vendor squabbles erupt. *Albuquerque Journal*, March 181.

———. 2003a. Council approves plans for Plaza gazebo. *Santa Fe New Mexican*, December 11, B1.

———. 2003b. Council waivers on Plaza gazebo design. *Santa Fe New Mexican*, October 12, B1.

———. 2003c. Mild makeover: Council approves plans for wider walkways and an expandable gazebo. *Santa Fe New Mexican*, October 9, A1.

———. 2003d. Vendors upset with rankings testify at hearing. *Santa Fe New Mexican*, March 6, B1.

Shields, R. 1989. Social spatialization and the built environment: The West Edmonton Mall. *Environment and Planning D: Society and Space* 7:147–164.

Short, J. R., L. M. Benton, W. B. Luce, and J. Walton. 1993. Reconstructing the image of an industrial city. *Annals of the Association of American Geographers* 83:207–224.

Showley, R. 1994. Coming of age: San Diego's development markets. *Urban Land* 53 (4):80–81.

Sibley, D. 1981. *Outsiders in urban society.* New York: St. Martin's Press.

Simmons, M. 2000. Trail dust: Soldiers monument on Plaza has survived repeated controversies. *Santa Fe New Mexican*, October 14, B1.

Singer, Joseph. 2000. *Entitlement: The paradoxes of property.* New Haven, CT: Yale University Press.

Smith, J. 1996. Geographical rhetoric: Modes and tropes of appeal. *Annals of the Association of American Geographers* 86:1–20.

Smith, N. 1996. *The new urban frontier: Gentrification and the revanchist city.* New York: Routledge.

Smolla, R. 1992. *Free speech in an open society.* New York: Knopf.

Sorkin, M., ed. 1992. *Variations on a theme park: The new American city and the end of public space.* New York: Hill and Wang.

Sparke, Matthew. 1998. A map that roared and an original atlas: Canada, cartography and the narration of nation. *Annals of the Association of American Geographers* 88:463–496.

Squires, J. 1994. Private lives, secluded places: Privacy as political possibility. *Environment and Planning D: Society and Space* 12 (4):387–401.

Staeheli, L. 1996. Publicity, privacy, and women's political action. *Environment and Planning D: Society and Space* 14:601–619.

Staeheli, L., and D. Mitchell. 2005. The complex politics of relevance in geography. *Annals of the Association of American Geographers* 95 (2):357–372.

———. 2006. USA's destiny: Regulating space and creating community in American shopping malls. *Urban Studies* 45 (5/6):977–992.

———. Forthcoming. Locating the public in research and practice. *Progress in Human Geography.*

Steinhauer, J. 2002. Ending a long battle: New York lets housing and gardens grow. *New York Times*, September 19, A1.

Stone, G., R. Epstein, and C. Sunstein. 1992. *The Bill of Rights in the modern state.* Chicago: University of Chicago Press.

Sugrue, T. 1996. *The origins of the urban crisis.* Princeton, NJ: Princeton University Press.

Sutro, D. 1989. Architecture: Urban space message for San Diego. *Los Angeles Times*, March 22, 5.1.

Teir, R. 1993. Maintaining safety and civility in public spaces: A constitutional approach to aggressive begging. *Louisiana Law Review* 54:285–338.

Tyner, J. 2006. *The geography of Malcolm X: Black radicalism and the remaking of American space.* New York: Routledge.

Van Deusen, R. 2002. Public space as class warfare: Urban design, the "right to the city," and the production of Clinton Square in Syracuse, New York. *GeoJournal* 58:149–158.

Vobejda, B., and J. Havemann. 1996. Large U.S. cities target homeless, advocates say. *Washington Post*, December 12, A23.

Waldron, J. 1991. Homelessness and the issue of freedom. *UCLA Law Review* 39:295–324.

Watanabe, T. 2006. Immigration forum gets intense: A discussion at L.A.'s Leimert Park about illegal immigrants and their impact on blacks escalates into a shouting match over jobs, housing and schools. *Los Angeles Times*, April 24, B3.

Weintraub, J. 1995. The theory and politics of the public/private distinction. In *Public and private in thought and practice: Perspectives on a grand dichotomy*, ed. J. Weintraub and K. Kumar, 1–42. Chicago: University of Chicago Press.

Whyte, W. 1988. *The social life of small urban spaces.* New York: Project for Public Space.

———. 1993. *Street corner society: The social structure of an Italian slum.* 4ᵗʰ ed. Chicago: University of Chicago Press.

Wildermuth, J. 2001. Heavy security planned for inaugural parade: Up to 20,000 protesters expected—Highest number since Vietnam War. *San Francisco Chronicle*, January 17, A3.

Williams, P. 1991. *The alchemy of race and rights.* Cambridge, MA: Harvard University Press.

Williams, R. 1997. *Problems of materialism and culture.* New York: Verso.

Wilson, C. 1997. *The myth of Santa Fe: Creating a modern regional tradition.* Albuquerque, NM: University of New Mexico Press.

Wilson, E. 1991. *The sphinx in the city: Urban life, the control of disorder, and women.* Berkeley: University of California Press.

Wilson, P. L., and B. Weinberg, eds. 1999. *Avant gardening: Ecological struggle in the city and world.* New York: Automedia.

Wolch, J., A. Rahimian, and P. Koegel. 1993. Daily and periodic mobility patterns of the urban homeless. *Professional Geographer* 45:159–169.

Wright, T. 1997. *Out of place: Homeless mobilizations, subcities, and contested landscapes.* Albany: SUNY Press.

Young, I. M. 1990. *Justice and the politics of difference.* Princeton, NJ: Princeton University Press.

Zukin, S. 1991. *Landscapes of power: From Detroit to Disney World.* Berkeley: University of California Press.

———. 1995. *The cultures of cities.* Oxford: Blackwell.

COURT CASES CITED

Bantam Books, Inc. v. Sullivan, 1963 372 U.S. 58.

Cantwell v. Connecticut, 1940 310 U.S. 296.

Clark v. Community for Creative Non-Violence, 1984 468 U.S. 288.

Cox v. New Hampshire, 1941 312 U.S. 569.

Fifty Years Is Enough, et al. v. District of Columbia, et al., n.d. http://www.civil-rights.net/a16/a16complaint.html (accessed 20 May 2005).

Hague v. CIO, 1939 307 U.S. 496.

Near v. Minnesota, 1931 283 U.S. 697.

Poulos v. New Hampshire, 1953 345 U.S. 295.

Pruneyard Shopping Center v. Robins, 1980 447 U.S. 74.

Shuttlesworth v. Birmingham, 1969 394 U.S. 197.

Virginia v. Hicks, 2003 539 U.S. 113.

INDEX